2004

Love 'Em and Lead 'Em

Leadership Strategies That Work for Reluctant Leaders

Tim Carman

A SCARECROWEDUCATION BOOK

The Scarecrow Press, Inc.
Lanham, Maryland, and Oxford
2002

A SCARECROWEDUCATION BOOK

Published in the United States of America
by Scarecrow Press, Inc.
A Member of the Rowman & Littlefield Publishing Group
4720 Boston Way, Lanham, Maryland 20706
www.scarecrowpress.com

PO Box 317
Oxford
OX2 9RU, UK

British Library Cataloguing in Publication Information Available

Library of Congress Cataloging-in-Publication Data

Carman, Tim, 1947–
    Love 'em and lead 'em : leadership strategies that work for reluctant leaders
    / Tim Carman
      p. cm.
    Includes bibliographical references (p.).
    ISBN 0-8108-4300-5 (cloth : alk. paper) — ISBN 0-8108-4298-X (pbk : alk.
paper)
      1. Educational leadership—United States. 2. Education—Standards—United
States. I. Title: Leadership strategies that work for reluctant leaders. II. Title.

LB2805 .C269 2002
379.1'58—dc21
                                          2002022170

∞™ The paper used in this publication meets the minimum requirements of
American National Standard for Information Sciences—Permanence of Paper
for Printed Library Materials, ANSI/NISO Z39.48-1992.
Manufactured in the United States of America.

Contents

Acknowledgments

I would like to extend my sincere appreciation to the many teachers, administrators, parents, and school board members who believed in me by giving me a chance to learn by working with them. These sorrel souls had the audacity to challenge me, the courage to care, and always the emotional sinew to say yes. And always a forgiving and compassionate heart.

I would also like to express my appreciation and gratitude to the colleagues who helped me to overcome and prevail. To Dr. Nancy Golden, who helped us to cast the first mold of the school improvement model (SIM) contained herein. Dr. Golden is easily the hardest working and most focused person I know, and she is the one who really created the SIM track and inspired in me the passion and hope to continue. And also to Dr. Pat Schmuck, who is so much more than my friend, my teacher, and my mentor. She is someone who writes with the same ease and grace that is used to create rainbows and clouds. Pat's example and high standards sometimes motivated me, but often her caring expectations were at once both intimidating and motivating.

Thanks to my friends and colleagues in Albany and North Clackamas who were a source of inspiration and support. To Dawn and Peter Tarzian, who taught me courageous honesty, I am deeply indebted. To Forrest and Shelly Reid, who walked by my side during the hard times, and to Jim and Garyann Linhart, who provided the kind of support that goes far beyond friendship. In fact, Jim provided the inspiration for chapter 8. You will notice reference in that chapter to his personal model for balance. To Albany leaders Martin Meyer, Erin Prince, Al Beltram, Dr. Janice Link Jobe, Jay Thompson, Pat Monson, Maria Delapoer, Doug Grimious, and Beth

Madison, who came to school early, stayed late, loved big, and taught me much about leadership in a standards-based school. To a giant of men, Ben Schellenburg, who taught me what I know about school district leadership, and to Dr. Terry Cassidy, who taught me how to align curriculum, measure success, remember names, and laugh at myself.

I am deeply saddened to report that Jim Linhart was lost to us in November 2001. I lost a dear friend and Albany lost a faithful servant. Jim became like a spiritual father to me as I struggled to recover from my stroke and to reshape a positive direction out of the job loss chaos.

I stepped down from my superintendent's position in Albany, and health was a contributing factor. When I left, the district had met or exceeded all goals. I enjoyed my years serving the community. The lessons that I learned and the memories that remain grow increasingly stronger each day. I would like to mention several people who contributed to my growth and good memories beyond those already mentioned: Kathryn Hedrick, Duane Barrett, Marcia Swanson, Ellen Carlson, Kathy Alden, Wayne Goates, Diane Smith, Maggie Decker, Peter Troumba, Jerry Bennett, and hundreds of parents, community members, neighbors, and students, teachers and other staff. Kathryn Hedrick, Dr. Jan Link Jobe, Marcia Swanson, Ellen Carlson, and Diane Smith provided guidance as we developed the principal proficiencies discussed in chapter 3.

I save the best for last, my family. With deep gratitude, I thank you family because without your support this journey would never have been possible. To Jami and Rick McKinney, who came to me with encouragement, empathy, understanding, and love. Without them, I would not be in a position to be writing this acknowledgment now. Thank you, Jami and Rick. You will never know how much your understanding and compassion provided the lubrication for this project to continue. A special thanks to Jami and Barbara whom I see with love and wonder. And a heartfelt thank you to my sisters, Pat, Joan, and Jean, who traveled great distances to provide support, love, and sometimes a kick in the pants. With sincere thanks to my parents, Edward and Ann, who taught me the value of hard work, persistence, and compassion. With deepest gratitude to my mother whose significant language skills and a critical eye provided an approving hug and smile early on. And a thank you to my constant companion, Holly, who somehow knew just when to provide a soothing nudge or a pesky prank.

And to you Barbara, what can I say. The ways you have helped are beyond description. Dr. Barbara May, (my person) you have been extraordinary. Thank you! You are an accomplished author in your own right. And you used that talent to become my full-time mentor, editor, coach, teacher, and friend. You always somehow knew what would, and would not, motivate me. You continually portrayed courageous patience, pacing, and cheering, precociously procuring new ideas and incentives to intermittently keep me going.

And, of course, I owe my greatest debt of gratitude to the Lord. I pray that I will express my thanks by helping others to learn and grow.

I pray Lord, that you will bless my life, indeed.
And, expand my chance to serve and lead,
And that your hand will be with me,
And, that you will keep me from evil.
—Adapted from the Prayer of Jabez (I Chronicles 4:9)
New Living Translation (paraphrase)

And finally, thank you to my friends at Scarecrow Press—to Cindy Tursman, who exercised immense patience with this novice; to Amos Z. Gunian, whose guidance significantly contributed to the quality of this work; and to Jessica McCleary, who taught me the ropes with care and concern.

Chapter One

The Potential for Standards-Based Response to Bully-Based Reform

There is no shortcut to any place worth going.

—Ken Blanchard, *Words to Lead By* (videotape)

Prior to the launch of Sputnik, the culture in a traditional educational system in America was calm, secure, and seldom challenged. All of that changed during the 1990s, when the standards-based movement (SBM) generated rigid accountability measures that were new and extremely threatening to educators. The SBM is difficult to define because each region of the country seems to have its own variations. When I use the term in this book, however, I am referring to SBM as it is defined in Oregon.

THE STANDARDS-BASED SCHOOL DEFINED

Specifically, in Oregon each standards-based school (SBS) is expected to demonstrate high academic standards through the use of performance-based tests. In the SBM, student success is determined through performance-based assessments. In a traditional system, promotion or graduation is often based on seat time or the number of credits earned. Student success in an SBS is defined by measured academic achievement. When teachers in an SBS become clear on what they want students to know or do, they design the curricula down from the expected academic outcomes called standards.

The Difference between an SBS and a Traditional School

To discuss how the SBS is different from the typical (traditional) system, I will mention several of the key differences taken from my thirty-two years of experience in this field. As I review the major tenets of the two systems, it is amazing to me that the traditional approach was ever embraced.

Because teaching is a very autonomous endeavor, there is no universal description that adequately addresses all of the many teaching variations in the traditional system. Therefore, while describing the differences in the two systems, my comments will remain at the conceptual level.

In a traditional classroom, teachers typically teach until the students reach some arcane saturation point. In a traditional classroom, the content standards just seem to quietly and magically emerge as the course content unfolds. In an SBS, however, the academic content standards are made clear to students before instruction begins. Students must learn the content and then demonstrate mastery of the content standards before they move on. Clear academic expectations (i.e., standards) are important. In my experience, when standards are made clear to students, they find a way to reach them.

The students may not meet these extraordinarily high academic standards immediately, but they will meet them in time, especially once the barrier is broken.

Defining the Standards-Based School

In a standards-based school (SBS), it is common practice to make content standards clear to students before instruction begins rather than after. Essentially, then, two of the major differences between the traditional school and the SBS are: (1) the academic content standards are clearly defined and made known to students before instruction begins, and (2) student mastery is determined through performance-based assessments at a specified time. In my view, there are distinct instructional advantages to such a system. For example, when students understand what the standards are, they can take more responsibility for their own learning and for ultimately meeting the academic standard.

Talking about academic standards reminds me of a story about the power of barriers. For many years, running a track mile in less than four minutes was an incredible international mental barrier. Since the beginning of track history, running a mile in less than four minutes had never been accomplished, and it seemed impossible even to the world's greatest track athletes. Then in 1954, Roger Bannister broke the four-minute mile for the first time in history. When Bannister broke the time barrier, he also destroyed the mental barrier. Subsequently, two other athletes also ran below four minutes in the next few months. The point is that when human beings understand a barrier (standard) and believe it can be broken, the likelihood of success is greatly enhanced.

Other advantages to the SBS are as follows: Students can progress at their own rate and use learning styles that best match their individual needs. In classrooms where more learning than teaching occurs, teachers facilitate learning and therefore meet the individual needs of the students more successfully. Bruce Joyce once observed that "In more effective classrooms, teachers give students more responsibility for their own learning by becoming guides on the side rather than sages on the stage."[1]

WHY A DIFFERENT
APPROACH TO SBM IS NECESSARY

While the SBM has real merit, all too often the standards have been set by policymakers for political reasons, with little input from those responsible for implementing them; therefore, the standards are often too high or too numerous. Further, in some cases the test score required to meet the standard is set too high for many students and schools. The unrealistic rigor of this top-down system, coupled with reduced funding, makes the whole movement appear politically motivated.

Some educators suspiciously believe that the real goal is aimed at tarnishing the reputation of the public school system rather than serving to improve it, thereby increasing the likelihood of tuition tax wavers or vouchers. For example, the language in Oregon's reform law indicates that "Oregon students will be the best educated citizens in the nation by the year 2000, and a workforce equal to any one in the world by the year 2010."[2] That is a lofty goal given that it coincides with a reduction in revenue for education and the erosion of local control. If the standards were practical, believable, and fundable, the SBM would have real merit. There is a kind of push-pull going on, though, because the successful development of such a system is at odds with the resources available to get it up and running. Despite these constraints, the SBM does have the potential to work. The premise of this book, therefore, is that the SBM is a solid concept that has real potential, but there will need to be a change in how the SBM is approached.

Even before the *Nation at Risk* report, and as early as the 1960s, public education was on the defensive in America. Some have viewed the repeated attacks as unfounded and politically motivated. From the educator's perspective, David Berliner eloquently set the record straight in his book *The Manufactured Crisis*. His point is that educators become understandably sensitive to the constant jokes and wisecracks about the failure of the public school system in America.[3] All of these attacks seem to coincide with the expectation to develop higher academic standards. High expectations are coupled with reduced resources, and that is perceived to be unfair. These conditions unnerve a culture that is already defensive and maybe even somewhat defiant. These forces combine to resemble a schoolyard bully.

A point critical to my thinking is simply that these conditions create an environment that was and continues to be insecure. How decisions are made is critically important in a high-stakes culture that is defined by mistrust and insecurity. When people perceive that their personal or professional life will be directly affected by school-based decisions, they need to be involved in the decision-making process. What type of decision-making structure is viable in an insecure and mistrustful environment? In my view, fear, panic, and failure damage morale and contribute to burn-out, a condition which only serves to impede the progress of a high-performance school. Further, stress, insecurity, and poor self-confidence can and must be managed to improve school effectiveness. Is it really true that stress and insecurity can actually reduce the effectiveness of a school and increase burn-out? Yes, it can, according to experts. In her in-depth treatise on burnout, Christina Maslock states that stress leads to "emotional exhaustion" and then to burn-out. She strengthens her point when she says that insecurity or a lack of self-confidence is part of the profile of a person who is "bound for burn-out."[4]

Centralized vs. Decentralized Decision Making

It is very important for the effective leader to determine whether centralized or decentralized decision-making structure is the most appropriate way to proceed in an SBS. Centralized decision making errs on the side of too much control and too little respect for those who will need to implement and monitor the decision. In other words, you can't mandate what matters. The more threatening the change, the less you can force it! Decentralized decision making is not without its shortcomings either. In my experience, decentralized decision making errs on the side of too little uniformity and an expensive duplication of effort. In an SBS, the standards are the same for every child. Policymakers have wisely insisted that the standards will be the same for all children even though they come to the public school with differences of race, ethnicity, religion, gender, ability level, and affluence. The competitive nature of life in a global society requires that all children need to meet high academic standards. All families should rightly insist on equity of opportunity (see chapter 2).

Both approaches to decision making have their advantages and disadvantages. While both the top-down and bottom-up strategies have probably always been necessary, the SBS is different in that high-stakes decision making requires the involvement of the people who will be directly affected by the decision-making process. Participatory decision-making strategies must be used so that the weaknesses of the system are mitigated. The integrated decision-making model takes advantage of both top-down and bottom-up approaches. Let me underscore a critically important point: in an SBS, public skepticism about the quality of education, along with runaway insecurity and the need for community support and understanding, creates conditions whereby strategic effort is required to deepen trust, understanding, and support through participatory decision making. The integrated decision-making model integrates participatory decision making into the overall schema. Four central assumptions that serve as parameters for the integrated model are as follows:

- The runaway insecurity in an SBS requires participatory decision making.
- Equity of opportunity is critically important in a free land (see chapter 2).

- People who are affected by high-stakes decisions need to be involved in the decision-making process.
- The best decisions are made at the point closest to implementation (see chapter 4).

Bully-Based Forces Defined

Webster's defines a *bully* as a blustering browbeater. I call these forces *bully-based*, because the pressure seems to be superimposed (top-down) on the system from the politicians, who allocate inadequate funds to support the reform. In my view, the forces that combine to create the bully-based image are fourfold: (1) high standards, (2) top-down decision making, (3) declining resources, and (4) accountability measures where the standards are perceived to be too high and too numerous for many schools and students. Collectively, these forces have had a negative impact on the efficacy of the educators, as well as the viability of the concept. I was discussing this thought with a retiring teacher over the summer, and he noted that when he attended social events many years ago, he would always proudly announce that he was a teacher and then quietly wait for the acclaim. In more recent years, however, he is reluctant to even mention being in education.

I believe bully-based forces of the SBM must be mitigated before the school community will seriously embrace the transformational changes of the SBS.

It is significant to note that parents excitedly support the higher standards until their children fail to meet them. Without parental involvement and support, the SBM will be hard-pressed to survive community-based resistance. The concepts presented in this book address how SBM can be made successful. While many educators support the standards, they argue that they need more time to prepare the curriculum, grade papers, and learn how to set up a standards-based classroom. What follows are processes and strategies that can mitigate the effects of bully-based reform and address how SBM can be successful. That is not to suggest that the ideas I discuss are new; in fact, they are not new and are being shared as a systematic way to proceed. This book is not intended to be a passive experience. As you work your way through it, you will find it to be interactive, because the success strategies that appear later in the book build on the ones that come earlier. It is my hope that school superintendents, principals, and site-based leadership teams will find these concepts useful and may choose to apply the strategies as appropriate to streamline their work.

A NOTE ON PERSPECTIVE

To provide perspective, it must be noted that public education has made tremendous strides in the twentieth century. Because of these advances, the United States has become a world leader in the percentage of its children who attend school and the percentage who go on to college.

Credit these improvements to two important factors. First, Americans have been generous in their support of public schools through increased taxes and volunteering. Second, schools and education have changed as society has changed. These strengths also carry with them a challenge. Although schools must change, they must do so in ways that create trust and community support.

As I think about perspective, I feel compelled to mention the incredible tragedy of September 11, 2001, which occurred just as I am writing this chapter. The attack will undoubtedly be viewed as one of the worst, most inhumane, and cruel acts the world has ever witnessed. I also fear there will be a backlash for Americans of Middle Eastern descent. If recent history is an accurate predictor, this issue will (along with many other social issues) undoubtedly be turned over to the schools to solve. I doubt if this prediction will occur immediately but it will develop just the same, over many years. This significant and challenging cultural need, while extremely important, will only serve to confuse the purpose of school even further. The schools of America are ill-prepared to successfully provide the moral remedy for America.

Public Education Needs to Improve

Clearly, schools need to improve if our children are to remain successful in a brutally competitive international marketplace where intellectual capital is now as valuable as investment capital. In the SBS, simply trying harder will no longer be good enough, either for school personnel or students. For the first time, effort is not the issue. Student success, as measured by standards, is what is important. Further, I believe that the SBS remains this country's best chance of making the transformational changes in public education that are necessary. I predict that the SBM will succeed only if the leaders involve people and address the human dimension, which is central to the culture of a school. I believe it is sheer folly to try to bully adults in the schoolhouse to implement a system that they do not understand or support.

When higher expectations are imposed by top-down strategies, and simultaneously resources are reduced, it is no wonder that the accountability system is perceived to be unfair. Then, to impose that system on schools when they receive less fiscal support in inflation-controlled dollars than they received at least ten years ago (in Oregon), it becomes clear that schools need to become more accountable. The approximately $5 billion the state of Oregon, for example, spent on public schools in 2001–2002 is clearly a sobering sum of money. In that regard, I believe that schools need to be more accountable and will successfully do so if bottom-up decision making is used to address the human dimension, along with or slightly before, the productivity dimension. Below are some of the key obstacles that we need to overcome, along with axiomatic strategies that leaders (superintendents, principals, and leadership teams) can use to enhance their chances of success.

The Cost of Vague Standards

We need clear standards for schools because vague or undefined outcomes test the credibility of the reform. I will use Oregon's experience to underscore how high-stakes testing has served to intimidate students, teachers, and parents in the nation and in Oregon. During the 1999 academic year, a new state law required the superintendent of education in Oregon to issue report cards to every school and district during that academic year! Of course, there were concerns expressed at every turn. Teachers protested, arguing they did not have the training or time to set up adequate standards-based classrooms.

The business community retorted that a little competition would solve the problem, and some politicians viewed charter schools as the answer. Superintendents in Oregon took a different track and argued that tax reform and funding shortfalls made the report card requirements nothing more than another political mandate, so undervalued that it could not even get support for funding. They also expressed that requiring higher standards while reducing funding could destroy or damage a reform movement that was, at the time, already having a positive effect on student achievement. That point was frequently stated during my tenure on the steering committee of Oregon Association of School Executives (OASE) in the spring of 1999.

When the state of Oregon began to issue school and district report cards for the first time, panic and fear began to reign. As late as one month before the reports were to be released, schools in Oregon were still unclear as to the exact grading criteria that would be used to rate the schools. School officials did have some sketchy information that schools would be rated in the following three major areas: (1) academic achievement, (2) student behavior, and (3) school demographics; however, they did not know how the state superintendent would arrive at their score. They also knew that there would be an overall rating, on a five-point rating scale, running from excellent (A = 1) to unacceptable (F = 5).

The growing anxiety increased when the specific variables that would be used to calculate the ratings remained unspecified until just days before the report cards were finally released. To be fair, the unrealistic time line that was demanded by the state legislature forced the Oregon Department of Education to design the report card quickly. In Oregon, the State Board of Education wisely insisted that the department get input from the field. The input, while critically important, slowed the process, forcing the late schedule. In any case, schools still did not receive the expectations early enough for the staff, in most cases, to incorporate them into their school improvement plans.

Have you ever thought how it might feel to be personally graded by standards that are unclear? To that end, I would like to use the following metaphor as an example of how the unfair nature of such standards might stimulate resistance and feelings of antagonism. To get into a metaphorical mind-set, please imagine that you are interested in being remembered (after your passing) for achieving a high degree of success during your life. You assume that you can leave that epitaph by having a high degree of status when you pass away. Assuming that the accumulation of wealth is a widely accepted measure of status in the United States, you proceed with your goal. Using unclear standards to define your status could be like measuring your success in life with a pop quiz designed around expectations that were kept a secret until the very last minute. For example, what if you did not know until it was too late that your generosity, rather than your accumulation of wealth, measured your status? Those with the highest status in life would be the poorest (not the wealthiest) because they had generously given their wealth away. Somehow, the new expectation would probably seem unfair, and your family would feel antagonistic. In like fashion, educators were also antagonized by the secrecy of the standards for schools (up until just the last moment).

Nonetheless, the lack of clarity of precise expectations seemed ironic because in a standards-based system (where the student standards are very clear), the standards for schools were not clearly pronounced until after all school improvement plans had been developed. In other words, schools were not given the chance to focus on the proper targets or standards because the grading criteria were unknown until the very last moment. Again, in fairness, the grading criteria were not actually being kept secret per se, but there was a perception of secrecy. Of particular concern, were:

- The type and date of the achievement data that was going to be used
- How academic achievement would be measured in schools with a high number of at-risk students
- The consequences, if any, of receiving a school or district rating of unacceptable (F)

As an advisor to the state school board from 1997 to 1999, I constantly heard principals and teachers request data that was longitudinal and current, expressing deep concern about what they believed was an unjust process to grade their school, a process that used archaic test data. This is only one example of how school and district report cards created an insecure environment. For example, many districts (including ours) defied the spirit of the new Oregon report card law and created their own reporting system with the intent of expanding on the positive measures that were reported locally. The Department of Education, equally concerned about how results would be received, did not discourage this strategy. As we were considering creating our district report card, I had several experiences that underscored how insecure the school culture was at the time. I remember expressing to our site councils (building-based leadership teams with legal authority in Oregon) that we would not "betray our dedicated teachers." To my surprise, I received a rather muted round of applause! I also remember expressing my favorable sentiment on developing our own reporting system to a principal who happened to be in one of our elementary schools with a high number of at-risk students. I was surprised at how strongly he voiced his support for the idea.

Schools with a high number of at-risk students have a more challenging task meeting standards than do schools that serve predominantly affluent students. This point is at the center of a contentious discussion being held between the schoolyard bullies and the education representatives; it makes the whole system seem inherently unfair. Simply said, the schoolyard bullies refuse to recognize that it takes more time and money to educate some students than it does others.

When children come to school unhealthy, undernourished, or abused, they cannot learn in the same way or at the same rate as students who do not have those disadvantages. It requires more resources to ensure academic and institutional success with children who come from disadvantaged home environments than it does with children who are advantaged. Who would have ever thought that children in America would have to choose between a teacher, a playground, or sufficient toilet paper?[5] Some schools have become more like surrogate homes (rather than schools) to address some of these challenging situations, and if it were possible to do both successfully, I would not quibble with the social-welfare focus. Other reputable educators have supported enhanced intimacy in the schoolhouse.

I once heard John Goodlad say that he admired high schools that were more like middle schools, and middle schools that were like elementary schools, and elementary schools that were more like an extended family. Indeed, if a school culture is like a family, then it is easy to understand why competition and other economic "survival of the fittest" principles of pure capitalism tend to produce deficiencies rather than capacities in schools. In light of these cultural challenges, it is imperative that leaders manage chronic stress and fear away from almost certain failure and toward confident success. To be successful in managing fear and stress, there are several axioms that are self-evident in nurturing a culture that is conducive to substantive change. I do not think we can change the world, but we can keep the world from changing us—and that is where the axioms come in.

Change Axioms for Standards-Based Reform Movement

Because educators and parents have been isolated and are correspondingly distrustful and threatened, they must be successfully recruited to participate (with sensitive and nurturing strategies) in the SBS, or this reform movement may fail to make the transformational differences necessary. It is important to understand that the SBM could not come at a worse time, unless the purpose of the reform is to generate resistance and alienate the public school. It is important to underscore that the SBS movement is coming at a time when the professional self-esteem of educators is at an all time low. I believe my own experience in Oregon (i.e., deputy superintendent for six years and superintendent for five years) typifies America's bully-based effort to change schools. Let me provide you with several examples using my leadership experience in Oregon. Change Axioms are truths that serve to guide the leader's direction. Axioms mitigate the damaging effects of the schoolyard bully and simultaneously shape the organization for positive change. Consider the following change axioms below. I will discuss each in more detail in this chapter.

- Change Axiom 1: School leaders must have the skills to be capacity-based.
- Change Axiom 2: Team training precedes decentralized decision making.
- Change Axiom 3: Team and community building come first.
- Change Axiom 4: The power of organizational success is through health and balance.
- Change Axiom 5: Alignment must come from within and without simultaneously.
- Change Axiom 6: There is power in moral purpose and positive discrimination.
- Change Axiom 7: Efficiency must precede effectiveness.

Change Axiom 1: School Leaders Must Have the Skills to Be Capacity-Based Capacity-based leaders focus on strengths rather than on weaknesses. If a leader can successfully motivate all of the high-performing individuals to perform at even higher levels then the organization will soar to even greater heights of success. It is an unwise investment of time to focus on the weaknesses of mediocre performers, helping them to excel in small incremental steps to an average performance level. "There is no alchemy for weaknesses. They can be removed but they cannot be transformed into strengths. The goal therefore is to manage weakness so the strengths can be free to develop and become so powerful they make the weaknesses irrelevant."[6] This change axiom is true for both schools and individuals.

Success Strategy 1: A Focus at the School Level   A strategy to get the whole school started using capacity-based leadership principles includes the following three-step process: (1) honor the past of the school, (2) challenge the present, and (3) envision the future. I will proceed to discuss each individually.

Step 1: Honor the past by looking for strengths and then systematically building on those strengths. Begin by interviewing each employee. Several questions that work well for the interview are as follows: What is it that we do better than anyone else here? What makes us champions (special)? What is it that we are especially proud of? What is it that makes this school a special place for students?

In addition, always work to create a participatory decision-making process. Bottom-up strategies are important because people who are affected by decisions in an SBS must be involved in the decision-making process because "you can't mandate what matters."[7] Substantive change cannot be top-down because the more complex and meaningful the change, the more it needs to rise and radiate out of the beliefs and skills of the individuals in the school. No one can expect to successfully dictate beliefs and new skill sets for someone else. Those who will be affected by the decision or change should be involved in the decision-making process. As an example, if there is going to be a change in the homework policy, the decision-making process should include teachers, parents, and students because all three groups will be directly involved in the implementation and evaluation of such a change.

Step 2: Challenge the present by asking questions such as "Why do we do this?" A good companion question is "If we weren't doing this already, would we begin now?" On occasion, educators do certain things just because it has always been done that way. It may not even make sense. A good example is the concept of social promotion. Why would a school agree to advance a student beyond his or her ability level, increasing the likelihood that the student will struggle or even fail in subsequent years? The SBS is increasingly calling the social promotion concept into question!

Step 3: Envision the future, but allow changes to take place naturally, over time. While the pace is sometimes important politically, it is important to be patient enough to allow the vision to arise from the core beliefs of the school community. Fullen makes a consequential point when he muses, "vision emerges from, more than precedes, action." [8] By honoring the history and culture of the school and asking fair, capacity-based questions, the vision is likely to radiate naturally from the core beliefs of the school community. When the vision grows out of the core beliefs of the people, then the vision enhances their understanding of and support for the change. Change can and should be built on the core values, beliefs, and strengths of the school community.

When one activates all three of these strategies simultaneously, the likelihood for transformational change is greatly increased.

Change Axiom 2: Team Training Precedes Decentralized Decision Making How decisions are made in a school, and how everyone works together, are critically important because teams enhance both productivity of and support for the school. To introduce this concept, I will focus on teamwork here, and then spend chapter 4 discussing integrated decision making. The elements of successful teamwork in a standards-based school system go beyond just working together. First, the leadership tends to rotate on a team or a site council (as they are called in Oregon), because the leadership tends to emerge based on who has the time and interest. In my experience, one should delegate based on interest or talent. In addition, the team must be given work that is both challenging and attainable. If the goals are set too low, it becomes a demeaning exercise. Occasionally, I have observed a district that was trying to do too much, too soon. I remember a district that attempted to move to performance-based graduation requirements before the community and staff were ready for the change, and the school community reacted with strong resistance. The district's public relations representative quipped, "We tried to go too far, too hard, too fast." In my opinion, this overreach caused a number of the board members in this Colorado district to be recalled.

More frequently, however, I have observed site councils taking on projects that are clearly beneath their talent or ability level. Two repeated examples are the annual attempt to re-stripe the high school parking lot and to purchase more playground equipment at elementary schools. Certainly, these efforts are noble and valuable, even important for safety (i.e., striping parking lots), but they distract from the mission of academic achievement. The American school cannot be successful reaching internationally competitive academic goals if we spend our time and money striping parking lots and assembling "big toys." We will never improve if these efforts are left solely to educators. Their teachers and some parents tell children that school is important. We need our communities to pull together around the core belief that academic achievement is as important as a championship basketball game. If school is important, then why do radio and television personalities go unchallenged as they often lament for our children when a summer or winter break is about to end? After spending months getting facilities, programs, and people ready and excited for the first day of school, I am always dismayed to hear a radio personality communicate that the fun is over because it's back to the books and the baloney of the classroom. It is even more devastating to hear a community leader tell a dedicated teacher, "Those that can do, and those that can't teach."

It is no wonder that our children appear confused when their ministers, parents, grandparents, neighbors, and older siblings communicate the importance of doing well in school and getting a good education, yet these values do not appear to be supported. Children and young adults in our schools can easily conclude that athletic prowess, trendy apparel, and owning a car, or at least having a job, is what really matters. Wouldn't it be wonderful if the U.S. Chamber of Commerce would communicate that for the good of international competition the chamber cannot support any business that promotes the hiring of school-age students during the academic year? I am sure that acceptable maximum work hours could be established, such as ten hours per week, two hours per day. The point is that our children respect us and pay more attention to what we do than what we say. "What you do speaks so loudly that I cannot hear what you say." The mixed messages children get from us are incredible, and it must be extremely confusing. If school is so important for success in life and we all want our children to be successful, then why should children be made to feel sad or nervous because school is about to begin? In my experience as a coach and a father, children generally feel excited about a new school year or sports season.

The point is that the natural inclination is for children to value school if only the school community would pull together for the sake of our children's future. The academic standards are very high so our effort must be community wide. As was noted earlier in this chapter, in Oregon the goal is to have students attain academic standards that are the highest in the nation by the year 2000 and second to no one in the world by the year 2010. The point is that we cannot achieve that lofty goal without the support of the whole school community.

Beyond being valued in the community, the work that site councils do must be both challenging and stretching. In addition, the team must decide how best to complete the work and also decide how the quality of the work should be measured. Ken Blanchard describes effective teamwork by using the metaphor "the way of the beaver, or taking control of the goal." Blanchard muses that when beavers build a dam, there is no single beaver giving orders, rather the beavers just begin working together to cooperatively finish the project. Each beaver just seems to know how best to assist in completing the task at hand.[9]

Success Strategy 2: The Power of Team Training   In my view, it is essential to provide training for the team and then invite the team to monitor its effectiveness over the course of the year. A team without training is a team without direction. One could begin by:

- Inviting each team to brainstorm the characteristics of an effective team
- Teaching the team brainstorming skills, team-building skills, consensus decision-making skills, and the art of balance and reflection
- Teaching consensus decision-making skills to the group by reaching consensus on the strongest characteristics of an effective team
- Having the team select a process observer whose job will be to provide periodic feedback to the team as measured against the effectiveness characteristics that have already been generated and posted in a public place like the staff lounge or media center or library

Note: See appendixes A and B for the team building and training material for brainstorming and consensus decision making.

Change Axiom 3: Team and Community Building Come First   A strategic effort should be made to enhance trust and support through community building and involvement. Capacity-based leaders understand that others give power to us, and that requires trust. Trust is critically important in a standards-based system because it is the lubrication that creates the capacity for change. I will discuss community building here and the communication component as part of decision making in chapter 4.

Success Strategy 3: The Power of Family   It is helpful to build a school or district culture where people feel valued and have a sense of belonging; therefore, this strategy is aimed at increasing the level of intimacy in medium- to large-sized districts or schools. I have always initiated this effort by comparing the district or school to a family; over time, I worked to recruit support for the concept. A successful, broad-based strategy to build support is as follows: begin by taking a photograph of every employee in the district and then create a slide show. Show the slides (or videotape) to the staff on a big screen at an annual staff event. I have always used elementary students to sing background songs that honor teaching like "Wind beneath My Wings" by Bette Midler. I now call the picture show "the family album" and show it annually, during our back-to-school rally. In addition, I make a point of welcoming new employees by welcoming them to the family. I do the same thing to welcome employees who have been on leave. Over the last five years I have been amazed at how frequently others have adopted the phrase "family." While this is a straightforward approach, the activity helped us to create a feeling of intimacy in a district with over one thousand full- and part-time employees. This same process could be adapted to a school as well.

Change Axiom 4: The Power of Organizational Success Is through Health, and Balance Is Essential   A discussion of this axiom begins with a focus on the power of balance and will conclude with a discussion of personal and organizational health in chapter 8. It is difficult to perform at high levels when one is sprinting at breakneck speed with little time for reflection. The SBS is not a revolution—it is an evolution. Transformational change takes time (eight to ten years) and we are only getting started. When we run at breakneck speed, solicitously attempting to improve the school, it has a least two consequences: it is not healthy to neglect everything in your life but work, and it communicates the misimpression that we are almost finished with the SBS.

It has been said that a well-known professional football coach told the following story to his players at critical times during the season. "When the sun comes up in the morning, the gazelle knows it must run faster than the fastest lion or it will be killed and eaten. The lion knows it must run faster than the slowest gazelle or it will starve and die. So no matter whether you are a gazelle or a lion, when the sun comes up in the morning, you better be running!"

Change will take time, maybe ten years, depending on the health of the organization and the curriculum alignment challenges that exist within the school or district. See chapters 6 and 7. Remember that "there is no shortcut to any place worth going." This type of substantive change will take self-discipline, policy-level support, and time. Even the concept of a marathon is too grandiose. It would be very difficult to maintain the necessary momentum while running a marathon over a ten-year period.

I think it is safe to assume that education will continue to attract good, solid people who are committed to children. I remember a time in the early 1970s, when I was a new, enthusiastic high school principal, and I would say, "We are ordinary people doing extraordinary things." At the time, I was working with a middle school principal who overheard me make the comment. Later that weekend, the principal and I had taken a drive to the Oregon coast to enjoy the beautiful fall. We were discussing the comment. After a number of minutes looking out over the ocean, he turned to me and said with anger in his voice and a tear in his eye, "I am an ordinary person, just trying to do the best job I can. I shouldn't have to be superhuman to do this work." Of course, he was right! School reform needs to function at the hands of people who are no more noble, intelligent, or hardworking than those who originally designed the common school system in America some one hundred years ago. We need to set a reasonable pace and conceive of this task as a marathon, not a sprint! Maybe it is more of a journey to be enjoyed, rather than a sprint to be endured. Educators have been frantically pursuing the standards as if they were running for their lives, causing considerable fatigue, burn-out, and cynicism.

Success Strategy 4: Leadership through Proximity (Closeness)   If balance is perceived as important, then leaders must systematically and proactively model a healthy and balanced lifestyle.

When I was a superintendent, I would visit each classroom two times every year (approximately nine hundred classrooms) and talk with teachers about how their students were doing relative to the standards. Two times a year, I would ask each teacher the same four questions. The first question was a warm up question:

- "How are your students doing academically?"
- Followed by a rather direct question, "How are your students doing as measured by the benchmark standards?"
- And then the question to assess the level of support they were getting from us, "What can we do to help you help your students reach the standards?"
- And then the final question to assess staff morale, "How is your stress level?"

In each and every instance, the staff communicated that they were experiencing acute levels of stress. At the time, it was hard for me to see that for the most part, our teachers did not have the tools or the time they needed to successfully create standards-based classrooms. That presumes we knew what that meant! Time, more than training, remains our biggest challenge. Performance-based assessments are very important, but they are not very pragmatic. Simply said, they require more time to design and rate than is realistically available, especially if interrater reliability is necessary. It is important to recognize that educators have a difficult time focusing on just a few tasks with the intent of doing them very well. Because the success of children is involved, educators unfortunately seem to try to do everything all at once. If teachers are going to do more of one thing, we need to give them permission to do less of something else. We need to help our schools and districts find a balance of mind, body, and soul.

I believe that each human being has a physical, spiritual, and emotional center. I once heard Ken Blanchard make the following comment: "We are not human beings having a spiritual experience. We are spiritual beings having a human experience." Every religion that I am aware of describes these domains in one form or another. To reach our peak performance we must maintain a healthy collective culture by, in part, finding balance in our individual lives.

Success Strategy 5: Your Health and Family Come First　Attempting to have people value healthy and balanced living is such a challenge in an organization focused on children that I recommend modeling the lifestyle. I suggest that you begin by making a list of things you can do for yourself that would help you be healthier. Select one and work on it for a month, then move to another for a month, then another, and so on. Invite others to follow suit and invite voluntary reports at meetings. Then invite principals to use the strategy with their staff as well.

Success Strategy 6: The Power of Humor   Consider hiring a humorist to address the staff at least annually. Serve only healthy refreshments. Use the opportunity to talk about the value of both exercise and healthy eating.

Success Strategy 7: What about a Health Walk?   Sponsor a health walk or run for the staff, before or after meetings, and give health-related rewards for participation.

Success Strategy 8: The Power of Setting Priorities   Consider what I call the "full plate" activity. The key point to this activity is a simple phrase to communicate, but a difficult one in which to motivate people to respond voluntarily and honestly. You are a dedicated and caring person who is already working too hard, and that is a bad example! The question is as follows: "If you are going to do more of one thing, you have to do less of something else. What can you comfortably take off your list?"

Ask principals to help you identify nonessential duties and stop doing them at all, or at least, do them less frequently. The criteria might be twofold: (1) how does it impact academic achievement of our students? (2) how does it align with or support the vision? I am always perplexed by the number of things that extremely well-educated, talented people expect of themselves. With few exceptions, the activities do not require a baccalaureate degree to complete. Consider asking the principals and district staff to replicate the activities for their staff and report back to the group what they are learning in the process. It is a valuable exercise because one can express a concern for hardworking individuals who are probably struggling with how, for the first time, to become a member of a high-performance team and also feel the economy of scale created by pulling together.

Often, the most valuable lesson learned is that, in some cases, more is not always better. I once heard Theodore Sizor say, "more is less."[10] It is extremely striking how difficult it is for individuals to take anything at all off the list. Even so, it is an important leadership function because it helps to teach the value of alignment and simultaneously create some economy of time and energy. Understand that this is a worthwhile activity, but pursue it with care. The roles people design for themselves are literally an extension of who they are as people. For some, this activity is like cutting off an arm, but do it anyway out of love.

I once shared this strategy with a group of district administrators and principals in an urban neighborhood in the Seattle area. When I completed describing the activity, the superintendent (a highly regarded friend of mine) then asked each individual to make a list of his or her most important functions as they relate to academic achievement. He asked each person to divide the list in two by making a horizontal line dividing the list based on just academic achievement. He reported that no one would henceforth be expected to do any task below the line. I observed that some of the participants were devastated by what was ostensibly an act of kindness, leadership, and caring.

Change Axiom 5: Alignment Must Come from within and without Simultaneously I will initiate our discussion of this axiom by discussing the power of recognition and then I will spend chapter 2 discussing vision building and alignment. It is important to develop intrinsic motivation in high-performance organizations. People are motivated by any number of incentives, including but not limited to, money, respect, enhanced authority, and recognition. High-performance schools have people who are self-starters and take the initiative. The key to developing that asset in the organization is to design intrinsic motivators. It has been said that Mohatma Ghandi said to his daughter, Indira Ghandi, "There are two kinds of people in the world, those who get things done, and those who take the credit. So I want you to always be in the first group, there is less competition." Recognition is a powerful motivator because it can help align the organization around the goals and vision. I like to call this concept "recognition density."

Success Strategy 9: Recognition Density Is an Inside-Out Alignment Strategy

1. Consider using the visioning techniques used in chapter 2 to identify the core beliefs of the community.
2. Set goals to achieve those core beliefs.
3. Design solid communication strategies to create an understanding of and deep support for academic achievement as measured by the goals.
4. Whenever possible, recognize students, staff, and parents for the achievement of the academic standards.
5. Try to find ways to recognize the work of students and staff. Recognition serves as a magnet to draw the organization toward the vision.

The kind of recognition we are speaking of is intrinsic in nature. Recognize students and staff for the achievement of the academic standards.

We called it Student and Staff All-Stars. This strategy is so powerful in making change that it is almost magical. In summary, this is a powerful three-step process:

Step 1: Publicly identify the community beliefs as important goals for the organization.

Step 2: Annually measure progress toward the goals and report the progress, then step aside.

Step 3: Allow the community to exert pressure to make the necessary changes to succeed in reaching the community's goals.

This three-step process requires administrators and others to step aside to insure that the recognition and affirmation fall on those who are successful in aligning the program to the organization's goals. This is a defining difference between a *leader* and a *manager*. *Leaders* use the core beliefs of the community in conjunction with recognition to energize the organization. *Managers* set goals, appoint committees, and delegate work to move forward.

Change Axiom 6: There Is Power in Moral Purpose and Positive Discrimination   The kinetic energy that erupts by putting children first (positive discrimination) is very powerful. We'll discuss the student-centered focus here, and follow it with a discussion of moral purpose in chapter 5. Educators often say that "everything we do in this school is for kids." With all due respect, I have observed that it is almost never true, especially in the most important areas. Take the school calendar for instance. Almost every district or school uses some type of process to surface community input on the annual school calendar. In the final analysis, vacation schedules, childcare issues, and administrative convenience are some of the pressures that actually drive the calendar. If that were not true, why then would we take three months off in the summer? As a superintendent and high school principal, I would always observe the expenditure of vast resources (when they were scarce to begin with) to start a new school year just to shut it all down as things were finally beginning to operate smoothly. For example, we would finally get the bus and food schedules running on time, the teachers assigned properly, and the union satisfied with the working conditions, and then we would shut the whole system down for three months just to start all over again the next fall. How do kids really fit into this picture? I seriously look for educators who really do discriminate and make their decisions based on what really is good for kids. When you find an organization that is organized more for kids than for adults, you will observe a high-performance school system. The following strategy will help to move a school to focus on students.

Success Strategy 10: The Power of One   I am reminded of a story about a boy who was born into poverty. The family was poor and hardworking, but not destitute. When he was three or so, his older sister died. When he was about middle school age, the boy's mother passed away. His father remarried, but not for love. The boy was becoming rowdy at school, getting in fights, skipping school, defying school officials, and generally practicing the at-risk behaviors that lead to school failure. The very next fall, a new young teacher expressed her belief in the boy and began to teach him to read. As he began to read, his confidence began to grow, and he quickly began to read everything he could get his hands on. He became a voracious reader. In short order, he began to believe in himself to such a strong degree that others did also. The level of community belief grew to such a degree that in 1860 the people elected this boy president of the United States. This story is about what miracles are possible when we believe in children. In this story, the child was Abraham Lincoln, but it could be any child in America.

What follows is a strategy to demonstrate the power of discriminating in favor of kids. What could happen if every adult in every school, from the custodian to the PTA president, decided to believe in a child who could not get that type of support from anyone else? Literally hundreds of children would feel loved and valued and possibly begin to experience success like the boy in the story. Through the "power of one" strategy, the school community could be taught how to put children first and begin to discriminate in favor of kids!

Change Axiom 7: Efficiency Must Precede Effectiveness   While the work that we do as educators is extremely noble and important, it must be understood that we cannot take ourselves too seriously. The stress of a standards-based system must be addressed by creating a workplace that is participatory, fun, and rewarding. The purpose is to create satisfaction in the workplace because it stimulates hard work, strong relationships, and higher academic achievement.

The nuts-and-bolts concept involves the basic structures of the SBS. Here, I will introduce the concept and several of the basics and spend chapter 6 discussing seven more nuts and bolts. If the school is not running smoothly (efficiently), then major changes, even for the positive (effectiveness), often flounder.

Success Strategy 11: The Power of Fun in the Workplace I recommend that each school develop a humor committee. Everyone should expect to experience a loud belly laugh each day as an official function of the humor committee. The humor committee should be charged with orchestrating a humorous or fun agenda item for each school day. It is important that the quality of life in the workplace be wholesome, supportive, positive, and fun.

SUMMARY

The relatively calm and secure culture of the traditional school changed during the 1990s in America because the standards-based reform movement (SBM) generated rigid accountability measures that were new and extremely threatening to educators. The standards-based school (SBS) is different from the traditional classroom in two ways: (1) the academic content standards are clear to students before instruction begins, and (2) student mastery of the content standards is determined through performance-based assessments. Students can progress at their own rate and use learning styles that match their needs as individuals. If the expectations are clear, teachers can more readily give students more responsibility for their own education.

For the last thirty years, public education in America has been under attack. These attacks seemed to coincide with the standards movement, which was superimposed on schools in a top-down fashion. These conditions unnerved a culture in public schools that was already defensive and even defiant. The forces were perceived as negative (called schoolyard bully). The forces that combined to create the bully-based image are (1) the high standards, (2) declining resources to put the changes in place, and (3) an accountability system where the standards are perceived to be too high and too numerous. The bully-based forces must be mitigated to insure the success of a good and necessary reform agenda. Most educators support the standards, but feel that the resources to make the needed changes are too limited. Clearly, schools need to improve if our children are to remain successful in a brutally competitive international marketplace where intellectual capital is now as valuable as investment capital. Public education has made tremendous strides in the last century, and America is now a world leader in the percentage of its children who attend school and go on to college. Even so, simply trying harder is not good enough, either for students or staff. Student success as measured by the standards, rather than effort, is what counts. It is important to note that the SBM remains this country's best chance of making the transformational changes to public education that are necessary.

It is sheer folly to try to bully the adults in the schoolhouse by imposing higher standards with fewer resources. The SBM will succeed only if the leaders address the human dimension. Below are some of the key axiomatic strategies that can assist leaders:

- Change Axiom 1: School leaders must have the skills to be capacity-based.
- Change Axiom 2: Team training precedes decentralized decision making.
- Change Axiom 3: Building community and teamwork comes first.
- Change Axiom 4: The power of organizational success is through health and balance.
- Change Axiom 5: Alignment must come from within and without simultaneously.
- Change Axiom 6: There is power in moral purpose and positive discrimination.
- Change Axiom 7: Efficiency must precede effectiveness.

The lack of clarity about what schools must do to meet the standards has caused frustration and panic, while negatively affecting the credibility of the SBM. Not all students come to school ready to learn. Schools with a high number of at-risk students have a more challenging task meeting standards than schools that serve children who are predominantly affluent. The fact that it takes more time and resources to educate some students than others is not recognized by the schoolyard bullies and remains a serious point of contention. Pressure tactics of the schoolyard bullies cause fear, panic, and failure, which damage morale and impede the progress of a high-performance school.

NOTES

1. Bruce Joyce, "Peer Coaching" (paper presented at the annual meeting of the Washington Association for Curriculum Development, Spokane, Wash., June 1972).

2. House Bill 2991, Oregon Legislature, June 1972.

3. David Berliner, *The Management Crisis* (Reading, Mass.: Addison-Wesley, 1995).

4. Christina Maslock, *Burn-Out: The Cost of Caring* (New York: Prentice Hall, 1982), 63.

5. Jonathan Kozol, *Savage Inequalities* (New York: Crown, 1992), 79.

6. Donald O. Clifton and Paula Nelson, *Soar with Your Strengths* (New York: Bantam Doubleday Dell, 1992), 73.

7. Michael Fullen, *Change Forces* (New York: The Falmer Press, 1993), 37.

8. Fullen, *Change Forces*, 28.

9. Ken Blanchard and Sheldon Bowles, *Gung Ho: Turn On the People in Any Organization* (New York: William Morrow, 1997), 83–93.

10. Theodore Sizor, "The American High School as a Compromise" (paper presented for the Institute for the Development of Educational Ideas, San Diego, 1971).

Chapter Two

Leading the Emotional Soul: The Secret of Capacity-Based Leadership

Success is never final. Failure is never fatal. It is courage that counts.

—Winston Churchill

Recent history suggests that adapting to the environment is an important trademark of a high-performance organization. Canter describes how vitally important it is for organizations to respond to their environment. Her book *When Giants Dare to Dance* describes the phenomena of large organizations needing to respond quickly and accurately to an environment that is changing at hyper-speed rates.[1]

Organizations need to have a clear sense of direction. This is another relatively new concept. In earlier years when the world was perceived to be stable, organizations attempted to remain calm, reliable, and predictable because their purpose seemed obvious, especially in a world that seemed unchanging and quite steady. The desire for stability has long since passed because all organizations, both public and private, are now expected to successfully adapt to hyper-speed changes in their environment, while still providing quality products and competitive results. Because the information age is defined by change, vision is more important in today's changing environment than ever before. Because organizations are forced to constantly change, a clear focus or vision is more significant today than ever.

In a school environment that is constantly rankled by the rumbling and racing to change, principals and superintendents are expected to create high-performance learning teams that share a commitment to a common purpose. To make matters even more challenging, schools and districts alike have become increasingly more democratic, where the expectation is that decision making is laissez-faire (decentralized and diffuse). While site-based governance is the norm in public schools, it also creates a tension between decentralized decision making and shared vision. In other words, in a standards-based system, the decentralized structure (bottom-up) is preferred because it empowers people who are feeling threatened to create their own destiny. Challenging or not, schools are compelled to become high-performance work organizations. Therefore, the tension between decentralized decision making and shared vision is a perplexing dilemma. Nonetheless, it is a powerful opportunity for educational leaders. The key is to ensure that each school owns and shares the mission of academic achievement. Once that is achieved, the school can determine how best to get there. The challenge is to create high-performance learning teams by working through people, and that thought brings me to a fundamental tenet. Power is not in position, but in relationships. Consequently, relationship building is a foundational skill upon which the SBS must be built. The relationship proficiency for leaders is defined and described in chapter 3.

THE POWER OF COMMON FOCUS AND VISION—TOUGH LOVE MUST COME FIRST

In my experience, the community, family, and government are doing less and less for children, while schools are expected to do more and more. Experience has taught us that it is less expensive and more productive to intervene early in a student's learning. If students are not ready to learn when they enter school, interventions are extremely expensive and much less effective. As I said in chapter 1, children who are unhealthy, poorly nourished, or abused cannot be expected to meet high academic standards in the same way or at the same rate as students who come to school ready to learn. It is clear that public policy must address this issue if all children are expected to have an equal chance to meet high academic standards. One of the richest countries in the world should be able to establish the public policy to resolve this challenge. The children cannot postpone the maturation process, therefore thousands of children enter school annually unprepared to learn. Consequently, out of a sense of compassion and unconditional love, educators organize the caring forces of education to intervene as a social service agency rather than a school. While this intervention is undoubtedly necessary, the school has not been designed to provide social services. The school, then, is distracted from its primary mission because social service support is well beyond the ability and resource base of the school. When schools focus on something other than academic achievement, they become less effective academically. I would like to underscore this point by sharing an experience that I found particularly poignant.

Without Vision the School Is Lost

When I was a superintendent, one of our schools was a low socioeconomic school (SES) that from time to time became confused about its academic focus. This elementary school had the propensity to shift from an academic focus to a social focus with regularity. This particular school had a clothes closet, which symbolized for me the shift in the purpose of the school from academic achievement to social support. It is important to add that schools serving poor neighborhoods are often shamed (by people in the community and the system as a whole) into becoming surrogate homes, with the primary goal of providing social support rather than basic academic skills. Everyone seems to understand that children who are not ready to learn when they come to school require more time and money than those children who do come to school ready to learn.

In the meantime, the students in this principal's school were so academically deficient, we had been notified that without significant academic gains, the school was in jeopardy of losing its Title I funding. As I recall, the fiscal impact was significant, maybe several hundred thousand dollars. Title I funds are additional resources that are available from the federal government through the state of Oregon. The federal government awards money (to teach basic skills) to high poverty schools that qualify through having high free and reduced lunch counts, high mobility, and poor attendance rates. After discussing the consequences of losing the federal money for reading and math, the principal was visibly upset. With a tremor in her voice and a tear in her eye, she observed, "We will have to become either a social service agency or a school, but we cannot do both." This precept is a powerful moral dilemma for the caring educators who face these choices. For example, if schools provide the social service support obviously needed, then the school will be distracted from its academic responsibilities and, in most cases, fewer of the students in the school will master the basic skills. This creates another cycle of poverty for future teachers and social service agencies to address. If, on the other hand, the school attempts to focus on academics when the students are not ready to learn, then the success rate is reduced as well. In either case, children who come from poverty do not have an equitable chance to experience academic success. With these grim choices in mind, educators often argue, "We need to feed, clothe, and support the child first, because he or she won't learn until those basic needs are met anyway!" The point is devilishly difficult to argue with. You will remember that Abraham Maslow's hierarchy of needs puts basic nutrition as a very high priority. One would think that an adequate and basic nutrition should be given a higher priority on any hierarchy of needs than basic academic skills.

So it is with great energy and unconditional love that the staff in the school collected the clothes, organized them by size and fashion, and proudly made them available to the children who were in need. Those children who needed a coat or mittens as winter quickly approached were encouraged to go to the clothes closet and simply pick out what they needed. While this type of support is clearly necessary and noble, it is consuming resources that schools need to use to meet high academic standards. The point is that it is becoming increasingly clearer that schools cannot simultaneously create a high-performance school (where students reach high academic standards) while simultaneously running a social service support system using resources meant for books and instruction. The choice is a perplexing moral dilemma for educators. But the simple fact is clear: educators do not have the training or resources to provide both.

In America, children are the largest cohort group living in poverty. According to the United Nations, there are 828 million people in the world living in hunger. Deplorably, a disproportionate number of people living in poverty are children. The United States is shamefully similar. In America, one of the most opulent, food rich nations in the world, 29 percent of our children are living in poverty.[2] This point is important because more and more children are living in poverty, and children who come from poverty have a more difficult time meeting high academic standards. In other words, children who come to school undernourished or hungry cannot be expected to learn in the same way or at the same rate as students who come to school ready to learn. It is critically important that students function at grade level as early as grade three, or their chances of success in school are significantly diminished. I recently heard Bill Blocker quote Richard Slavens when he said, "Students who do not read at grade level by the third grade are unlikely to graduate from high school."[3] Therefore, interventions need to begin early.

In my experience, basic math skills need to be added to reading as these are the two subjects that are the most difficult for students to master and for teachers to teach. I believe it is important to emphasize that students need to master the basic skills in reading and math by the end of grade three or they have a significantly diminished chance of being successful through high school. This is the crux of a major public policy debate that could frame the context for America's survival as a nation and culture. This issue is one of the defining challenges that face this republic. As de Tocqueville once instructed, "It cannot be doubted that in the United States the instruction of the people powerfully contributes to the support of the democratic republic; and such, must always be the case . . . where the instruction enlightens the understanding not separated from the moral education which amends the heart."[4]

America's diversity has historically been a powerful strength because the public school system has served to assimilate all children into a single yet diverse culture. The collective culture that has emerged is more powerful than any individual culture because of the beliefs, values, and basic skills that everyone, in a relatively equitable way, learns at school. Almost all Americans have shared this common experience. Therefore, America has been able to harness the power of a diverse culture by maintaining the unique qualities of each ethnic group by building on the group's strengths. Our history as a republic suggests that this lofty goal was attained with much pain and sacrifice by a variety of ethnocentric groups. We need to take the steps necessary to insure that our republic is not forced to repeat this cycle of brutality and belligerence.

I am trying to underscore the point that if this fundamental equity question is not resolved, then two school systems could well emerge; one school system for the rich and another one for everybody else. Kozol truculently portrayed the resource gap when he wrote that "One would never have thought that children in America would ever have to choose between a teacher or a playground or sufficient toilet paper. Like grain in a time of famine, the immense resources which this nation does in fact possess go not to the child with the greatest need but to the child of the highest bidder—the child of parents who, more frequently than not, have enjoyed the same abundance when they were school children."[5] The consequences of destroying the great middle class in America should be obvious to all, but these deeply knotty issues of equitable educational opportunity seem to languish as if the public school system will come to the rescue. We insanely expect the school to simultaneously and miraculously make transformational changes to the whole educational program, while affably putting high academic achievement within the grasp of each American child. The hope is grandiose and well meaning, but entirely unattainable given current funding levels, knowledge, and skills. The goal of having every child reach high academic standards will not happen if it is left to only the educators and the politicians.

My statements are not intended to suggest that educational equity of opportunity is not important, but rather to define for policymakers what is possible by clearly articulating the limits of the educational system. The limits of the system cannot be stated with more elegance and grit than by the principal who knew that the school would loose its funding if the site council didn't focus on academic achievement when she said, "I feel guilty to say so, but we cannot be both a school and a family, so we must be a school first." Today's academic standards are so high that schools need to focus on academic achievement, or they will fail to meet them. Therefore, let me be clear, equity of opportunity is beyond just important! I believe it is central to America's survival as a great and exalted republic. The issue of equity of educational opportunity tugs at the very fabric of the ideals personified by our leaders as most sacred. President Lincoln underscored the point of equity of opportunity in his now putative Gettysburg Address which was, at the time, received more as a prayer (about the soldiers who died on the battlefield) than a political address. The spectators were assembled on the Gettysburg battlefield where Lincoln intended to revere the brave men "living and dead, who hallowed that sacred ground . . . in their deathly fight for freedom," when he said, "Four score and seven years ago, our forefathers brought forth on this continent a new nation conceived in liberty and dedicated to the proposition that all men are created equal. Now we are engaged in a great civil war testing whether that nation or any nation so conceived and so dedicated can long endure." President Lincoln took this somber time to underscore that equity of opportunity is not optional in a nation so conceived and so consecrated. In my view, there is no choice but to ensure that all children are given equity of opportunity to master the basic academic standards and therefore break the destructive cycle of poverty and dependency. To do less is un-American!

The principal who knew that her school had to be a school first had real social needs. Of 177 elementary schools in Oregon, it was seventy-seventh from the bottom, as measured by SES. At last check, the school had made good choices, focused on academic achievement, selected a new principal and had also retained Title I money. There is no choice but to insure that these poor children master the basic academic standards and therefore break the destructive cycle of poverty that creates this hostile condition in the first place.

What is true is that the academic standards in the SBM are so high that schools need to either focus on the standards or they will fail to meet them. The point is clear; schools must persistently develop a strong single-minded focus on the vision of high academic standards or their students will fail to meet them. Decentralized decision making is a powerful vehicle if there is a *school system* with a shared sense of academic focus, rather than a *system of schools* each with a unique purpose and direction.

As the role of the family, community, and church seems to erode further year after year, I do worry about the need to educate the whole child. In a culturally diverse democracy, where basic academic skills should go beyond reading, writing, and math to include citizenship, respect, service, and concern for the common good, schools will need to find a way to strike the balance between the acquisition of basic academic skills and the attainment of human decency that promotes the common good above self. The issues of moral purpose and character education will be discussed in chapter 5.

These issues of poverty need to be resolved at the public policy level. If the schoolyard bullies do not recognize that some students require more resources, time, and unconditional love to succeed in the SBS, the consequence will be that some students will be condemned to academic failure, simply because of their economic background. Public policy must change or it is increasingly likely that these children will be condemned to repeat the same cycle of poverty as their parents. If the policymakers continue to fail to recognize that position, the credibility of the whole standards movement will fall into question and likely fail. I fully recognize that these are strong words, and my words might put the credibility of my thinking in jeopardy. Nonetheless, it remains the cornerstone of school-based resistance to bully-based reform. Schools with proper resources have the capacity to develop and attain a vision that successfully addresses the standards for all students. Every child in America should have an equitable chance to succeed both in school and in a world that is increasingly calling for well-educated knowledge workers.

The Importance of Vision

The Bible gets quickly to the point regarding vision: "Where there is no vision, the people perish."[6] Unfortunately, it is quite possible, even probable, that some educators will be solicitously seduced into committing to a nonacademic purpose. The critical point I am making is that there is much to obscure the educator's focus (more than just poverty), and there are consequences for that lack of direction in an SBS. Simply said, when schools do not focus on the academic standards, their students fail to meet them. If educators do not remain disciplined, they lose their sense of purpose and direction. In my experience, the most common call for help is a plea from teachers and site councils to help them in setting and focusing on priorities. When I ask what I can do to help, the most common response is, "Just help us to focus because we are trying to do too much." As has been noted, this is a very important issue because experts suggest that students who do not master the academic basics early in their schooling years have a significantly diminished chance of graduating from high school.

Schools are easily seduced into committing to goals beyond their scope. It is unusually painful for educators to admit that if their school doesn't focus on the content standards, their children tend to experience less success in meeting them. We have come to believe we can do it all, and frankly that was probably true prior to the SBS. At that time, the academic expectations were lower, and there were no high-stakes tests to hold students and schools accountable. It is true that the standards in reading and math are so high that many schools and children will not reach them, especially if school leaders or leadership teams do not give the staff and students the opportunity to focus on the school's vision of academic excellence. Let it be clearly understood that, for this author, the issue is not a lack of commitment, or the work ethic of the teacher, or the questionable ability of the students, but rather the issues are limited resources, time, training, and sometimes a lack of visionary leadership.

The point is that to be effective in meeting these high academic standards, a school has to have a clear sense of purpose that grows out of the core beliefs of the people. It is important, then, that the people believe in themselves. It is for that reason that a leader must be a dealer in hope. In a deficiency-based culture, "some will always ask if the people believe in the leader"; in a capacity-based culture, the proper question is, "Does the leader believe in the people?"[7] It is easy for all of us to build artificial limits. As John Gardner taught in his book *Self-Renewal*, "We build our own prisons and serve as our own jail-keepers."[8] Deep ownership comes from being involved in vision-building processes. Realizing that the vision is an extension of the core or beliefs of the individual is critical. The school's vision helps to create that clear purpose and thus direction. If clear purpose (vision) exists, educators can spontaneously align their program strengths and beliefs with the vision. When the staff owns the vision, a significant precondition for success has been met. This is another one of the defining differences between *leaders* and *managers*. Leaders establish a compelling, collective vision, then step back and let the power of the human spirit move the school forward. Managers, on the other hand, decide what to do, develop committees, and delegate responsibilities. The leadership proficiency of visioning will be addressed in the next chapter.

Steven Covey tells the following story that helps to underscore the necessity of having a clear and common sense of purpose. According to Covey, a world-class team was drawn together to cut down trees. It was notable that this team was exceptional at cutting down trees. Now this team had the strongest, best-trained, and motivated group of lumberjacks that had ever been drawn together. In addition, their leaders had retained the most advanced and sharpest tree-cutting equipment that was available anywhere in the world. This tree-cutting team was proceeding to rampage through the forest, cutting more trees per day than any one else in history. Unfortunately, when the leader scaled the tallest tree in the area to assess their work (progress on their vision), he was dismayed to discover that they had been cutting trees in the wrong forest.[9] This story amplifies the point that the vision must be shared and owned because if the vision is unclear, individuals will not be able to align their work to support the vision. And like the lumberjacks who are felling trees in the wrong forest, the activities of the people become isolated from the vision. It has been my experience that when individuals understand where the school is going and why, they seek to align their personal and program goals to those of the school's vision. Leaders who create a shared sense of purpose energize the emotions of the school community and harness the power of the human spirit.

Those who cannot create a shared vision are compelled to manage the power of the human will. Managers who do not create organizational clarity are forced to manage a school of overworked adults who have an "add-on mentality." In other words, no matter how noble the vision is, if the vision is not owned by the people, the vision can feel superimposed and therefore an unnatural and unwelcome extension of the beliefs and values of the adults in the school. The culture of a school is such that each task is an extension of a personal agenda or belief of the people. Because resources are scarce and the people do not own the visioning activity, it becomes layered on top of the strongly held preexisting activities of each individual. A school is a complex mix of personalities, core beliefs, values, and needs, and without clear direction, the school can become riddled with chaos. Schools without clear direction experience a kind of organizational vertigo. As the Cheshire Cat said in *Alice in Wonderland*, "If you don't know where you are going, any road will get you there."[10] The visioning process described here assumes that the environment inside the school is in chaos.

Mark Cain once observed, "There are those who travel, and those who are going somewhere. They are different, yet they are the same. The success has this over his rivals: he knows where he is going."[11]

THE POWER OF VISION AS AN EXPRESSION OF CORE BELIEFS

When I first began to think about the power of shared vision, it appeared to me as if vision and strategic planning should come before alignment and action. Now I realize that vision building must come later. As has been noted, I contend that ownership is critically important. Therefore, the vision of the school needs to come later because a viable vision must grow naturally out of the values and core beliefs of the school or district. It takes time and careful listening to allow the vision to emerge from, rather than precede, the core beliefs of the school.

Vision as a Moving Target

If a vision is that important, then why is it that so many schools appear to experience chaos because they don't seem to have a clear sense of purpose? This is a substantial question and there are at least two possible responses.

The first reason that shared sense of purpose is unusual in a school is that adults who work in schools are isolated from each other. This may well be the most serious challenge we face. Schools were designed like American factories. In 1911, Frederic Taylor unveiled the principles of scientific management that brought new ideas to American industry to increase efficiency and profits. The centerpiece was the assembly line. Like the assembly line, each classroom was intended to develop the child by specializing in a specific content area or grade level. Over the years, teachers became isolated from each other, and there was less and less of a connection between the individual parts, especially the curriculum. The human connections in a school are more difficult to see than the connections between manufactured products in a factory. To illustrate the point, the individual components that make up the automobile are tangible and therefore observable. The academic connections between grades or subjects are somewhat more obscure. The academic connections can and should be observable. The point is that educators have long been isolated from each other, and for that reason we do not automatically value working closely together as a team. Therefore schools are not necessarily structured for teamwork, nor does it seem familiar. As a result, teachers teach in a very private setting. I once heard a humorist quip that "Teaching is the second most private act that adults engage in, in America!" The isolation is poignant not only for teachers but also for principals, superintendents, and other educators.

The second reason that shared sense of purpose is unusual in a school is that the school community is covertly chaotic, the beliefs in the school are constantly changing and evolving. Therefore, the vision should be changing to reflect the differences as the school evolves through different stages of development. In many ways the vision must be like the phrase "ready, fire, aim!" The sequence of that phrase suggests that visioning is a fluid and dynamic process rather than a linear and sequential one. There is no perfect order! Even with a very clear sense of direction, a school is almost never perfectly on course. Because of the chaotic environment, the vision needs to be in a constant state of flux. That thought reminds me of a personal experience that illustrates the point that visioning requires hitting a moving target.

The personal experience is my attempt to keep our small sailboat precisely on an exact compass heading while at sea. As we sail up and down the West Coast, I observe that we are almost never precisely on course. For example, if the desired heading is 183 degrees south, the wave action on a small boat forces one to constantly correct the direction of the boat which, in turn, changes the compass reading from ten to fifteen degrees off course. Those adjustments to the waves cause the compass needle to swing radically from one side of the proper compass heading to the other. The net effect is that the boat is almost never on the precise compass heading because the person at the helm is constantly correcting for the action of the waves and the swing of the compass needle. Yet, the boat still arrives at the exact destination. How can a boat that is on course only a small percentage of the time still arrive at an exact location? It is, of course, because the direction of the boat is constantly being adjusted to the correct compass heading, like the course of a school adjusting to the vision. I believe that this sailing metaphor is comparable to a school in pursuit of its vision. Carl Schurtz underscores the point when observing, "Ideals are like stars, you will not succeed in reaching them with your hands. But like the seafaring person on the desert of waters, you use them as your guides and follow them until you reach your destiny." [12]

What Is Vision and How Is It Different from Mission?

I have frequently observed that *vision* and *mission* are used interchangeably. To avoid any confusion, I will define how the terms are used in this book. I define a *vision* as a description of the best that can be imagined in five years. In other words, the vision is a description of the ideal destination.

The historical use of the term *mission* has been military in nature. Given the military context, mission is used to clarify why we exist and how to get there. Therefore the route is used to get to the vision or destination.

The philosophy is a statement of shared beliefs or how we do things. In other words, the vision is the ideal destination, while the mission is why we exist and the route to take to get to the vision. In this model, the philosophy is used to create the vision.

The mission does not have the same allure as the vision. When vision is portrayed in literature it seems to generate a kind of mystical, even evocative, kind of discussion. Historians approach the visionary leader as if vision is a function of creative genius. The aura of something as mystical as vision seems out of reach for the ordinary person. I am not so sure it is all that alluring. One does not have to be omnipotent to crystallize a vision. Common people with good listening and empathy talents can, and do, galvanize the vision.

For example, I recall hearing President Kennedy's inaugural address when he presented his vision of putting a man on the moon by the end of the decade. At the time Kennedy gave the address, I doubt if he knew for sure whether the country had the will or the resources to pursue and attain the vision. Probable or not, that vision caught the imagination of the American people.

A quick review of history will reveal that the visioning strategy was more a function of good listening and common sense than creative genius. Clearly, President Kennedy was not an ordinary person. At the time, however, the American people were somewhat paranoid about the spread of Communism and the growing power of the USSR and the Communist bloc nations. The American people were concerned that the Soviet Union would catch up to us economically, militarily, and scientifically. The USSR surprisingly discovered the secret of the atomic bomb just four years after the end of World War II. It was portrayed by the Communist bloc nations as if it were a great victory for the Communist form of government. In that same year 1949, China, the most populated nation in the world, fell to Communism, bringing approximately two-thirds of the world's population under that form of government. In addition, Sputnik, the Soviet's basketball-size satellite, beat America's first satellite into orbit. The USSR also successfully sent the first man into space and brought him back to earth safely, beating the United States a second time. In the early 1960s, the American people were defensive and competitive, and they wanted to remain first in the world, especially in space.

Was Kennedy's vision a stroke of pure genius? Probably not, but it did suggest that he was listening carefully, and therefore he was able to reflect a vision that was valued by the American people. The vision enabled Kennedy to crystallize a lofty goal, while building on America's strengths and beliefs. When the people own the vision they will either find a way to reach it or make a way!

For example, the vision was anything but easy and attaining it certainly required extra effort. The Atlas rocket that made the first moon walk possible was not even conceived when Kennedy made his statement. After much research and testing, the new Atlas V rocket was ready. The rocket was easily the largest and most complex in the world, with its three stages and three million parts reaching skyward, higher than the Statue of Liberty, while having the capacity to travel 24,000 miles per hour.

Like many other visions, this project encountered serious setbacks requiring changes in the initial vision plus a "can-do attitude" to make a way for the United States to reach the vision. Sadly, during the first few seconds of the initial test flight, three of America's astronauts were burned to death while the rocket was still on the launching pad. Not to be deterred and with a good deal of grit, the NASA team completely retrofitted the Atlas rocket with fire-retardant materials. The new version of the Atlas V rocket successfully and safely delivered three astronauts to the surface of the moon and home again, on schedule and ahead of any other nation.

Arthur Blumberg and William Greenfield summarize by observing that vision is a kind of "moral imagination . . . the ability to see that the world need not remain the same—that it is possible for it to be otherwise, and to be better."[13] The vision reflects the character, values, and beliefs of the people and the leader.

The Attributes of Vision

In my experience one need not be omnipotent to crystallize a vision. If ordinary leaders listen and observe the culture and then use that information to frame a short vision statement that captures the imagination and creates drama, a motivating vision can be developed. Vision statements should be bold, and never wimpy—challenging, but possible. A vision for a school district would start with group development in one or more sessions and end with school board involvement. A formal process designed to surface the core beliefs is listed below. The characteristics of a vision statement are as follows:

- It is short.
- It creates drama.
- It captures the imagination.
- It is compelling.
- It is bold and never wimpy.
- It is challenging, but possible.

Success Strategy 12: Vision Building through Listening

Phase 1: Consensus on core values:

Step 1. Meet with a random selection of all of the stakeholders whom you need to involve. Although that group would be different in every culture, work with your strongest leadership group to select a diverse group that adequately represents your community (i.e., a stratified random sample). As a minimum, let me suggest that you consider the following groups:
- Community leaders including, but not limited to, key communicators and school ambassadors (defined as basic structures in chapter 11)
- Community leaders including, but not limited to, parent club leaders, business partner leaders, student leaders, leaders from the ministerial association, local police and youth correction representatives, youth club leaders, real estate brokers, Chamber of Commerce officials, fund-raising group leaders (United Way, Boys and Girls Club, Rotary, Kiwanis), and tax reform activists
- Staff leaders including certified, classified, and administrators (meet with principals and district staff as a group)
- School club leaders, coaching representatives, union leaders, site council leaders, and department heads or grade-level leaders, if you have them

Step 2. Submit all of the data collected from this process to the school board for their use in developing the vision statement. The data should come to the board in the form of core beliefs with several sample vision statements.

Vision Heuristic

Using the following word formula write a vision statement.

Directions:

Webster defines a heuristic as "something to help discover." To write the first draft of your vision statement, simply substitute the correct word or phrase into the following word formula.

Word formula:

Who _____ takes what action _____ in order to do what _____ based on what beliefs _____?

Who <u>East School</u> takes what action <u>uses high academic standards and community support</u> in order to do what <u>to insure that all students reach their potential</u> based on what beliefs <u>so all children will succeed because the whole community is their partner and support.</u>

Example:

East School uses high academic standards and community support to insure academic success for each student because children reach their potential when they feel support.

Sample statements but not necessarily models:

* "Pacific Northwest Bell is in business to serve the information movement needs of our customers and to serve related markets where our expertise and resources enable us to meet our fundamental objective of enhancing the return to our investors."
* Clackamas School District: "Education for tomorrow . . . today."
* Battleground School District: "To make the pursuit of educational excellence of paramount importance for parents, students, staff, and community."
* The Greater Albany Public Schools: "To ensure high academic success for all students by focusing on standards, promoting character development, retaining exceptional staff, emphasizing safety, and fostering community partnerships."

Success Strategy 13: Vision as a Vehicle of Direction   Use brainstorming and consensus decision-making techniques with all groups to complete the heuristic above. As you begin to develop a vision in an SBS, it is extremely important to have discussions that are carefully aimed at student achievement. From my experience, that is not a stretch because most agree that academic achievement is a central goal of a school.

Learner outcomes: To assist the stakeholders in maintaining a focus on what students should know or do, begin by creating community consensus on academic standards. The student will:

Step 1:   Brainstorm what the school or district does (action).
- Word
- Phrase
- Concept

Step 2:   Brainstorm what the action should generate in terms of student learning (outcome).
- Word
- Phrase

Step 3:   Brainstorm the beliefs that the work was based on.
- Concept

Step 4:   Putting it all together: Select the best work to create a sample vision statement. The results are actions that generate student outcomes based on what beliefs should be used by the site council or board as they articulate the vision statement.

Step 5:   Invite principals and other unit managers (food service, transportation) to replicate the process to create school and unit vision statements. Use this framework as is, or modify it as necessary.

Summary of Using Core Beliefs to Generate a Vision Statement

Step 1:   The student will be able to know or do (what learner outcome) because of (?).

Step 2:   Brainstorm what the school does to generate outcome.
Activity: Brainstorm the core beliefs regarding the inputs (what the school does to generate results) and the schooling process (inputs or what the school does to generate the outcomes).
- Word
- Phrase
- Concept

Step 3:   Pull it all together and reach consensus on the beliefs relative to the learner outcomes that have the highest priority. Keep the core beliefs separate for board use at a later date. Conclude the activity by appointing a committee to generate a sample vision statement to be drawn from the core beliefs. Allow the board to craft a vision statement from the core beliefs and the sample vision statements.

Step 4:   Create and implement a communication plan for the vision statement aimed at three outcomes:
  • Enhance the understanding of the SBS and the purpose of the vision statement.
  • Create an image of a high-performance school by focusing on what students and staff do well.
  • Recruit support for the vision of an SBS.

Step 5:   Invite principals and other unit managers to replicate the process to create building and unit vision statements.

Step 6:   Repeat an abbreviated process annually to allow for appropriate changes.

Example Vision Statements

• The student will be able to maximize his or her potential (outcome) because the staff is highly competent and caring (action).
• The student will be able to experience success in school (outcome) because the community is loving, businesses are supportive, and academic standards are high (action).

SUMMARY

It is only in recent history that adapting to the environment has become an important trademark of a high-performance organization. That organizations need to have a clear sense of direction is another relatively new concept. Vision is more important in today's changing environment than ever before. In an environment that is constantly changing, school leaders are expected to create high-performance learning teams who share a purpose or a common commitment. To make matters even more challenging, schools and districts have become more decentralized where decision making is almost laissez-faire.

The community, family, and government are doing less and less for children, while schools are expected to do more and more. Children who are unhealthy, poorly nourished, or abused cannot be expected to meet high academic standards in the same way or at the same rate as students who come to school ready to learn. It is less expensive and more productive to intervene early. Children who come from poverty do not have the same equity of opportunity as those children who come from affluence. The United States, one of the richest countries in the world, should be able to establish the public policy to resolve this challenge. If the United States fails to do so, the consequences are serious. America's diversity has historically been a powerful strength because the public school system has served to assimilate all children into a single culture. Therefore, America has been able to harness the power of a diverse culture. The fear is that if this fundamental equity question is not resolved, then two school systems could emerge: one school system for those perceived elite and another for everybody else. The consequences of destroying the great middle class in America should be obvious to all. These issues need to be resolved at the public policy level. If the schoolyard bullies do not recognize that some students require more time and resources to succeed in an SBS, some students will be condemned to failing to meet the standards, simply because of their economic background. Unfortunately, it is also possible that the children who experience school failure will be condemned to repeat the same cycle of poverty as their parents.

Schools are easily seduced into committing to goals beyond their scope. The academic standards are so high that if schools do not focus on them they will fail to meet them. The concern is not a work ethic issue, but rather one of limited resources, time, and training. To be effective, a school has to have a clear sense of purpose. Ownership comes from being involved in the vision-building process. The school's vision helps the school community to create that clear purpose and direction. When the people own the vision, a significant precondition for success has been met. Leaders establish a compelling vision that is owned by the people, then step back and allow the power of the human spirit to move the school. Because the vision needs to spring from the core beliefs of the people, it takes time up front to establish the involvement. As a result of the environment constantly changing, the school is almost never perfectly on course. The school community is complex and constantly changing, and the vision should also be changing or evolving. For this reason, leaders need to be able to tolerate ambiguity.

By definition, the vision is a description of the best that can be imagined in the future. The mission, on the other hand, is a military term that describes how the organization can get to the vision (i.e., the route to be taken). The vision seems illusive because it is often portrayed as mystical and even evocative. The skills to identify a vision are not mystical or even magical, but do require careful listening and well-organized processes. Therefore the vision is a powerful precondition for success.

NOTES

1. Rosabeth Canter Moss, *When Giants Dare to Dance* (New York: Simon and Schuster, 1989).

2. Deborah Watson, United Nations agencies document, *Mounting World Hunger.* http:/www.wswsw.org/article/1999/food [October 13, 2001].

3. Bill Blocker, *How to Get Children to Read* (paper presented at the Institute for the Development of Educational Activities, Harvey Mudd College, Claremont, Calif., July 9–14, 2000).

4. Alexis de Tocqueville, *A Democracy in America* (New York: Vintage Books Random House, 1835).

5. Jonathan Kozol, *Savage Inequalities* (New York: Crown Publishers, 1991), 79.

6. Prov. 28:18, *New Living Testament.*

7. John Gardner, "Self-Renewal" (paper presented at the Aspen Institute for Humanistic Studies, 1983), 9.

8. Gardner, "Self-Renewal," 2.

9. Stephen Covey, *The Seven Habits of Highly Effective People* (New York: Simon and Schuster, 1989), 101.

10. Lewis Carroll, *Alice in Wonderland* (New York: Gilbert H. McKibbin, 1899).

11. Wynn Davis, ed., *The Best of Success* (Lombard, Ill.: Celebrating Excellence, Inc., 1992).

12. Davis, *The Best of Success.*

13. Larry Lashaway, *Leading with Vision* (Eugene, Ore.: House of Educational Management, 1997), 8.

Chapter Three

The Changing Nature of Educational Leadership

Children are the gift we send to an era we will never know.

—Neil Postman, *The End of Education: Redefining the Value of School*

Public school education is being challenged by a variety of forces. During this time of accountability, uncertainty, and doubt, public education needs strong leadership. It is quite clear that public education is at the center of a volatile debate that is only likely to get worse. Public skepticism, rebuke, and scrutiny are likely to be constant companions of school leaders. Student performance is being portrayed as low and getting worse. Yet public schools are built on a foundation of tradition and recidivism. Many who observe the educational construct as a whole appear pessimistic about future attempts to revitalize what is considered to be an inflexible, unimaginative institution. This consideration is not new. In fact in the late 1960s Carl Rogers observed, "Can the system as a whole, the most traditional of our time . . . come to grips with the real problem of modern life? Or will it continue to be shackled by the retrogression, added to its own traditionalism?"[1] As a whole, schools have been difficult to change. In fact, most of the research on effective schools looks at the individual attributes of schooling rather than the school as a whole. John Goodlad, in his school reform primer observed that "There have been few attempts to study schools as total entities. . . . Researchers criticize schools but tend to study students, teachers, or methods of teaching."[2] While Goodlad addresses the lack of research on the school as a whole, and Rogers addresses the rigid nature of the educational culture, I believe the real key rests with the quality of leadership. Peter Drucker underscored the point when he noted, "In human affairs, the distance between the leader and the average is constant. If leadership performance is high, the average will go up. The effective executive knows that it is easier to raise the performance of the leader than it is to raise the performance of the whole mass."[3] If Drucker is correct, then it follows that the performance of the superintendent, principal, and site council is critically important to the success of the SBS. Therefore, we will focus on leadership in this chapter.

How do the best school leaders in the country successfully create a high-performance SBS? The answer ranges on a continuum from "we don't really know" to a barrage of cluttered and conflicting ideas and theories. It is really no different in the general area of leading and managing. The myriad of answers ranges from the bizarre to the sublime. "In 1975 there were two hundred books which were published on the subject of leading and managing. By 1997 that number had more than tripled. In fact, over the last twenty years authors have offered up over nine thousand models, systems approaches, and silver bullets."[4] It is easy to understand why there have been few clear and compelling leadership theories informing leaders and leadership teams in schools. The evolution of the high-stakes accountability of the SBS has made the crisis of viable leadership models in education a clear emergency.

To begin our study of educational leadership, I will overview some of the recent theories of leadership. I will do that to show how the theoretical framework presented in this chapter builds on previous work. Since the 1960s, I submit that the literature on leadership has fallen into three schools of thinking:

- School 1: Characteristics of leaders
- School 2: Behavioral patterns of leaders
- School 3: Beliefs of leaders

Drucker's work represents a widely circulated discussion of leadership, and in my view, it also represents school thinking about leadership that tends to focus on the characteristics of leaders. I will call this school of thinking school 1 because in my view Drucker's work generally precedes the others and tends to focus on the characteristics of effective leaders.

Douglas McGreggor developed an interesting and useful theory of management that he called theory x and theory y, which tends to focus on the second school of thinking (behavioral patterns of leaders). For example, theory *x* describes a type of leader who is monocratic and bureaucratic, while theory *y* describes a leader who is pluralistic and collegial. As has been noted, this research was different from Drucker's in that it represented a focus on what leaders did to achieve success rather than the characteristics of the people.[5]

An example of the third school of thinking (beliefs of leaders) is William Ouchi's brilliant characterization of leadership, which tends to emphasize what effective leaders believe, rather than who they are or what they do. In his book, *Theory Z*, Ouchi describes a leader who is very concerned for the welfare of the people who work within the organization.[6] I believe that more effective leaders secure their practice with beliefs, principles, and values. Thomas Sergiovanni underscored that point when he wrote, "Authentic leaders anchor their practice in ideas, values, and commitments, exhibit distinctive qualities of style and substance. And can be trusted to be morally diligent in advancing the enterprise they lead. . . . Authentic leaders, in other words, display their character . . . ground their practices in unique purposes and ideas and then act with courage and fortitude to advance those ideas."[7]

In more recent work, Steven Covey addresses the last two schools of thinking in his widely read books. Covey emphasizes behaviors of highly effective people (school 2).[8] His other book focused on the beliefs of leaders (school 3).[9]

If McGreggor's theory *x* and theory *y* are helpful in initiating the discussion of leadership, then the next step is to conceptualize the importance of blending efficiency with relational support to maximize success. Jack Welch (the highly esteemed CEO of General Electric) supported McGreggor's theory during an interview on *Sixty Minutes* when he told Lesley Stahl, "I kick butt and hug!" The definition of leadership seems to be evolving:

- From who leaders are (characteristics),
- To what they do (behaviors),
- To what leaders believe (beliefs and values).

In summary, I believe that the contemporary literature on leadership in schools is still in the process of evolving. This thinking is my attempt to begin to forge a new and viable direction that is practical and useful to educational leaders and leadership teams.

THE CAPACITY-BASED LEADER: TOWARD
A NEW INTEGRATED THEORY OF LEADERSHIP

Leadership is continuing to evolve as the world and people change. Educators have generally taken their leadership models from the military, business, or corporate sector. I believe that is unfortunate, because the knowledge and the skills necessary for leadership in a school or a district does not correlate well to leadership in business. The concept of leadership in education is best articulated with the phrase "servant leadership" or "leading from behind." Many educational leaders feel strongly that leadership in the private sector is different from the business or corporate sector. Clearly, the role of leader in corporate America is neither more nor less difficult than it is in education, but simply different from business.

One of the key differences relates to how cuts in business are received as opposed to cuts in education. Business responds differently to cuts required because it is seemingly understood that competition in the new world economy both gives and takes in cycles. Competition can force business to reduce its payroll costs by downsizing. Downsizing, a concept taken from the business sector, means the organization is getting smaller. To my knowledge that term is not routinely used by educators because, at least in part, when educational leaders are forced to reduce the teaching force, class sizes get larger. Therefore, the process of staff reduction is quite different for the human element in education. Everyone in the community perceives that they are being hurt, including staff, parents, students, and business. The striking difference in the private sector is how matter-of-factly—even happily—many elite workers are taking their reduction in force notices. According to Daniel McGinn and Keith Naughton of *Time* magazine, the elite do so well because, "After years of near continual downsizing (many due to merger), many workers have come to accept the risk of layoff as the price of admission to the 'new economy.'"[10] "It's almost a right of passage," says Dale Klamforth, a vice president at the outplacement firm of Drake Beam

Morin. "'If you haven't lost at least one job in your career today, you haven't taken enough risks.'"[11]

A second important difference is how decisions are made. The decision-making structure is also quite different. In education, the chain of command is very diffuse, slow, and usually democratic. That is true, at least in part, because of the bipolar phenomena previously described. Power is neither centralized nor decentralized; rather, it is both centralized and decentralized, and consequently it is very diffuse. The custom of electing school boards, which hire their professional school executive, raises the obvious question, "Who is the leader?" This school community organization often has the largest budget, food service, and transportation system in the town so it is no small matter for elected citizens to share that significant community leadership responsibility. Therefore, elected board members become susceptible to fierce community pressures. The point is that unlike the private sector, the democratic will of the people is strongly represented. It is recognized that the private sector has to answer to stockholders or at least a board of some type. Nonetheless, direct democracy (representing the voice of the people, informed or otherwise) in schools is a different structure altogether. Therefore the checks and balances in school systems are extremely unique.

Unfortunately, the balance of power is so diffuse that it is sometimes difficult to get a decision made. It is even more problematic to get a decision in areas that are unpopular or controversial. For example, when districts have tried to economize by downsizing and closing a small or remote school, the battle is excessive! Oregon is a good example (but certainly not unique) of the diffuse governance structure in education.

In some states, the governor appoints the members of the state school board and they, in turn, work with an elected (at large) state superintendent. That structure parallels the local process where superintendents are appointed by school boards that are elected by their community, as are members of the school-based site council (a governance structure in Oregon with legislative decision-making authority). While the locus of school authority is clear in Oregon statute, in application the system is as tangled as the Gregorian knot. That tangle makes providing leadership for the principal, superintendent, board, or site council difficult at best. That is *not* to say that leadership in education is more or less difficult than anywhere else. Simply said, it is just different.

Participatory Governance Is Required in Public Education

Since public education requires participatory governance, the leadership literature that is drawn from the business or corporate sector is only helpful in a general sense. As a result, educators need to think about and design leadership models that find their genesis in education rather than in the private sector. The diffuse nature of school leadership requires educational leaders to lead by working through others. In schools and districts, I believe that only through innovation and creativity will public education keep pace with rising expectations, rapidly changing conditions, and severely reduced resources (conditions that are faced in both the public and the private sectors alike) by leading from the inside out. The consequences of decentralized decision making are, to be sure, at times slow and ponderous. Innovation and creativity by their very nature tend to require decentralized decision making. Innovation needs to be small, tentative, and flexible for it to materialize into a synergistic success.

The SBS utilizes the following forces that I have labeled bully-based. Those four forces include (1) high standards, (2) top-down decision making, (3) academic standards that are often too high or too numerous, and (4) reform that, in general, has not been funded. The net effect of the bully-based reform effort is that the school community is hyper-insecure. Any decision affecting the classroom can have a dramatic effect on how a teacher is perceived by colleagues, students, parents, and the community. Therefore, people should be involved in decisions that affect them because the individual will be held accountable. In addition, the effective leader must build strong and lasting relationships. Strong relationships are essential because they build trust, which generates the lubrication and lucidity for change. Trust is also the emotional glue that sustains the culture through changes that appear intimidating and unfair. In education, before a leader focuses on improvement he or she must successfully pinpoint the delicate balance between threat and challenge. The leader or leadership team must find a way to strike that balance or run the risk of failure (see chapter 1). I call this general school of thought the *integrated leadership model*, which grows out of capacity-based beliefs rather than deficiency-based beliefs.

The key premises of this model are threefold:

• It is a much more productive use of time to use the strengths of the high performers to set the performance standard, rather than to work with mediocrity, hoping to motivate them to perform at average levels.

• If one intends to use people as a resource, they need to be involved in the decision-making process.

• Every effort should be made to mitigate the feelings of insecurity and threat by creating a tough love challenge.

Capacity-Based Leadership Defined

Maybe it is the nature of their work, but coaches seem to inherently understand capacity-based leadership. I believe that the former Chicago Bulls coach Phil Jackson understands and uses capacity-based principles of leadership in his coaching. While he probably doesn't use that label, I observed him use the strategy in developing his star forward Scotty Pippin. For instance, I was especially intrigued to observe Coach Jackson (then the coach of the three-time NBA champion Chicago Bulls) use Michael Jordan to set the standard of play for the team. Scotty Pippin responded to the standard that was set by Michael Jordan and subsequently developed into one of the league's most productive players as well. With both Pippin and Jordan performing at extremely high levels, the Bulls set a new NBA record by winning three back-to-back championships. That is not to suggest that Michael Jordan wasn't an extraordinary talent. Simply said his performance standard made everyone else better, and Pippin proved that is was possible to rise to a higher level.

Managers focus on deficiencies or weaknesses and use critical feedback approaches to push the mediocre staff to higher levels. Leaders build on the capacities of the high-performance people by letting them set the performance standards that pull others along, as if their work standard was an engaging type of performance magnet. In my view, it is one of the critical differences between leaders and managers. An excellent explanation of the strength-based (capacity-based) approach to leadership is voiced by Don Clifton (1992) when he writes that studying strengths results in productive conclusions and studying weaknesses results in ineffective conclusions. The key point about building on strengths is nicely underscored when Clifton states, "The study of strengths leads to the understanding of the difference between good and great." In summary then, "There is no alchemy for weaknesses. They can be removed, but they cannot be transformed into strengths."[12]A strength is characterized by yearnings (often from early in life), great satisfaction, rapid learning, glimpses of excellence, and total performance of excellence.[13] According to Clifton a weakness is more than just a bad habit (submitting to the urge to eat chocolate) or something you don't do very well (keeping a tidy office). Rather, it is something that you do that either damages your self-image or makes your strengths invisible. It is not that weaknesses are ignored. Weaknesses should be managed so that the strengths will be allowed to soar to new heights of effectiveness.

In his book, Clifton presents the following story to demonstrate the powerful results of building on strengths. Clifton reports that the Chinese had been the world champions in table tennis for many years. After winning the gold in 1984, reporters asked the Chinese coach to describe his training philosophy. The coach responded by saying that the team practiced by working on its strengths for twelve hours a day. The reporter was surprised and asked why they never worked on their weaknesses. In explanation, the coach reported that the team's strongest player only practices his forehand and never his backhand. In fact, this world champion table tennis player did not even possess an adequate backhand. Even though the rest of the table tennis world knew that he had an ineffective backhand, he still never wasted any time practicing it. Because his forehand was so invincible, it made his lack of a backhand irrelevant.[14]As has been previously noted, the world has been changing at hyper-speed rates. Certainly those changes have affected leadership in significant ways. John Naisbitt dramatically chronicles these changes in his best selling books entitled *Megatrends* and later *Megatrends 2000*. He graphically summarizes the changes as follows:

Table 3.1.

From	To
Industrial society	Information society
Forced technology	High tech/high touch
National economy	World economy
Short-term	Long-term
Centralization	Decentralization
Industrial held	Self-help
Representative democracy	Participatory democracy
Hierarchy	Networking
North	South
Either/or	Multiple choice

Many have examined these changes and their implications for educational leadership. In all of this work, I find that there are two elements missing and they are crucial to my discussions here.

First, Naisbitt is correct in his assertion that many organizations have moved from a centralized to a decentralized system in recent years. In education, however, that trend is only partly true. In education, both centralization and decentralization are occurring simultaneously. A kind of centralized and decentralized bipolar movement has affected school boards, superintendents, and schools at the same time. For example, in many cases, school boards and superintendents have lost authority to the state legislature (centralized) as well as to local school-based councils (decentralized). Further, the standards and the accountability system in the SBS movement are typically superimposed on local districts from the state. In addition, local site-based leadership teams are responsible for implementation; their effort is then graded by the state, leaving the local school board somewhat impotent. The board's legitimate authority has been shifted in both directions (i.e., centralized and decentralized). The shift concerns me because no local group is focused on policy-level direction. School boards would like to think they cover the policy issue, but policy development always seems to come after the politics of funding, decision making, and marketing. In my own experience of being a superintendent of a small district of approximately eight thousand students, I didn't get around to policy development until the fifth year of a five-year plan, and only then with the unenthusiastic support of staff and the half-hearted interest of the board. I was less than comfortable with the truncated model that was presented to us by a policy development organization with a kind of handshake and wink that meant that the job would be accomplished expeditiously. We finally agreed to a truncated policy approval process where policies were approved as a group. In this process, only the staff and two of the five board members gave the policies a deep review. Policy level direction is critically important in any organization that is changing at a speed-of-light pace. The point is that decentralized decision making creates a *system of schools* with unbridled latitude rather than a *school system* with collective vision (direction).

It is interesting to note that this strange, confusing, and antithetical movement in education is not an anomaly. In fact, it seems to parallel a global trend. In Europe for example, nations are coming together individually and collectively, while others are dissipating or imploding, and these shifts are happening simultaneously. I first thought about this phenomenon when Margaret Thatcher (then–prime minister of England) described the development just before she was defeated for another term of office. The point she made was that a new federalism and a growing sense of nationalism were occurring concurrently. For example, the world witnessed the Soviet Union implode, at the same time as new nations emerged in the Balkans. Since she has made her comments, the observation has advanced even further as the multinational European movement continues to move to a single currency, the euro.

Second, the literature on leadership is devoid of any discussion of power. Bennis underscored that point when he observed, "there is something missing from all the 'new age' formulations [of leadership]—one issue that has been systematically neglected without exception: *power*, the basic energy to initiate and sustain action translating intention into reality."[15] Educational power is decentralized or diffuse and integrated throughout. There is no real power per se. The most one can hope for is influence, which is based on trust, relationships, and respect. As was pointed out in chapter 1, leadership in education is diffuse because school-based teams are primarily responsible for making the needed changes. As we view current events, we see a very different kind of world changing at hyper-speed rates. These forces, along with the unique structure in education, dictate that a new leadership structure must continue to evolve. My purpose here is to initiate that evolutionary process. In education, real power is not in position, but in relationships. In other words, the changing world and the diffuse decision-making structure in education, coupled with the emergence of the standards-based school system, dictate that the nature of leadership be reexamined. The environment is not just changing, the culture has already changed. The education community is evolving a new way of looking at work. In my view, today's educators tend to value:

Table 3.2.

People	over	Institutions
Individualism	over	Conformity
Participation	over	Authority
Quality	over	Quantity
Diversity	over	Uniformity
Experience	over	Education

Student leaders	over	Student followers
Teacher leaders	over	Teacher followers
Student safety	over	Student rights
Academics	over	Athletics
Great teachers	over	Great coaches

High performance organizations work at being excellent by responding to the changes around them. They are simultaneously results-oriented and sensitive to the human element. It is significant to emphasize that two dimensions of leadership, productivity and relations, need to cross-fertilize and support each other within the environment or culture of the school.

Standards Cannot Be Forced: The Runaway Insecurity of the SBS Requires Teamwork and Tough Love

It is important for leaders and leadership teams to understand the disparate culture of the school in the standards-based movement (SBM). It is especially important because during this time of superimposed (i.e., top-down) change, I believe that the nature of the high-stakes mandate of the SBM has created a culture that is experiencing a precariousness that has, heretofore, been alien to schools. To be successful, a standards-based school (SBS) needs to be simultaneously results-oriented and sensitive to the human element. It is important to note that productivity is built on a foundation of trust, which results when relationships are strong and lasting.

Teachers tend not to be motivated by the usual incentives of the workplace. Teaching is a very private endeavor that is performed in public. Good teaching comes from good people. While I realize that statement sounds trite and sanctimonious, it is nevertheless true. Beyond the academic content, teachers teach who they are as people (their beliefs). What teachers teach and how they teach it is the literal extension of their very essence as human beings. Great teachers come to the vocation of teaching for reasons of the heart, spirited by passions of helping children. Therefore teachers will not be forced to implement something that they believe to be threatening to children. Ethical lessons are taught by the best teachers inferentially if not directly. The best teachers have the ability to communicate that "While I care about you, I also have very high academic and behavioral expectations for you." Let me call that kind of caring *tough love* (or a kind of unconditional love). For the best teachers that phrase galvanizes the pedagogical framework defined by high expectations that are necessarily balanced with a safe and nurturing environment. Good teachers know that students must be given the opportunity to try and fail without the loss of self-esteem. Some would argue that there is nothing wrong with a little failure because that is what happens in life.

The caution is that every good teacher has learned that students learn to be successful, not by experiencing failure, but by experiencing success. This powerful and highly desirable outcome occurs when students successfully achieve rigorous standards through hard work and perseverance. We will discuss education as a moral purpose in chapter 9. However, educational psychology professes that if students fail to meet high standards, it is much less than helpful in terms of their future success. There can be no doubt that failing is a very important part of learning. Therefore, students must be given the opportunity to try and fail without feeling threatened or diminished.

The most challenging job a teacher has in a standards-based classroom (SBC) is to help students distinguish between challenge and threat. We have all seen the out-of-control soccer coach who behaves as if he were coaching in the World Cup. In an SBS, the teacher needs to create an environment that is safe, wholesome, and nurturing. If students view the atmosphere as threatening, then they may also view it as hostile and potentially destructive. Every parent and teacher knows that a child will refuse to do anything that may cause embarrassment in front of family or friends. In a threatening environment, a student's perceptions are narrowed to the object of the threat. Little can occur that is positive if a student views the school as hostile. One of the trademarks of an SBS is efficiency. The efficiency occurs in an SBS because the academic expectations are known to all, and the staff in the school works as a team to ensure that the students can achieve standards. It simply does not follow that because a school is well organized and efficient, it is necessarily inhumane and cruel. Teachers easily sense the concern that some of their students may experience threat, so it can become threatening for the staff as well. Therefore, the staff are extremely reluctant to participate in making the necessary changes. Teachers, and only teachers, can create that delicate balance between challenge and threat. That idea is threatening for teachers. In other words, teachers need to create a culture that is safe, wholesome, and nurturing for their students just as leaders need to create a culture that is safe, wholesome, and nurturing for staff.

As has been discussed earlier, the key concern is that students will perceive the notion of accountability as a threat. Therefore, it is the goal of the leader or leadership team to create an environment that is challenging yet as threat free as possible. There is probably no environment that is totally threat free, and a bit of natural tension is probably necessary and healthy. Because student success is of central importance, these approaches cannot be forced. People who will be affected by decisions need to be involved in the decision-making process. To use power as a change strategy is unwise because it does not honor those who will ultimately be responsible for the success of the change. The point is that participatory decision making tends to create understanding, which also helps to mitigate the concerns of parents, teachers, and administrators, thereby generating harmony, cooperation, and sharing. To make the needed changes, leaders and leadership teams must build on the strengths or capacities of the district or school, rather than focus on the deficiencies of the organization or school. I believe that can be accomplished by creating balance between productivity and relational domain. Specifically, I am referring to what I call the formulaic integrated leadership model.

Leadership Style Defined and the Evolution of Leadership Theories Analyzed

Your leadership style is a pattern of behavior (not characteristics) that grows out of your beliefs that identifies you as a leader. What follows is a description of the evolution of several contemporary theories of leadership.

This leadership overview is not intended to be all inclusive. Rather, the evolution of contemporary leadership theory is being presented to demonstrate how the capacity-based leadership model builds on previous work. Theories of leadership have been evolving probably since recorded history, or even before. I will detail just several contemporary leadership theories that focus on the interplay between the following two dimensions:

- a concern for *production*, and,
- a concern for *people*.

The first theory taken under study is called the leadership grid and it theorizes that dimensions of productivity and people interact together to create a leadership style. As early as 1964, Blake and Mouton's leadership grid became a pivotal contributor to the literature because it went beyond the characteristics of leaders to their behaviors.[16] The model was a two-dimensional model which held that a leader's behavior was a function of either of two variables: a concern for people or a concern for getting things done.

The One Style Only Theory

Initially, theorists believed that a leader's style would be dominated by task (productivity) or relationship (people), but not both simultaneously.[17] The theory is based on the concept that leaders vary—from one to nine—in their concern for people (relationships) and in their concern for getting things done (productivity or task). It was believed that a leader would be either high relationship or low task (see figure 3.1, quadrant I), low relationship and high task (quadrant III), or even low relationship and low task (quadrant II).

The Best Style Theory

After identifying task and relationship as the two central aspects of leadership behavior, numerous practitioners and writers tried to determine which of the four styles was the most effective style of leadership. At one point high task/high relationship (quadrant IV) was considered the most effective style, while low task/low relationship was considered the least effective style.[18] In these instances, the theorists considered the variables (task and relationship) of equal weight. The leadership model presented in figure 3.1 is built on this thinking. Therefore, the contention that both productivity (P) and relationships (R) are important is a significant contribution to the capacity-based leadership theory. The capacity-based theory begins to deviate at this point. While both P and R are important, they are not of equal significance in an SBS. Leaders in an SBS are able to be productive as a function of the relationships they nurture; therefore, R is more important because it became the multiplier. In fact, the stronger the relationships, the more productive the individual or team becomes. Further, possessing a relationship orientation is at least two times as important as having a task orientation.

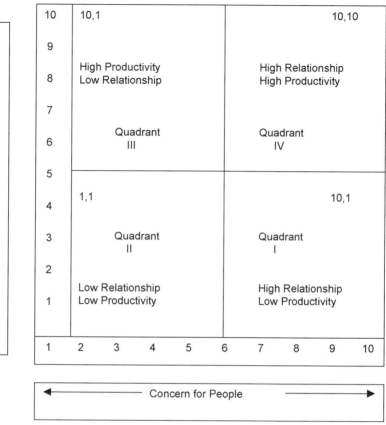

Figure 3.1.   The Best Style Theory
The managerial grid: Concern for production (R. R. Blake and J. S. Mouton, The Managerial Grid, Houston, Texas Gulf Publishing. Douglas McGregor, "The Professional Manager." New York: McGraw-Hill Book Co.

The capacity-based leadership theory builds on all of the grid system work in another way. The theoretical framework presented here goes on to define the general dimensions of productivity and task.

Situational Leadership Theory Also Expands Best Style Theory

Then in the 1970s, Hersey and Blanchard began to advance the theory of situational leadership where "Successful leaders are those who can adapt their behavior to meet the demands of their own unique environment." "If the effectiveness of a leader's behavior style depends on the situation in which it is used, it follows that any of the four basic styles may be effective or ineffective depending on the actual situation."[19] Therefore leadership effectiveness depends on the degree to which the leader is able to match the independent dimensions of task or relationship to the situation at hand. The situational leadership framework suggested that the effectiveness of a leader was dependent on the match between the leadership style and the situation (environment). This theory counters the notion that there is a universal, all-purpose leadership style. The work of Blanchard and Hersey is significant and mentioned here because it contributed another dimension to Blake and Mouton's grid theory by including a third dependent dimension (variable), which was environment.

Therefore, Blanchard and Hersey built on the existing leadership framework when they added the third dimension of situation (culture) to Blake and Mouton's concern for people (relationship) and a concern for getting things done (productivity*)*. Blanchard and Hersey put their finger on a problem we confront when we attempt to quantify all of the variables that could affect the success of a given leadership style. Creating an all-purpose model that is applicable to schools and their unique and ever changing culture is difficult, if not inane.[20]

School leaders were intrigued by the theory of situational leadership. The theory was widely supported, at least in part, because it explained leadership in pragmatic terms that could be applied to almost every leader and culture. My reading of situational leadership suggests that the theory was developed as a model intended to be used to deepen our understanding of leadership in a general sense. In that way, the theory of situational leadership has been monumentally helpful because it broke the mold of two equal, dependent variables. Therefore, I have elected to build on the situational leadership model. The concepts are not intended for exclusive use in education. The culture of organizations varies dramatically, of course. As I pointed out earlier, generic leadership models do not adequately address schools. Therefore, to say that a successful leadership style in a school can range from dictatorial to democratic at one time and from collegial to autocratic at another is, I submit, highly improbable. To conclude that the combination of two independent variables (relationship and productivity) should have equal weight is unrealistic. Fortunately for educational theorists, we are left with the task of building on the previous work of leadership in developing a leadership concept unique to SBS. I believe the theory of situational leadership may have been an appropriate theoretical framework for the traditional school.

Alchemy of Capacity-Based Leadership: Integrating Relationship, Productivity, and Professional Efficacy

A useful leadership model for school leaders can and should be built on the foundation of the aforementioned theoretic leadership models. I would submit that the culture of a school community in the standards-based movement is not a variable, but a constant. Schools create a unique culture because both the product and the customer are people. Additionally, the product (an educated child) is the most complex and precious product in a community. The culture of a school community is people-centered and therefore primarily relational.

PROFESSIONAL EFFICACY
REQUIRES PARTICIPATION

Efficacy or belief in self is a core value that comes to educators quite naturally. Efficacy requires a participatory leadership style. Educational leaders (i.e., principals and teachers) come to their work for reasons of the heart, with a modicum of love for children thrown in. Therefore in the SBS, productivity is not independent of culture. P depends on R. Those who study ethnology define culture as shared, learned behavior. Therefore, the leader must create the circumstance where a shared, learned behavior includes strong relationships and tough love, the very elements we want for our children in the school.

In an SBS, the culture needs to be built on a foundation of strong relationships. The SBS is considered more efficient because the expectations are clear. The academic standards are often high enough that many children will necessarily be challenged to the very limit of their ability. Some argue that a tough academic challenge is good for a child. In theory that is correct because challenge (not failure) is an important part of learning. In reality, however, it is only constructive if students, when they fail, feel challenged rather than diminished. If students feel diminished, then the academic rigor of the standards can easily be interpreted by families as a threat. Clearly, mistakes are an important part of learning, but if academic challenge is viewed as threat and therefore diminishing, our children will not reach their potential. The point is that teachers, parents, and administrators have learned that there is a very delicate balance between challenge and threat. We have learned that children do not thrive in a threatening environment. Therefore, educators know that their task is to challenge children in a nurturing, safe, and wholesome way. For that very reason, the task of the leader is to create a safe, wholesome, and nurturing environment for the staff so they can experience the same culture (for the same reasons) that they need to create for children. In a classroom where students feel safe, it doesn't necessarily follow that a well-organized and efficient school is also inhumane and cruel. Actually, the exact opposite can be true. If children know precisely what the expectation is and they get support, they will, more often than not, find a way to meet the standard. Happily, self-confidence is a function of success. Productivity of school leaders is built on a foundation of strong and lasting relationships. There is no attempt here to minimize the importance of productivity in this era of accountability. Because productivity is a realistic expectation, it must be multiplied by strong relationships to generate a high-performance, standards-based school. Therefore, both variables (P and R) are interactively important to generate a school that is performing at peak capacity. Please be reminded that we are not talking about an individual when we use the term leader in an SBS. Our focus could be diverse teams of people who come together from vastly different backgrounds to create quality schools.

Therefore, the relationship domain for high-performance school administrators and leadership teams is not a variable. It is a fundamental requirement. In successful schools, the relationship talent of leaders does not often vary from high to poor and still consistently generate excellent results. School research simply does not support the notion that people or teams with poor relationship skills can also be highly effective. There is some variation, of course, in that it may take some time and experience because leaders or teams may begin with a slow relationship, high task approach, but effective leaders and teams evolve over time. I was discussing these phenomena with a highly respected chief administrator who worked for one of the most prestigious districts in our area. He pointed out to me that he routinely interviewed some of the most incredibly capable, aspiring principals because many wanted to work in this district. He reflected that these new hires almost always made the same initial mistake. He mused that they were always so grateful to have been selected that they tried to convince everyone that they were the right choice. He lamented that without any hesitation and against his best advice, they all attempted to do too much too soon and were relegated to the struggle of the earth school (experience driven). Of course, experienced school leaders vary their approach from time to time and evolve to quadrant IV (high relationship, high task) over time. To lead high performance over the long term, strong relationships are the foundation on which productivity is built. In fact, I cannot cite a single instance where a leader in a high-performance SBS who was high task and low relationship was successful over the long term.

Sara Lawrence Lightfoot (1983) said of her study of school leaders that all had a focus on nurturance and support. Six of these principals were male, but they all described the feminine sides of their natures when talking about leadership in schools, touching upon listening, a sense of community, relationships, and support. According to Lightfoot's work, a successful school principal's leadership would not fall anywhere on a continuum from monocratic and bureaucratic, to pluralistic and collegial. One more significant point to underscore about relationships follows. The most important resource we have is not technology or even pedagogy, but people.[21] One can convert an environment of scarcity to an environment of abundance if we rely on our human capital. The prerequisite for the belief in and use of human capital is building relationships. Trust is a keystone to the success of any endeavor involving people because trust is a constant in creating a winning formula.

In *Primal Leadership,* authored by Daniel Goldman, Richard Boyatzis, and Annie McKee, Goldman suggests that specific emotional skills and real caring are at the heart of an effective leader. On the first page of the book, Goldman and McKee say it this way: "Great leaders . . . ignite our passion and inspire the best in us. When we try to explain why they are so effective, we speak of strategy, vision, or powerful ideas. But the reality is much more primal: Great leadership works through emotions."[22]

I agree that managing positive relationships is a specific emotional skill that is critically important to leaders in an SBS. Trust is the lubrication that creates the capacity for change; further, trust is the emotional glue that holds an organization together in the transmutation of the school culture. The importance of relationship and trust in a learning community is of central importance to reach the vision. With limited resources, one will need to rely on human capital. I see quadrants I through IV of figure 3.1 as evolutionary stages that school leaders are likely to experience as they evolve toward the necessary balance of capacity-based leadership.

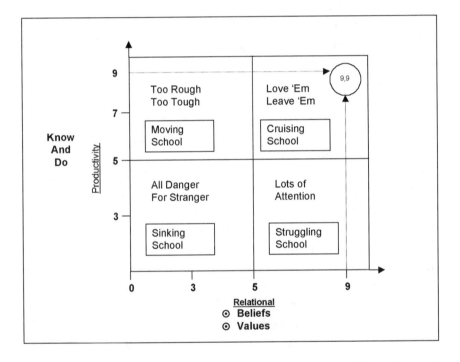

Directions:

- On a scale from 1 to 10, rank yourself on the vertical axis, or Productivity Domain.
- On a scale from 1 to 10, rank yourself on the horizontal axis, or Relational Domain.
- Extend both notations horizontally and vertically until they intersect.
- Repeat the process after completing the questions for preservice principals.
- Use the equation above to determine your rankings. Plot your PC.

Figure 3.2.　Domain Balance

Figure 3.2 is a two-dimensional model that allows one to conceptualize both a positive and a negative capacity. It also helps one determine where leaders are in relationship to the different evolutionary stages of leadership development.

Please be reminded that we are pursuing a leadership framework that is the most effective over the long term in the unique culture of an SBS. I have observed that high-performance principals or teams in an SBS work at being excellent. They are simultaneously productivity-oriented and sensitive to the human element. I will discuss this further later in this chapter. First, however, I would like to define productivity and relations in much more detail. Capacity-based leadership includes two leadership domains defined below.

Integrated Leadership Domains Defined

- Productivity domain—what leaders know and do
- Relational domain—what leaders believe and value

PRINCIPAL AND TEAM PROFICIENCIES

Providing leadership for the standards-based reform movement requires the emphasis of the human dimension, while not losing sight of productivity. When I was a superintendent, we thought it might be useful to quantify the proficiencies of such a leader. Therefore, Pat Schmuck and I created and directed a process that generated the proficiencies and rubric (scoring guide) that follow. See figure 3.3.

Success Strategy 14   To develop the proficiencies that serve to define the capacity-based leadership model, first we studied the research on school leadership. Then, all of the building leaders and the district office leaders were divided into groups of five and asked to reach consensus (using the consensus guidelines in appendix A) on the two following questions given on the standards-based school:

- What do principals need to know and do to provide leadership to insure that the school is productive?

- What are the most important beliefs that principals need to sustain re- lationships? The group as a whole reached agreement on the proficien- cies to be included in each domain. The results follow for your analy- sis and use.

The productivity domain was defined as the skills and knowledge that principals needed to be successful.

Productivity Domain (P)

The seven proficiencies that were addressed by our formal leaders in the productivity dimension (know and do) are as follows:

- Knowledge of what it takes to develop an SBS
- Instructional and managerial expertise
- Ability to hold school and self accountable
- Ability to systematically respond to change flexibly
- Skills to be resourceful
- Skills to provide support
- Strong cognitive and effective communication skills

Relational Domain (R)

The *R* domain was defined as the beliefs and values necessary for the leader to be proficient in a standards-based school (see figure 3.4). The three proficiencies on which our formal leaders reached consensus in the *R* dimension (beliefs and values) are as follow:

- Belief in the power of relationships and ability to publicly nurture and sustain them
- Ability to develop and value trust
- Belief in the precondition of vision and ability to let the vision emerge from the core beliefs of the school

The rationale for including each of the proficiencies and the definition for each follows.

Productivity Domain

• Leadership Proficiencies

Rationale for and Definition of Knowledge   Knowledge is on the productivity axis because a school leader must have a clear knowledge of the content standards. In addition, the leader must understand curriculum alignment strategies, data-based decision making, and school improvement planning. At a minimum, the principal must know and be able to do these things in an SBS.

We defined knowledge proficiency in the following way: Building administrators who are proficient in this area have a clear understanding of what it takes to develop a standards-based school and classroom. They have a thorough knowledge of the content standards and eligible content. They also understand the science, art, and craft of teaching and work with their staff to make the necessary improvements. They understand people and systems and provide a safe and wholesome environment for students and staff.

Notice that the substance of the definition defines the elements of setting up a standards-based school, while still expressing concern for the *R* dimension. Again, you will observe in this definition the need to balance challenge and threat by creating an emotionally safe environment for both students and staff.

Rationale for and Definition of Expertise   Expertise is located on the productivity axis because a clear understanding of how to provide leadership in aligning content and academic standards to the school's curriculum is essential. In addition, the leader must have the ability to set high expectations and measure program effectiveness. It is also important for the leader to have the ability to locate instructional materials that correlate to the aligned curriculum of the school.

To that end we defined expertise in the following way: Building administrators who are proficient in this area understand academic standards so as to facilitate the development of curricula that match state standards and eligible content. They also have the ability to set high expectations, they can design assessments or processes to measure program effectiveness, and they can select instructional materials.

Rationale for and Definition of Accountability   Accountability was located on the productivity axis because the SBS is intended to make everyone more accountable. There has been a public policy clamor for more accountability, and that is a realistic expectation where tax dollars are concerned. Principals must model accountability and also formulate measures to assure that the program is held accountable. They also need to supervise their staffs so as to help them stretch their strengths to perform at their peak capacities.

Building administrators who are proficient in this area are able to formulate and develop measures around high academic standards for students. They establish measurable goals and routinely make a self-assessment as measured against preestablished criteria. They understand and plan effective supervision of staff in their area of responsibility.

Rationale for and Definition of Flexibility   Flexibility was included under the productivity axis because decisions must evolve from the core beliefs of people in the school. That is to say, those people affected by a decision need to be involved in the decision-making process. This leadership proficiency is characterized by leading from behind. Therefore, it is not a point-and-tell mentality. Principals trust the staff and use the staff as human capital to insure success. In other words, principals are persuasive and use the ideas of others to move the school. In many cases, the school is not only in transition, but also immersed in decentralized decision making, so they are running a dual program. For this reason, it takes flexibility to continue running some aspects of the traditional system, while evolving through decentralized decision making to a new SBS.

Building administrators who are proficient in this area spontaneously observe thoughts, feelings, and proposed actions from the viewpoint of patrons, faculty, and students. This person remains sensitive, is aware, and adjusts accordingly. This person is capable of developing a systematic response to change. He or she understands there is a variety of ways to reach the goals of the school. He or she constantly looks for ways to work through others and remain open to new ideas and change.

Rationale for and Definition of Resourcefulness   Resourcefulness was placed on the productivity axis because to make the transformation to the SBS, one either has to acquire new resources or use those that are already available, but in different ways. This proficiency is unique and emerged primarily because the standards are mandates that also came with funding shortfalls. I predict that education will never have all of its varied needs funded, so this proficiency is intended to go far beyond getting more money and other capital resources. This proficiency in its fullest development describes a leader who uses the strengths and interests of each staff member to leverage the human capital as a resource.

Building leaders who are proficient in this area make it a point to find out the strengths and interests of each staff member in order to extend responsibilities in a way which helps each staff member grow (the use of human capital). The leader begins with the problem, not the individual. The leader is creative and imaginative in dealing with a difficult situation. He or she is good at delegation, finds out what the faculty members do well, and delegates accordingly, constantly looking for resources to support the staff and the school improvement plan.

The Relationship Domain

Rationale for and Definition of Relationships Relationships were placed on the relationship axis for relatively obvious reasons and also because this proficiency is, more than any other, a foundational value which is required in an SBS. Education is a people-dependent endeavor. Therefore, building leaders must care for and have a concern for people. They believe that real power is not in position, but relationships. This develops the trust necessary to use people as a resource (human capital).

Building administrators who are proficient in this area express care and concern for people. They make it a point to be close to their school community (students, parents, and staff), as well as other district administrators. They want to be liked because they know that they can get more done for students if they are liked by the school community. Further, they have a specific process to develop team and personal relationships. They also understand how to use critical feedback for the benefit of students and staff.

Rationale for and Definition of Support Support was included in the productivity axis because building administrators must make a personal commitment to the success of each staff member in an SBS. More than that, they have to take action to insure the success of the staff. They consistently get personal satisfaction out of seeing individual staff members grow. Support is one of the interventions that is particularly valuable when people feel threatened, which is all too often the case in an SBS. Support is a tangible way one shows care for others. Support is given only when it is consistent with the vision.

Building administrators who are proficient in this area receive satisfaction from the personal and professional growth of the staff members. This person helps staff members experience success and finds fulfillment in the achievement of each person's goals. This person is constantly looking for ways to provide staff with the tools to help them help students to be successful. He or she focuses on the problem, not the person. He or she serves as a facilitator when a staff member is meeting with concerned parents.

Rationale for and Definition of Vision   Vision was included on the relationship axis because it is an important precondition for success. Vision creates the conditions where the human energies of the organization are aligned toward a common end, which is a significant precondition for success. Proficient building administrators have a clear understanding of where the school is going. They also have an uncanny way of knowing just what step to take next.

Building administrators (principals and vice principals) and leadership teams who are proficient in visioning have a clear understanding of their own values regarding education, are focused on them, and meet educational goals based on those values. They communicate those goals consistently to teachers and to parents by their actions and their statements. They are able to influence the climate of a school and achievements of the staff and students with their vision of education.

Rationale for and Definition of Trust   Trust was included in the human domain because trust is the lubrication that makes everything else possible. Trust is the by-product of all the other proficiencies in the human domain combined. Relationship and trust building are the precondition for building on human capital. Trust is the first and most important ingredient in creating a high-performance school. Trust is earned in paltry amounts and accumulates, but trust is delicate and can be damaged by even the smallest of inconsistencies. And most importantly, others give trust only after it has been earned. Some would state that the people should trust the leader. As for this definition, the leader must trust the people. Certainly, mutual trust is important, but this proficiency implies that the leader must trust the people first.

Building administrators who are proficient in the area of trust understand that they need to delegate based on interest and talent. They recognize that others give power to them, which requires trust. They believe in the people and work continuously to bring out their best by focusing on their capacities. They are good listeners and seek direction when appropriate. They understand that trust is earned and delicate to maintain. They are predictable and work to sustain a high level of trust. They rely on trust as a vehicle for making positive change.

Rationale for and Definition of Communication Communication was placed in the productivity domain because it addresses two-way communication. Communication used herein is intended to aid in collecting information about what people know and how they feel. Communication is both sending and receiving messages. Communication is also cognitive and affective. The focus of cognitive communication is on sending and receiving information, and the focus of affective communication is listening for feelings. This proficiency is in the human domain because the core of this proficiency is listening for feelings beyond just content.

Building administrators who are proficient in this area excel in two-way communication; they are equally adept at sending and receiving messages. They choose the form of communication that best fits with the purpose of, and audience for, the message. At the highest level of proficiency they assist other staff members to excel as communicators.

SELF-ASSESSMENT INSTRUMENT FOR PRACTICING BUILDING ADMINISTRATORS

Enclosed is a self-assessment instrument that includes the aforementioned proficiencies along with a rubric or scoring guide. The proficiency indicators stair-step up (i.e., from simple to very complex) through the six levels of Benjamin Bloom's cognitive taxonomy.

The levels are defined as follows:

Level 1 (Beginning): Includes the simplest level of the cognitive domain (knowledge)
Level 2 (Developing): Includes level 2 of the cognitive domain (comprehension)
Level 3 (Maturing): Includes level 3 of the cognitive domain (application)
Level 4 (Strong): Includes the complex application level of the cognitive domain
Level 5 (Exemplary): Includes the most sophisticated level of the cognitive domain (synthesis and/or evaluation)

PRINCIPAL PROFICIENCY #1

Expertise:
- Instructional
- Managerial

Building administrators are proficient in instructional leadership when they understand the academic standards so as to develop curricula that matches state standards and eligible content. They have the ability to set high expectations; they can design assessments or processes to measure program effectiveness; and they can select instructional materials that correlate to the curriculum.

Proficiency Level Indicators:

Level 1 (Beginning)	Level 2 (Developing)	Level 3 (Maturing)	Level 4 (Strong)	Level 5 (Exemplary)
Knowledge: ability to identify, recognize, recall	Comprehension: ability to translate, explain, transform	Application: ability to apply solutions to real-world predictable and unpredictable problems	Synthesis: ability to create, compare, design	Evaluation: ability to discriminate, appraise, consider
INSTRUCTIONAL • Knowledge of State Content Standards • Knowledge of assessment theory and validity	• Guides staff through application of State Standards	• Guides staff through application of State Standards	• Merges State Standards with District Curriculum	• Evaluates State Standards with District Curriculum
MANAGERIAL • Knowledge of physical plan operations and maintenance	• Guides custodial and maintenance staff in all dimensions of operations	• Anticipates needs; plans for contingencies with plan operations, staffing, and personnel	• Coordinates all staff and personnel with student learning, and academic and athletic goals	• Evaluates school effectiveness and is able to adjust to meeting ongoing student needs

Figure 3.3. Principal Proficiencies

PRINCIPAL PROFICIENCY #2	
Relationships	Building administrators who are proficient in this area express care and concern for people. They make a point to be close to teachers and other district administrators. They want to be liked because they know that they can get more done for students if they're liked by students, parents, and staff. Further, they have specific processes to develop team and personal relationships. They also understand how to use critical feedback for the benefit of students and staff.

Proficiency Level Indicators:

Level 1 (Beginning)	Level 2 (Developing)	Level 3 (Maturing)	Level 4 (Strong)	Level 5 (Exemplary)
Knowledge: ability to identify, recognize, recall	Comprehension: ability to translate, explain, transform	Application: ability to apply solutions to real-world predictable and unpredictable problems	Synthesis: ability to create, compare, design	Evaluation: ability to discriminate, appraise, consider
• Acknowledges that positive relationships between people can create a more productive work environment. • Understands that trust is necessary to build positive relationships.	• Converts beliefs about relationships into a plan to create a culture of positive relationships into a productive work environment. • Explains how to create trust.	• Shows how positive relationships can create a more productive work environment. • Shows how trust can build positive relationships. • Explains how recognizing strengths is an asset.	• Efforts to develop positive relationships with students, staff, and parents are successful. • Staff, students, and parents trust the word and works of the administrator.	• Efforts to develop positive relationships are learned and practiced by students, staff, and parents. • Creates an environment in which individuals trust one another.

Figure 3.3. (*Continued*)

Level 1 (Beginning)	Level 2 (Developing)	Level 3 (Maturing)	Level 4 (Strong)	Level 5 (Exemplary)
• Understands that positive relationships encompass more than work-related issues. • Understands that recognizing individual strengths and talents is a good thing. • Knows that listening to others will increase understanding and build relations. • Considers the impact of a process on the individual.	• Rearranges schedule to be available anytime to staff during a crisis. • Can give examples of how listening to others will increase understanding and build relationships.	• Shows how listening can be used to increase understanding and build relationships.	• Knows and relates to individuals on both a personal and professional level. • Is able to spot individual strengths and talents, celebrate them, and build a program around them. • Listens authentically and communicates effectively around personal and professional relationships. • Puts people first and process second.	• Creates an environment in which individuals feel sensitivity to, and take into account, the whole person. • Is able to nurture the growth and development of new areas of talent and strength. • Models authentic listening in such a way as to create open and responsive culture in environment. • Creates processes that respect individuals.

Figure 3.3. (*Continued*)

PRINCIPAL PROFICIENCY #3	
Accountability	Building administrators who are proficient in this area formulate and develop measures around high academic standards for students. They establish measurable personal goals and routinely make a self-assessment as measured against pre-established criteria. They understand and plan effective supervision of staff and program evaluation in their area of responsibility.

Proficiency Level Indicators:

Level 1 (Beginning)	Level 2 (Developing)	Level 3 (Maturing)	Level 4 (Strong)	Level 5 (Exemplary)
Knowledge: ability to identify, recognize, recall	Comprehension: ability to translate, explain, transform	Application: ability to apply solutions to real-world predictable and unpredictable problems	Synthesis: ability to create, compare, design	Evaluation: ability to discriminate, appraise, consider
• Understands the need for professional accountability. • Understands importance of personal and professional goal-setting. • Identifies program criteria.	• Recognizes and communicates the need for professional accountability. • Shares the importance of personal and professional goal-setting.	• Applies standards of professional accountability to situations involving coworkers, students, and community. • Practices personal and professional goal-setting.	• Creates an environment that supports high standards of professional accountability with coworkers, students, and community. • Creates environments conducive to setting personal and professional goals.	• Maintains an environment of outstanding professional accountability among coworkers, students, and community. • Models personal and professional goal-setting.

Figure 3.3. *(Continued)*

Level 1 (Beginning)	Level 2 (Developing)	Level 3 (Maturing)	Level 4 (Strong)	Level 5 (Exemplary)
• Is aware of appropriate professional performance. • Knows how to supervise staff.	• Understands importance of using established criteria to evaluate program effectiveness. • Communicates supervision information to staff.	• Uses established program criteria to evaluate program effectiveness. • Plans for and carries out effective supervision of staff.	• Supports a culture where program criteria are used to make evaluative decisions. • Uses effective supervision methods to enhance pedagogical practices.	• Initiates and participates in assessing programs against clearly established criteria. • Displays a high standard of professional performance. • Supports an environment in which staff supervision is a positive part of professional growth.

Figure 3.3. (*Continued*)

PRINCIPAL PROFICIENCY #4	
Communication	Building administrators who are proficient in this area excel in two-way communication; they are equally adept at sending messages and receiving them. They choose the form of communication that best fits with the purpose of, and audience for, the message. At the highest level of proficiency, they assist other staff members to excel as communicators.

Proficiency Level Indicators:

Level I (Beginning)	Level 2 (Developing)	Level 3 (Maturing)	Level 4 (Strong)	Level 5 (Exemplary)
Knowledge: ability to identify, recognize, recall	Comprehension: ability to translate, explain, transform	Application: ability to apply solutions to real-world predictable and unpredictable problems	Synthesis: ability to create, compare, design	Evaluation: ability to discriminate, appraise, consider
• Recognizes a lack of understanding. • Listens 80% and is aware of the listening percentage. • Anger clouds conversation. • Uses words that sometimes offend. • Integrity starts.	• Listens 85% of the time. • Recognizes anger is a problem. • Realizes interests are needed. • Recognizes mutual trust is missing. • Looks for solutions.	• Develops agreements. • Listens 90%. • Controls anger. • Chooses words wisely. • Integrity builds. • Develops interest. • Equal at times. • Takes time to understand.	• Listens 95% of the time. • Recognizes anger and adjusts. • Distinguishes between words that build integrity and those that harm. • Recognizes when to listen and when to speak.	• Creates a climate of mutual understanding. • Listens almost 100% of the time. • Keeps anger in check. • Attempts to never offend. • Integrity always.

Figure 3.3. (*Continued*)

Level 1 (Beginning)	Level 2 (Developing)	Level 3 (Maturing)	Level 4 (Strong)	Level 5 (Exemplary)
• Focuses on position.		• Probes for common points.	• Can develop trust with members of the school community.	• Focuses on interests.
• Top-down/bottom-up.		• Trust is felt.	• Recognizes that empathy is important in developing integrity.	• Horizontal—equal always.
• Advises before understanding.		• Understands how others feel.		• Understands before advising.
• Few or no common points.		• Develops win/win techniques.		• Speaks from common point of reference.
• Low mutual trust.		• Express it—then do it.		• High trust and good feeling.
• Feels as they feel (sympathy).		• Beginning to balance emotions.		• Understands how they feel based on how they see the world (empathy).
• Recognizes win/loss.				• Always end on win/win terms.
• Express it.				• Do it before saying it (walk the talk).
• Emotion—too little/too much.				• Always balanced.

Figure 3.3. (Continued)

PRINCIPAL PROFICIENCY #5
Vision	Building administrators who are proficient in this area have a clear understanding of their own values regarding education and are focused on and meet educational goals based on those values. They communicate those goals consistently to teachers and parents by their actions and statements. They are able to influence the climate and goals of the school and the achievements of the staff and students, given their vision of education.

Proficiency Level Indicators:

Level 1 (Beginning)	Level 2 (Developing)	Level 3 (Maturing)	Level 4 (Strong)	Level 5 (Exemplary)
Knowledge: ability to identify, recognize, recall	Comprehension: ability to translate, explain, transform	Application: ability to apply solutions to real-world predictable and unpredictable problems	Synthesis: ability to create, compare, design	Evaluation: ability to discriminate, appraise, consider
• Recognizes the importance of clearly defining one's values. • Recognizes the need for forming personal vision. • Identifies the need to set goals and prioritize tasks that benefit children. • Recognize the importance of climate in meeting a school's goals.	• Ability to explain one's own values. • Ability to explain vision. • Ability to explain importance of setting goals that are driven by a vision. • Ability to describe a desired school climate.	• Set priorities—conduct self based on values. • Carry out actions that reflect personal vision. • Set goals into action plans that are in harmony with school vision. • Communicate the importance of desirable climate to staff/community.	• Create systems that reflect values. • Help create a school vision that is congruent with own vision. • Develop programs to meet goals. • Create with staff a school climate in harmony with vision.	• Discriminate among systems given input from others and further information. • Foster vision throughout the school. • Analyze programs—monitor and adjust. • Foster throughout the school a commitment to maintaining a desirable school climate.

Figure 3.3. (Continued)

PRINCIPAL PROFICIENCY #6	
Trust	Building administrators who are proficient in this area have a clear understanding of their own values regarding education and are focused on and meet educational goals based on those values. They communicate those goals consistently to teachers and parents by their actions and statements. They are able to influence the climate and goals of the school and the achievements of the staff and students, given their vision of education.

Proficiency Level Indicators:

Level 1 (Beginning)	Level 2 (Developing)	Level 3 (Maturing)	Level 4 (Strong)	Level 5 (Exemplary)
Knowledge: ability to identify, recognize, recall	Comprehension: ability to translate, explain, transform	Application: ability to apply solutions to real-world predictable and unpredictable problems	Synthesis: ability to create, compare, design	Evaluation: ability to discriminate, appraise, consider
• Knows that honesty builds trust. • Knows that acting on morals, values, and principals is a good thing. • Is aware of areas of weakness.	• Understands that honesty builds trust. • Can explain how acting on morals, values, and principles is a good thing.	• Can translate knowledge of trust into action. • Applies strong personal moral code to leadership role. • Can adjust areas of weakness to establish trusting relationships.	• Is honest in dealing with people and issues. • Acts on a set of principles, morals, and values which can be identified and articulated. • Acknowledges publicly errors, weaknesses, and shortcomings. • Uses life experiences to support individual's life and work issues.	• Creates an environment in which people feel safe, acting honest, even when errors are made. • Creates an environment built on mutually identified and held principles, morals, and values. • Allows team to share talents so that weaknesses and errors are supported by talent strengths. • Encourages life experiences of individuals in the organization to support.

Figure 3.3. *(Continued)*

PRINCIPAL PROFICIENCY #7	
Knowledge	Building administrators who are proficient in this area have a clear understanding of what it takes to develop a standards-based school and classroom. They have a thorough knowledge of the content standards and eligible content. They also understand teaching and work with their staff to make necessary improvement. They understand people and systems and provide a safe and wholesome environment for students and staff.

Proficiency Level Indicators:

Level 1 (Beginning)	Level 2 (Developing)	Level 3 (Maturing)	Level 4 (Strong)	Level 5 (Exemplary)
Knowledge: ability to identify, recognize, recall	Comprehension: ability to translate, explain, transform	Application: ability to apply solutions to real-world predictable and unpredictable problems	Synthesis: ability to create, compare, design	Evaluation: ability to discriminate, appraise, consider
• Understands the need for a standards-based school. • Knows the content standards and eligible content. • Is aware of appropriate teaching practices.	• Communicates the need for a standards-based school and classroom. • Provides information regarding content standards and eligible content to staff and the school community.	• Works to align school practices with standards-based instruction and evaluation. • Motivates staff to teach to content standards and eligible content. • Provides focused feedback on appropriate teaching practices.	• Creates an environment that recognizes and rewards standards-based efforts. • Shares data that communicates progress toward standards and informs staff of the next steps needed to bring all students to standard.	• Discerns levels of ability to create a standards-based classroom learning environment. • Motivates staff to assume leadership roles in the design and implementation of standards-based practices.

Figure 3.3. (*Continued*)

Level 1 (Beginning)	Level 2 (Developing)	Level 3 (Maturing)	Level 4 (Strong)	Level 5 (Exemplary)
• Understands the importance of a safe and wholesome environment for students and staff.	• Provides descriptions of appropriate teaching practices. • Shares the vision of a safe and wholesome environment with students and staff.	• Addresses behaviors that undermine a safe and wholesome environment.	• Provides individualized learning opportunities and feedback to support teachers in utilizing best teaching practices. • Provides recognition and incentives to support and enhance a safe and wholesome environment. • Utilizes data to evaluate school practices and environment.	• Maintains an environment of accountability for student attainment of content standards. • Provides meaningful incentives for students to strive to attain content standards. • Models and reinforces best teaching practices in interactions with staff and students. • Promotes professional dialogue among staff with respect to standards-based teaching and related best instructional practices. • Provides an environment where students and staff actively engage in activities designed to maintain and enhance the safe and wholesome environment.

PRINCIPAL PROFICIENCY #8
Support	Building administrators are proficient in this area when they receive satisfaction from the personal and professional growth of some of the staff members. This person helps staff members experience success and finds fulfillment in the achievement of each person's goals. This person is constantly looking for ways to provide staff with the tools to help them help students be successful. They focus on the person, not the problem. They serve as a facilitator when a staff member is meeting with concerned parents.

Proficiency Level Indicators:

Level 1 (Beginning)	Level 2 (Developing)	Level 3 (Maturing)	Level 4 (Strong)	Level 5 (Exemplary)
Knowledge: ability to identify, recognize, recall	Comprehension: ability to translate, explain, transform	Application: ability to apply solutions to real-world predictable and unpredictable problems	Synthesis: ability to create, compare, design	Evaluation: ability to discriminate, appraise, consider
• Recognizes personal and professional growth among staff. • Is aware of opportunities for staff to improve student achievement and program effectiveness.	• Explains importance of personal and professional growth. • Shares opportunities to improve student achievement and program effectiveness. • Understands the need for administrative support for staff and students.	• Encourages experiences that lead to personal and professional growth for all staff. • Supports staff in their efforts to improve student achievement and program effectiveness. • Looks for ways to support all facets of the school community.	• Creates an environment in which staff anticipates and celebrates personal and professional growth. • Encourages staff to examine methods that could improve student performance and program effectiveness.	• Maintains culture in which personal and professional growth are encouraged and expected. • Determines when staff is not making growth and sets out on course to support effort and provide direction.

Figure 3.3. (*Continued*)

Level 1 (Beginning)	Level 2 (Developing)	Level 3 (Maturing)	Level 4 (Strong)	Level 5 (Exemplary)
• Identifies situations in which staff and students need administrative support.	• Encourages staff and students to communicate about areas for building, program, and personal improvement.	• Examines how to support staff and students in identified areas for improvement.	• Develops a caring behavior among staff and students that strengthens interpersonal relationships and enhances personal and professional growth.	• Enhances school culture through collegial analysis of student and program needs. • Focuses on both short-term and long-term solutions that strengthen the school community. • Maintains a strong supportive environment for staff and students that encourages risk taking and celebrates personal and professional fulfillment.

Figure 3.3. (*Continued*)

PRINCIPAL PROFICIENCY #9	
Flexibility	Building administrators are proficient in this area when they spontaneously observe thoughts, feelings, and proposed actions, from the viewpoint of patrons, faculty, and students. This person remains sensitive, is aware, and adjusts accordingly. This person is capable of developing a systematic response to change. He or she understands that there is a variety of ways to reach the goals of the school. He or she constantly looks for ways to work through others and remain open to new ideas and direction.

Proficiency Level Indicators:

Level 1 (Beginning)	Level 2 (Developing)	Level 3 (Maturing)	Level 4 (Strong)	Level 5 (Exemplary)
Knowledge: ability to identify, recognize, recall	Comprehension: ability to translate, explain, transform	Application: ability to apply solutions to real-world predictable and unpredictable problems	Synthesis: ability to create, compare, design	Evaluation: ability to discriminate, appraise, consider
• Can recognize the need for flexibility. • Understands the importance of being flexible with students, parents, and staff. • Is familiar with members of the school community who are not proficient in the area of flexibility.	• Understands how flexibility supports the principles of good leadership. • Explains why flexibility is an important trait in a fast-paced world. • Understands how to develop a systematic response to change.	• Has the ability to be flexible in real-world predictable and unpredictable problems. • Uses a number of ways to reach the goals of the school. • Looks for ways to remain open to new ideas. • Communicates support for new approaches and ideas.	• Ability to create workable and flexible responses to new ideas and actions. • Arranges professional life for flexibility and leadership. • Recognizes the role that flexibility can play in leading a school.	• Discriminates when flexibility is the appropriate response to a problem or new idea. • Revises a plan to more ably solve a problem. • Questions the value of flexibility when nonnegotiable values are at stake.

Figure 3.3. *(Continued)*

Level 1 (Beginning)	Level 2 (Developing)	Level 3 (Maturing)	Level 4 (Strong)	Level 5 (Exemplary)
• Understands how flexibility can play a positive leadership role.	• Understands there are a number of ways to reach the goals of the organization. • Understands how to spontaneously observe thoughts, feelings, and proposed actions.	• Supports the unexpected change in perceptions of patrons, faculty, and students.	• Recognizes how flexibility can be used to support school improvement. • Accepts the responsibility to be flexible and to model flexibility. • Integrates responses to problems that demonstrate flexibility.	• Verifies with trusted colleagues that flexibility is an appropriate response. • Proposes solutions that are flexible and supports the vision of the school.

Figure 3.3. (*Continued*)

PRINCIPAL PROFICIENCY #10	
Resourcefulness	Building administrators who are proficient in this area find out the strengths and interests of each teacher in order to extend responsibilities in a way which helps each staff member to grow. This person begins with the individual, not the problem. This person is creative and imaginative in dealing with a difficult situation. He or she is good at delegation and finds out what the faculty members do well, and delegates accordingly—constantly looking for resources to support the staff and the school improvement plan.

Proficiency Level Indicators:

Level 1 (Beginning)	Level 2 (Developing)	Level 3 (Maturing)	Level 4 (Strong)	Level 5 (Exemplary)
Knowledge: ability to identify, recognize, recall	Comprehension: ability to translate, explain, transform	Application: ability to apply solutions to real-world predictable and unpredictable problems	Synthesis: ability to create, compare, design	Evaluation: ability to discriminate, appraise, consider
• Is able to articulate the importance of resourcefulness. • Values resourcefulness as a leadership quality in others.	• Understands the importance of resourcefulness. • Estimates the consequences of innovative solutions to difficult issues.	• Is able to apply creative and imaginative solutions to real-world predictable and unpredictable problems.	• Interrelates a variety of ideas to a single creative workable solution to complex problems.	

Figure 3.3. *(Continued)*

Level 1 (Beginning)	Level 2 (Developing)	Level 3 (Maturing)	Level 4 (Strong)	Level 5 (Exemplary)
• Understands the importance of creativity and innovation in leadership positions. • Knows how to identify creative solutions to difficult problems.	• Translates difficult problems into creative solutions. • Selects solutions that creatively support staff and school improvement. • Defines solutions in creative and innovative ways to help students learn.	• Resolves complete problems by combining many ideas into one creative solution. • Explains how innovative solutions can support school improvement.	• Identifies individual staff strengths and interests to extend their responsibilities so as to assist staff members to grow.	

Figure 3.3. (*Continued*)

Directions This instrument is designed to be used as a self-assessment guideline for practicing building administrators or leadership teams. If you are a practicing administrator (or team) the activity will allow you to reflectively assess your progress toward the stated proficiencies. Rate yourself or team from one to five in each of the ten areas, then review the results to determine if you are satisfied with the outcome.

CAPACITY-BASED LEADERSHIP AUDIT FOR BUILDING AND SCHOOL LEADERS

This activity is also for people who may aspire to a position of leadership, but have questions about how the role may fit them.

Directions Assume that you are involved in each of the following ten scenarios. To prepare for the activity, thoughtfully read each of the definitions and rationale for the ten proficiencies. Then read each question carefully and think about how you would respond, given those exact circumstances as articulated in the question. For each situation, interpret and respond based on your understanding of the proficiencies and your role as a school administrator. Then circle the letter of the alternative that best describes your behavior or belief and transfer the results to the data table on page 95. Maintain a consistent frame of reference as you respond to each question. Each situation is being used to catalog what you believe and what you would do in each situation.

1. If the morale of your staff was at an all-time low and beginning to affect the way the staff responded to children in need, what step would you take to address the issue of low staff morale?
   A. Meet individually with each staff person to praise his or her work.
   B. Become much more visible in the school so individuals will have informal access to you.
   C. Strengthen your relationship with each individual by spending time with him or her.
   D. Pressure policymakers to provide a salary increase or some other incentive.
2. A varsity athlete is suspended from play for breaking training rules. A legitimate question emerges as to how long the suspension should

last. The athletic director recommends the maximum suspension possible, while the student's parents appeal the decision to you favoring the shorter suspension. What course of action would you take?

A. Elect to support the student because students should always come first.

B. Support the staff to affirm that high behavioral standards are an important part of the vision.

C. Support the staff, but make restitution available to shorten the time served.

D. Support the parents because community support is critically important to the success of the school.

3. You have just been appointed principal of Hard Castle High School. Your predecessor recommends that you articulate your beliefs to the staff at your first faculty meeting. What would you do?

A. Reject his advice, not wanting to appear too egocentric.

B. Ask the staff to articulate their expectations of you instead.

C. Accept his advice and present your core beliefs about education in a concise statement, asking for feedback.

D. Communicate to him that you would prefer to allow the beliefs to unfold naturally over time.

4. The staff asks you if they can have "flexible Friday" and leave for home immediately after they finish teaching their last class, to beat the weekend traffic. You allow the request, and it is quickly brought to your attention that the staff has been trading teaching assignments, so as to get an early tee time at the country club. What would you do?

A. Tell the staff what you have been told, and when they admit it is true, eliminate flexible Friday to protect the professional image of the school.

B. Confront the offender and withhold the appropriate pay.

C. Maintain flexible Friday, but monitor it more carefully.

D. Publicly reprimand the violator.

5. A staff member stops in to see you late one evening and indicates that he is seeing another woman behind his wife's back. What would be your reaction?

A. Listen at first and then try to get the staff member to see his minister.

B. Listen with energy and interest for the feelings of the staff member.

C. Try to reason with the staff member.

D. Ask the staff member to stop by when you both have more time.

6. The staff asks you to redo the hall supervision schedule because it seems unfair and conflicts with other duties. What would your reaction be?

A. Not agree to make any changes.

B. Agree to take all requests over again and publish a new supervision schedule to model flexibility.

C. Ask the staff to get their preference in earlier next year so conflicts can be avoided.

D. Invite the staff to make a new schedule and submit it to you for approval.

7. The third-grade teachers have already exceeded their annual allocation for instructional materials. They recognize that fact and still ask you if they can go to the PTSA with a request to purchase new science materials, even though the PTSA has made it clear that they want resources to go for a new "big toy" for the playground. What would you do?

A. Not support the request to the PTSA because you know it will be rejected.

B. Ask the staff wanting science materials if they would like to convert their field trip money to instructional materials. Ask if the staff can come up with other ideas that are resourceful.

C. Ask the teachers to try to plan a bit more carefully in the future.

D. Agree to give their request a high priority if the school receives additional resources.

8. The parents' organization asks you if you would be willing to allow the staff to evaluate you. The staff hears about the request and opposes it because they say that teachers will be next. What would your reaction be?

A. Support the concern of the teachers and deny the request.

B. Agree to the staff evaluation because you believe in accountability.

C. Not feel that staff is really qualified to evaluate you so you deny the request.

D. Feel that teachers are not perceived to be objective enough, so you deny the request.

9. The staff objects to having to develop a written school improvement plan, arguing that it takes more time than it is worth. What would your response be?
   A. Understand the frustration of the staff and agree that the school improvement plan could easily become a multiyear document.
   B. Express your understanding of the frustration, but communicate that the annual plan is vitally important because the standards are still in constant flux.
   C. Ask the staff to develop a proposal of their idea, leaving the door open for an alternative to their annual plan.
   D. Agree and make a request to the superintendent to wave the annual requirement, because of the frustration your staff is feeling.

10. The staff is very excited about a reading program that Bill Blocker is going to present in Orlando, Florida. They ask if they can go and if you will come along as well? You have a conflict because the superintendent has just asked you to be on call to fill in for emergencies (she has to attend a series of meetings on funding and there have been several safety issues in the district of late). The dates are the same time as the reading conference. In addition, the district has just cut one position because of funding problems. What would you do?
    A. Feel forced to deny the request because it would be politically unacceptable to go to a national conference during staff cuts.
    B. Approve the request and agree to go along because you want to know as much about reading instruction as is possible.
    C. Approve the teachers' request, but stay at school because filling in for the superintendent would be good experience.
    D. Deny the request because a respected colleague has told you that the program was a waste of money.

Directions Transfer your answers to the data table (see figure 3.4). *R* is equal to your total responses in column B, and *P* is equal to column C.

Therefore, leadership could be viewed on a continuum from monocratic and bureaucratic to pluralistic and collegial. The purpose of this next activity is to generate an ideal versus an actual comparison of how you perceive your preferred style compared to how you answered the questions beginning on page 91 through 94. Follow the directions below to gener-

	A	B	C	D
1				
2				
3				
4				
5				
6				
7				
8				
9				
10				
Relational Axis				
Productivity Axis				

Figure 3.4.   Data Table for Scoring Proficiencies

ate two results: (1) Ideal style compared to actual style (2) Actual style based on the ten questions for preservice principals.

As we moved into the fourth year of our standards-based effort, the district leadership team (cabinet) and I realized that our role was changing, and we wanted to know more about how others viewed our changing role. During the summer of 1999, we studied the literature on effective district leaders. I then discussed these concepts with a number of superintendents across the nation.

Voices from the Field

I initially began to grapple with these issues of school leadership from the top some ten years ago. Specifically, in 1988, I interviewed twenty-eight Oregon superintendents representing a combined 185,000 students and 10,300 teachers. Included in the sample were seven small districts (fewer than one thousand students), fourteen medium-sized districts (from one thousand to five thousand students), and seven large districts (more than seven thousand students). I did those interviews to find out what Oregon superintendents believed to be (1) the critical issues for administrators, and (2) the role of the principal in transition. A summary of the results follows.

Summary

(1) What is the critical issue (external challenge) for administrators?
    Of the twenty-eight superintendents interviewed, the most significant
    external challenge reported was the politics of funding. In close prox-
    imity were (in order): leadership development, instructional leader-
    ship, and long-range planning.

(2) What is the role of the principal in transition?
    Twenty-six out of twenty-eight principals maintained that the role of
    the principal was going through a transition, but that the trend seemed
    to lack any type of definition. A superintendent summarized the gen-
    eral sentiment when he said, "the role of the principal is going
    through a transition of some kind, but the trend seems to lack any
    kind of definition."

Directions   Using the formula $R^2 \times P = PC$, determine your PC Index,
where PC = peak capacity (see figure 3.5). R is equal to column B and P
to column C. Plot that number on axis A. Are you satisfied with the result?

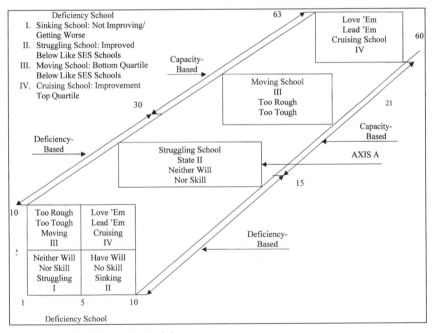

Figure 3.5.   Peak Capacity Model

SUPERINTENDENT AND
DISTRICT OFFICE ADMINISTRATORS

With all of those developments in mind, I began to work with the staff to develop proficiencies and a rubric for the district office administrators. By way of process, we started with the proficiencies for district administrators, then we moved to the standards-based proficiencies for principals the second year, and for teachers the third year. I will not submit the teacher proficiencies here because it is beyond the scope of this theoretical framework. In addition, a significant work has already been published by Charlotte Danielson and is available in print for your consideration.[23] The principal's formulaic construct created balance between the productivity and relational domain. The data that we generated suggested that the central office administrator's proficiencies took a modestly different direction from the principal's proficiencies.

The data suggested that the central office administrator needed to be more of a technician with highly developed and important interpersonal skills. Therefore, the formulaic integrated leadership model is somewhat different for central office administrators than for principals. There was a stronger emphasis on the technical side. I can only speculate why that might be true. With decentralized decision making now in place in school systems, the decision-making role of central office administrators has been significantly diminished. Therefore, the technical skills have become more important in the district administrator's ability to serve schools effectively. I suspect that this trend will evolve until the central office administrators will be housed in a mobile van, and they will need advanced technical skills or become obsolete. I found it fascinating that the data generated a heightened appreciation for relational skills in central office administrators as well.

To adequately reflect the data, the formula for central office administrators is marginally similar, but still somewhat different in that more technical expertise is expected without any reduction in the relational domain. As with building-based leadership, the same two domains emerged. The same two-step process follows for central office administrators as for building leaders. First, practicing district leaders can choose to generate their perceived dominant leadership domain and then compare it to their actual dominate domain.

Capacity-Based Leadership Audit for Preservice District Leaders

Directions Assume that you are involved in each of the following scenarios. First, read each of the definitions and rationale for the ten proficiencies with great care. Then, read each question and respond given the exact circumstances as articulated in the question. Circle the letter of the alternative that best describes your projected behavior or belief. For each situation, interpret and respond based on your understanding of the proficiencies and on your role as a district office administrator. Then circle the letter of the alternative that best describes your behavior or belief, and transfer the result to the data table that follows. Use the data on the table to fill in the values of R and P and complete the equation. Then, plot your peak capacity as done earlier in the domain balance figure (figure 3.2).

Maintain a consistent frame of reference as you respond to each question. Each situation is being used to catalogue what you believe and what you would do in each of the following situations.

1. You are taking a course in leadership and for the final exam you must write some goals you might consider using as a first-year superintendent or district office administrator. The professor, whom you admire and respect, advises you not to write nonmeasurable goals for the class assignment because he believes that such an artificial constraint (of measurable goals) will force you to avoid goals that are truly meaningful. He also asks you to provide him with a rationale for each goal. In the meantime, you have just been moved to the central office as the superintendent or assistant superintendent and you find that you are required to write five goals. The professor recognizes that you are busy and indicates that you can turn in your actual goals if you like. What would you do?
   A. Write measurable goals and use them for both your new job and the class.
   B. Write both measurable and nonmeasurable goals.
   C. Write a set of measurable goals for work and another for class.
   D. Write nonmeasurable goals for your new job and for the class.
2. You have just been appointed to take an emergency vacancy as a district leader in Frostbite Falls. The previous superintendent was termi-

nated because he had an affair with his secretary. The staff is upset because they feel that the proceedings were unfair and he was a much-loved leader. Morale is so low that it is beginning to impact students. What would you do?

A. Talk about the issue with the cabinet.

B. Make it a point to spend as much personal time as possible with the staff.

C. Ask the human resources department to come up with a solution.

D. Work with the union to develop its involvement in the solution.

3. The parents want to start an academic booster club at your premier high school. The coaches and staff are resisting the parents. You are asked to come to a club meeting to look into the matter. What would you do?

A. Agree to the meeting and communicate that you support the staff because they know what is best for the students.

B. Communicate your regrets and ask the building staff to handle it.

C. Attend the meeting and just listen to the parents, but do not make any commitments.

D. Ask the board to explore the possibility of writing a policy that would allow academic booster clubs.

4. The United Way executive director asks you if you will chair the annual fund-raising drive. What would you do?

A. Tell the director no because you just do not have the time.

B. Agree to help even though you are busy because you want to model community involvement.

C. Indicate that you will help if the United Way will support an ongoing effort in the district.

D. Indicate that you do not have time, but will work with the United Way to increase giving in the district.

5. The instruction team plans a technical assistance program to schools and they ask you if you would like to participate. How would you respond?

A. Decline the offer because your time with the board has limited your flexibility.

B. Accept the offer because you want to be visible.

C. Enthusiastically agree because you want to model your interest and expertise in the technical aspects of leadership.

D. Encourage the idea and ask members of the board if they would like to participate.

6. You just accepted the job as assistant superintendent to the Hassle View district. You are having your first meeting of principals, and the union president asks you how you would work with a principal who is struggling and has lost the support of the staff and the community. How would you respond?

   A. Indicate that you would set goals with the person in question and then give critical feedback.

   B. Indicate you would consider a transfer to a less troublesome school.

   C. Work with the principal to address the concerns, by working through the strengths of the individual.

   D. Indicate you would consider a transfer to a school with a less troublesome staff.

   E. Indicate to the principal that you would give him one year to turn it around, then move him to the curriculum department.

7. The teachers' union asks if you would move the starting time for the high schools from 9:00 A.M. to 7:30 A.M., giving students more time to work after school. The community and a majority of the board are strongly behind the proposal. The research indicates that the sleep patterns of adolescence make earlier starting times problematic. What would you do?

   A. Support the suggestion because community support is critical in passing the school tax levy in the spring.

   B. Create a study team to bring a recommendation to you for board consideration.

   C. Deny the proposal because the research indicates that an earlier starting time is negative for high school age students.

   D. Support the proposal when the local chamber of commerce and city council vote to support the change as well.

8. The high school principal whom you supervise is invited to present a paper on school improvement at a national symposium (out of state) that is scheduled to conflict with parent–teacher conferences. The principal wants to attend because she is excited about the quality of the program. The parent club expresses concern because it has scheduled her to meet with the parents of students who are at risk. They

also wonder where the money would come from, given recent budget cuts. How would you respond?

A. Discourage the trip because parental support is critically important.
B. Encourage her to go because you believe her personal growth is an important precondition for the improvement of the school.
C. Discourage the trip because the board is concerned about the rising dropout rate.
D. Deny the request because out-of-state travel would fly in the face of recent budget cuts.

9. The chairman of the board has a son who graduates with a degree in teaching and applies for a vacancy at one of the schools. He advises you that he expects you to find him a job so he can live at home for just a few more years. The selection committee at the school selects someone else because their first-choice candidate is just uncommonly good. They communicate that the board member's son is a very close second and would normally have gotten the job, except for the candidacy of this exceptionally talented first choice. The committee asks you to support their nomination. How would you respond?

A. Indicate that you cannot support their recommendation because the board member's son is also very good and certainly will not do any harm.
B. Accept the recommendation and instruct the human relations department to find a job for the board member's son.
C. Reject the recommendation (accepting the political risks) because you believe in hiring the very best.
D. Reject their recommendation and reopen the position.

10. The board returns from a national convention and asks you to set a goal to improve the district's athletic program. How would you respond?

A. Ask the athletic director to develop an improvement program for board consideration.
B. Agree because all of the programs in the district should be exceptional.
C. Reluctantly take the matter under study because you do not want to shift the focus away from academic excellence just now.
D. Ask the booster clubs to take an active hand in the improvement effort.

RELATIONAL SQUARED TIMES
PRODUCTIVITY EQUALS PEAK CAPACITY

To generate the framework, we studied the research on leadership. Then we asked all of the building leaders and the district office leaders to reach consensus on the following two questions:

1. What do central office leaders need to know and do to provide leadership insuring that the school district is productive?
2. What are the most important beliefs that the district leaders need to sustain the relational foundation?

Productivity Domain

The productivity domain was defined as the skills and knowledge that district administrators need to be successful. The seven proficiencies that surfaced in the productivity domain (know and do) are as follows:

1. Purpose and mission
   The district leader (DL) has a clear vision of how to develop an SBS.
2. Continual improvement
   The DL models continual improvement through professional development.
3. Accountability
   The DL uses personal and organizational accountability to impact the quality of education for students.
4. Communicate effectively
   The DL communicates effectively in both the cognitive and affective domains.
5. Technical expertise
   The DL exhibits technical expertise in designing systems that help students meet academic standards.
6. Professional efficacy
   The DL demonstrates professional efficacy in impacting the quality of education for students.
7. Effective instructional systems
   The DL designs effective instructional systems that meet academic standards.

Human Domain

The human domain was defined as the beliefs and values necessary for the district leader (DL) to be proficient in a standards-based school district.

1. Relationships
   The DL develops strong, personal, and lasting relationships.
2. Service
   The DL is service oriented.
3. Capacities
   The DL develops capacities in others by working from others' strengths, talents, and ideas.

SELF-ASSESSMENT INSTRUMENT FOR PRACTICING DISTRICT OFFICE ADMINISTRATORS

The definition of each proficiency and the rationale for including each follows.

Definition and Rationale: Accountability   District leaders who are proficient in this area formulate accountability measures around what is good for students relative to the academic standards. They establish measurable personal goals and continually perform reflective self-assessment as measured against preestablished criteria. In addition, they understand and apply effective supervision and program evaluation in their area of responsibility.

Accountability is located on the productivity axis because accountability is personal in a system defined by high standards and high-stakes assessment for students and schools.

Definition and Rationale: Communicate Effectively   District leaders who are proficient in this area excel in two-way communications; they are equally adept at sending and receiving messages. They communicate cognitively (for meaning) and affectively (for feeling). They choose the form of communication that best fits the purpose and audience of the message. At the highest level of proficiency, they lead the rest of the district's staff members to excel as communicators.

Communicating effectively is included as proficiency because communication skills are the core tools for leaders to succeed. Everything that needs to be accomplished in the leadership arena occurs through some form of communication, so this proficiency was deemed to be critically important.

Definition and Rationale: Technical Expertise District leaders demonstrate a thorough understanding of the culture and characteristics of individual schools. Through their expertise in academic programs and school systems, they are a valuable resource for schools in the planning and implementation of school goals and programs.

Technical expertise was included as a proficiency because schools want to work with DLs who understand and appreciate the uniqueness of each individual school. They also want, and expect, DLs to help them with their technical expertise.

Definition and Rationale: Professional Efficacy District leaders who are proficient in this area have courage to take charge and make things happen. They facilitate the work of individuals and groups. They understand the power of delegation and working through others. They show initiative and are willing to take risks to impact student success. They have a high level of productivity and engender significant levels of trust and credibility through personal integrity.

Personal and professional efficacy was included on the productivity axis because having a sense of efficacy (potency) as a DL is critically important to making a difference for students and staff.

Definition and Rationale: Effective Instructional Systems District leaders who are proficient in this area design and implement systems that help students meet academic standards. They help others understand the importance of a curriculum that matches state standards and progresses logically K–12. They have the ability to set expectations through participatory processes and design assessments to identify what programs are working for students.

Effective instructional systems were included because building administrators value technical expertise. Because the stakes are so high in the SBS, building administrators want DLs who can help them technically be successful.

Human Domain

The human domain was defined as the beliefs and values necessary for the district leader to be proficient in a standards-based school district.

Definition and Rationale: Relationships   District leaders who are proficient in this area express care and concern for people. They make it a point to be close to principals and other district administrators by spending time working with them. They are available and work hard for others. Finally, they balance ego with humility as appropriate.

Relationships were included as a proficiency because positive relationships are the culminating effect of all of the proficiencies working together. Relationship is in the same proportion to trust as hard work is to success. Relationship itself is an axis.

Definition and Rationale: Service   District leaders who are proficient in this area exhibit two distinguishing characteristics: (1) they assist the work of the board, district staff members, and the community as a way to provide effective education for our students, and (2) they enjoy providing effective service. At the highest level of proficiency, they lead the rest of the district staff members to provide service that improves the education for our students.

Service was included on the relational axis because it is one of the defining beliefs of effective DLs in a standards-based district. Providing meaningful service is a powerful way to build strong and lasting relationships.

Definition and Rationale: Capacities   District leaders enhance the professional effectiveness of colleagues through capacity building. They recognize the strengths and talents of others. Through personal and purposeful strategies, they enhance the growth of those strengths and talents.

Developing the capacities of colleagues by building on their strengths is the keystone to relationship building. Capacity-based leadership techniques create powerful and lasting relationships.

SELF-ASSESSMENT INSTRUMENT FOR PRACTICING SUPERINTENDENTS AND DISTRICT LEADERS

Following is a self-assessment instrument that includes the aforementioned proficiencies along with a rubric or scoring guide.

The proficiency level indicators stair-step up (from simple to very complex) through the six levels of Bloom's taxonomy.

The level indicators are defined as follows:

Level 1 (Beginning):   Includes having knowledge or knowing; it is the simplest level of the cognitive domains.

Level 2 (Developing):   This level goes beyond simple knowledge to un-
                          derstanding or comprehension.
Level 3 (Maturing):   This level goes beyond knowing and understand-
                          ing to applying.
Level 6 (Strong):   Level four is analysis—the ability of the individ-
                          ual to break down information into its component
                          parts.
Level 7 (Exemplary):   Level five is synthesis—the ability of the indi-
                          vidual to put together elements or parts to form a
                          new whole.

Directions   Use the leadership indicators, proficiencies, and scoring
guides that follow to rate yourself in each of the ten proficiency areas (see
figure 3.6). You might ask several administrators whom you trust to evaluate you as well. Then use the results to see if there is a discrepancy between how others see you and how you see yourself. Review the outcome
to determine if you are satisfied with the results. Use the outcome to help
you improve. See proficiency instrument.

CAPACITY-BASED ASSESSMENT FOR PRESERVICE
SUPERINTENDENTS OR DISTRICT LEADERS

Directions   Assume that you are involved in each of the ten following
scenarios. To prepare for the activity, read with care and thought each of
the definitions of the proficiencies. Then read each question carefully and
think about how you would respond given the exact circumstances as articulated in the question. Think carefully about how you would respond to
each situation exactly as written. For each situation, interpret and respond
based on your understanding of the proficiencies and your role as a district administrator. Then circle the letter of the alternative that best describes your behavior or belief and transfer the results to the data table in
figure 3.7.

Be sure to maintain a consistent frame of reference as you respond to
each question. Each situation is being used to catalogue what you believe
and what you would do in each of the following scenarios:

LEADERSHIP PROFICIENCY #1	Relationships
District Leadership Team members develop strong relationships.	DLT members who are proficient in this area express care and concern for people. They make it a point to be close to principals and other district administrators by spending time working with them. They are available and work hard for others. Finally, they balance ego with humility as appropriate.

Proficiency Level Indicators:

Level 1 (Beginning)	Level 2 (Developing)	Level 3 (Maturing)	Level 4 (Strong)	Level 5 (Exemplary)
Knowledge: ability to identify, recognize, recall	Comprehension: ability to translate, explain, transform	Application: ability to apply solutions to real-world predictable and unpredictable problems	Synthesis: ability to create, compare, design	Evaluation: ability to discriminate, appraise, consider
• Recognize that it is important to express care and concern for people. • Know that it is important to balance ego and humility.	• Explain why strong and lasting relationships help leaders to help students. • Rearrange schedules to be available to people.	• Organize a system that allows routine expression of care and concern for people. • Apply balance of ego and humility to personal and professional work.	• Consider additional ways of expressing care and concern for people. • Consider additional ways of being available to people.	• Organize an annual schedule to be available (visible) to people in the school community. • Evaluate own ability to balance ego with humility.

Figure 3.6. District Office Leadership Proficiencies

Level 1 (Beginning)	Level 2 (Developing)	Level 3 (Maturing)	Level 4 (Strong)	Level 5 (Exemplary)
• Recognize opportunities to spend time with school leaders. • Identify feelings of humility and ego-driven feelings.	• Explain the importance of spending time with school leaders. • Translate feelings into expressions of care and concern for others.	• Organize time to be available to others. • Design and implement specific strategies in developing strong mutually supportive relationships.	• Design short- and long-range plans aimed at being close to school leaders. • Compare outcomes of different relationship-building strategies. • Consider the perspective of school leaders and demonstrate an ability to articulate those concerns.	• Discriminate between perceived levels of care and concern among others. • Consider new ways of reaching others who present relationship challenges.

Figure 3.6. (*Continued*)

LEADERSHIP PROFICIENCY #2	Purpose and Mission
District Leadership Team members demonstrate commitment to purpose and mission of the district.	DLT members who are proficient in this area understand that their fundamental purpose is to impact the quality of education for students by working through others, often principals. Further, they recognize that power is given to them by others, which requires trust. They also balance new ideas with academic standards and existing workload of district staff. They have the ability to prioritize tasks and make decisions that are centered around what is important for students. They have tenacity and critical thinking ability.

Proficiency Level Indicators:

Level 1 (Beginning)	Level 2 (Developing)	Level 3 (Maturing)	Level 4 (Strong)	Level 5 (Exemplary)
Knowledge: ability to identify, recognize, recall	Comprehension: ability to translate, explain, transform	Application: ability to apply solutions to real-world predictable and unpredictable problems	Synthesis: ability to create, compare, design	Evaluation: ability to discriminate, appraise, consider
• Recognize that student achievement comes first. • Know that power is not a matter of position, but rather trust.	• Transform priorities into results for kids. • Explain why academic standards are important.	• Solve problems based on what is good for students. • Make decisions based on what is good for students.	• Create systems that impact academic achievement for students. • Develop programs to help students meet standards.	• Discriminate among those programs that impact students most significantly. • Analyze the organization for ways to impact student achievement.

Figure 3.6. *(Continued)*

Level 1 (Beginning)	Level 2 (Developing)	Level 3 (Maturing)	Level 4 (Strong)	Level 5 (Exemplary)
• Identify ways that others impact the quality of education for students. • Recognize the basic skills involved in working through others.	• Explain the importance of balancing the work of implementing new ideas with the existing workload. • Prioritize tasks for greatest impact on student learning.	• Organize work to include others for maximum impact on student learning. • Apply knowledge of student learning to work related decisions. • Make inferences about the connection between academic standards and own area of self-responsibility. • Distinguish between the programs that impact students positively and those that do not. • Demonstrate the ability to articulate the purpose and mission of the district.	• Create relationship stability over time to enhance trust. • Compare new ideas against potential gains for effective decision making. • Create the capacity in others to articulate the purpose and mission of the district.	• Discriminate among effective organizational strategies to determine the best of the best. • Consider the district's purpose and mission in designing organizational work. • Make operational the district's purpose and mission.

Figure 3.6. (Continued)

LEADERSHIP PROFICIENCY #3	Leadership through Service
District Leadership Team members are service oriented.	DLT members who are proficient in this area exhibit two distinguishing characteristics: (1) they assist the work of the board, district staff members, and the community as a way to provide effective education for our students, and (2) they enjoy providing effective service. At the highest level of proficiency, they lead the rest of the district's staff members to provide service that improves the education of our students.

Proficiency Level Indicators:

Level 1 (Beginning)	Level 2 (Developing)	Level 3 (Maturing)	Level 4 (Strong)	Level 5 (Exemplary)
Knowledge: ability to identify, recognize, recall	Comprehension: ability to translate, explain, transform	Application: ability to apply solutions to real-world predictable and unpredictable problems	Synthesis: ability to create, compare, design	Evaluation: ability to discriminate, appraise, consider
• Are familiar with the principles of effective service. • Understand the concept that district staff members (including the DLT), schools, and departments are service organizations.	• Understand how a specific action fits or doesn't fit the principles of effective service. • Enjoy providing effective service. • Understand how a specific action fits or doesn't fit the goals established for the district by the school board.	• Apply the appropriate service principles to specific predictable and unpredictable situations. • Communicate the importance of effective service to other district staff members. • Carry out specific actions to fulfill the goals established for the district by the school board.	• Develop plans that apply appropriate principles of effective service. • Develop plans to communicate the importance of effective service to other district staff members. • Develop plans to fulfill the goals established for the district by the school board.	• Foster throughout the school system the appropriate application of the principles of effective service. • Foster throughout the school system a commitment to fulfilling the goals established for the district by the school board. This includes

Figure 3.6. (*Continued*)

Level 1 (Beginning)	Level 2 (Developing)	Level 3 (Maturing)	Level 4 (Strong)	Level 5 (Exemplary)
• Are familiar with goals established for the district by the school board. • Are familiar with the goals of each district school and department. • Are familiar with the goals of major community organizations (governmental and nongovernmental).	• Understand how a specific action fits or doesn't fit the goals of a specific district school or department. • Understand how a specific action fits or doesn't fit the goals of a specific community organization.	• Carry out specific actions to enable a district school or department to fulfill its goals. • Carry out specific actions to enable a specific community organization to improve education for our students.	• Develop plans to help district schools and departments fulfill their goals. • Develop plans to help community organizations improve education for our students.	a commitment by schools and departments to coordinate their goals development and help each other fulfill their goals. • Foster throughout the school system a commitment to helping schools and departments fulfill their goals. • Foster throughout the school system a commitment to involving community organizations in efforts to improve education for our students.

Figure 3.6. (*Continued*)

LEADERSHIP PROFICIENCY #4	Professional Development
District Leadership Team members model continuous improvement through professional development.	DLT members model personal and professional growth in a rapidly changing, standards-driven system with improved student achievement as the goal. They consistently and actively seek opportunities which support continuous learning for themselves and others.

Proficiency Level Indicators:

Level 1 (Beginning)	Level 2 (Developing)	Level 3 (Maturing)	Level 4 (Strong)	Level 5 (Exemplary)
Knowledge: ability to identify, recognize, recall	Comprehension: ability to translate, explain, transform	Application: ability to apply solutions to real-world predictable and unpredictable problems	Synthesis: ability to create, compare, design	Evaluation: ability to discriminate, appraise, consider
• Identify the critical relationship between personal growth and improved student achievement. • Identify growth opportunities which are relevant and realistic for self and others. • Recall salient issues of school improvement models as they relate to professional growth.	• Describe the measurable aspects of the connection between personal growth and improved student achievement. • Distinguish among a variety of growth opportunities to determine which ones are realistic for self and others. • Translate professional growth opportunities into school improvement	• Apply new learning to programs that inculcate and foster increased student achievement. • Integrate new strategies and skills into individual and group performance. • Mentor others in the use of school improvement practices that have professional growth as a foundation.	• Design professional plans based on self-analysis and student needs which demonstrate academic knowledge, action research, or other acceptable research methods. • Create plans for professional growth, which include significant representation from members of the school community.	• Evaluate professional growth plans which impact academic standards and make recommendations which are effective and representative or research-based best practices. • Model continual learning and growth by demonstrating evidence of extensive reading, participation in professional organizations, and

Figure 3.6. *(Continued)*

Level 1 (Beginning)	Level 2 (Developing)	Level 3 (Maturing)	Level 4 (Strong)	Level 5 (Exemplary)
• Recognize the importance of school, district, and community mores when pursuing professional development for self and others. • Seek information which will be beneficial for personal and professional growth.	practices which are measurable and authentic. • Explain the nature of local mores and how professional improvement works in concert with the culture of the community, state, and nation. • Appreciate the nature of continual learning for pleasure.	• Analyze the major factors which drive local mores and interrelate these with specific professional growth options. • Value the variety of mores and laws that shape a local culture.	• Formulate professional growth plans so that school improvement practices which demonstrate growth and effectiveness in a standards-driven system are the norm. • Plan for the immediate, short-term and long-term academic needs of the community using professional growth as one of the vehicles to meet those needs. • Support the importance of self-reflection as a process in professional development.	current knowledge of educational theory and practice. • Provide leadership in the design and implementation of professional improvement programs that foster consistency between educational philosophy and pedagogy. • Design, implement, and assess a professional growth plan consistent with local, state, and national needs using cultural awareness as factor. • Differentiate among complex issues relating to professional growth and revise action plans as needed.

Figure 3.6. (Continued)

LEADERSHIP PROFICIENCY #5	Accountability
District Leadership Team members use personal and organizational accountability to impact the quality of education for students.	DLT members who are proficient in this area formulate accountability measures around what is good for students relative to the academic standards. They establish measurable personal goals and continually perform reflective self-assessment as measured against preestablished criteria. In addition, they understand and apply effective supervision and program evaluation in their area of responsibility.

Proficiency Level Indicators:

Level 1 (Beginning)	Level 2 (Developing)	Level 3 (Maturing)	Level 4 (Strong)	Level 5 (Exemplary)
Knowledge: ability to identify, recognize, recall	Comprehension: ability to translate, explain, transform	Application: ability to apply solutions to real-world predictable and unpredictable problems	Synthesis: ability to create, compare, design	Evaluation: ability to discriminate, appraise, consider
• Recognize the value of setting measurable personal goals. • Recognize the value of measurable performance goals	• Explain personal goals in area of responsibility. • Set goals that help students meet academic standards.	• Organize programs for personal and organizational accountability. • Organize evaluation and measurement	• Create evaluation strategies that reflect an understanding of the relationship between staff performance and student achievement.	• Appraise the effectiveness of evaluations in moving the organization toward higher levels of achievement for students.

Figure 3.6. (*Continued*)

Level 1 (Beginning)	Level 2 (Developing)	Level 3 (Maturing)	Level 4 (Strong)	Level 5 (Exemplary)
in supervising others. • Understand the need for and purpose of accountability in the school organization. • Articulate to others the value of goals and accountability.	• Translate goals into program, department, or service outcomes that impact students. • Help others set goals that impact student achievement.	strategies around preestablished criteria. • Apply goal implementation to real-world predictable and unpredictable problems. • Analyze performance through self-reflection and interpretation of data.	• Design accountability systems for self and others which lead to continuous improvement. • Infer cause and effect from actions and outcomes. • Revise goals as necessary to respond to changing conditions.	• Discriminate between core and tangential information in analyzing data for decision making. • Engage in self-reflection and positive self-support. • Synthesize the most effective strategies for high personal achievement based on accountability measures.

Figure 3.6. (*Continued*)

LEADERSHIP PROFICIENCY #6	Assisting School Leaders in Reaching Their Goals
District Leadership Team members develop capacities in others by working from others' strengths, talents, and ideas.	DLT members enhance the professional development and effectiveness of colleagues through capacity building. They recognize the strengths and talents of others. Through personal relationships and purposeful strategies they enhance the growth of those strengths and talents.

Proficiency Level Indicators:

Level 1 (Beginning)	Level 2 (Developing)	Level 3 (Maturing)	Level 4 (Strong)	Level 5 (Exemplary)
Knowledge: ability to identify, recognize, recall	Comprehension: ability to translate, explain, transform	Application: ability to apply solutions to real-world predictable and unpredictable problems	Synthesis: ability to create, compare, design	Evaluation: ability to discriminate, appraise, consider
• Recognize the value of a professional growth model that builds upon strengths and talents rather than deficiencies. • Identify specific strategies for capacity building. • Recognize the value of strong interpersonal relationships as a	• Understand and explain the growth process, and distinguish between capacity-building strategies and deficiency strategies. • Understand and explain processes and strategies for professional growth based on capacity building.	• With individuals, apply capacity-building strategies to recognize their talents and strengths. • With groups, apply capacity-building strategies to recognize their dynamics and capacities. • Apply interpersonal skills to enhance the effectiveness of	• Assess specific individuals' capabilities, and design or implement capacity-building strategies to optimize performance. • Assess specific work groups or staff capability and design or implement capacity-building strategies to optimize performance.	• Continually evaluate the effectiveness of oneself and peers to gain direction for determining capacity-building strategies. • Continually evaluate interpersonal relationships to be aware of others' growth and utilize to develop capacity-building strategies for their growth.

Figure 3.6. *(Continued)*

Level 1 (Beginning)	Level 2 (Developing)	Level 3 (Maturing)	Level 4 (Strong)	Level 5 (Exemplary)
component to building capacity in colleagues. • Recall which strategies assist in recognizing the professional strengths and talent of peers.	• Understand and explain the importance of personal relationships and trust in working with others and developing capacity in others. • Understand and explain the strengths and talents of peers and peer groups.	professional growth efforts with individuals through mutual trust and respect. • Apply group interaction skills that allow effective intervention with groups in helping groups grow in productivity.	• When working with and encouraging others' performance and growth, incorporate knowledge of the organization and its needs, so that the effort is channeled in a focused manner. • Establish long-term relationships that enhance others' desires to grow and give recognition for the growth steps they take.	• Appraise the strengths and status of the organization as a means of enhancing the effectiveness of others in helping to achieve the organization's goals.

Figure 3.6. (*Continued*)

LEADERSHIP PROFICIENCY #7	Effective Communication
District Leadership Team members communicate effectively.	DLT members who are proficient in this area excel in two-way communication: they are equally adept at sending messages and receiving messages. They communicate cognitively (for meaning) and affectively (for feeling). They choose the form of communication that best fits the purpose of, and audience for, the message. At the highest level of proficiency, they lead the rest of the district's staff members to excel as communicators.

Proficiency Level Indicators:

Level 1 (Beginning)	Level 2 (Developing)	Level 3 (Maturing)	Level 4 (Strong)	Level 5 (Exemplary)
Knowledge: ability to identify, recognize, recall	Comprehension: ability to translate, explain, transform	Application: ability to apply solutions to real-world predictable and unpredictable problems	Synthesis: ability to create, compare, design	Evaluation: ability to discriminate, appraise, consider
• Are familiar with communication theory and the steps in the communication process. • Support the concept of two-way communication. • Know techniques for communicating cognitively and effectively.	• Understand how a specific communication fits or doesn't fit the components of communication theory. • Enjoy two-way communication with specific audiences. • Understand the cognitive and affective elements of	• Apply the appropriate components of communication theory to specific communication. • Control the cognitive and affective elements of specific communication. • Apply the right techniques to specific communication.	• Develop a communication plan that incorporates the appropriate components of communication theory and the appropriate techniques of oral, visual, written, and multimedia communication. • Develop plans to encourage systemwide	• Appraise and foster throughout the school system the appropriate application of communication theory and the appropriate use of oral, visual, written, and multimedia communication. • Appraise and foster throughout the school system the

Figure 3.6. *(Continued)*

Level 1 (Beginning)	Level 2 (Developing)	Level 3 (Maturing)	Level 4 (Strong)	Level 5 (Exemplary)
• Know techniques of oral, visual, written, and multimedia communication.	understanding of a specific communication. • Understand the techniques used in a specific communication.	• Respond appropriately to unexpected dynamics in two-way communication.	and support for two-way communication. • Develop plans to encourage system-wide understanding of the cognitive and affective elements of communication. • Develop plans to communicate system-wide during unpredictable situations.	understanding of and support for two-way communication. • Appraise and foster throughout the school system the understanding of the cognitive and affective elements of communication. • Appraise and foster systemwide the ability to communicate effectively during unpredictable situations.

Figure 3.6. (*Continued*)

LEADERSHIP PROFICIENCY #8	Technical Expertise
District Leadership Team members exhibit technical expertise in designing systems that help students meet academic standards	DLT members demonstrate a thorough understanding of the culture and characteristics of individual schools. Through their expertise in academic programs and school systems, they are a valuable resource for schools in the planning and implementation of school goals and programs.

Proficiency Level Indicators:

Level 1 (Beginning)	Level 2 (Developing)	Level 3 (Maturing)	Level 4 (Strong)	Level 5 (Exemplary)
Knowledge: ability to identify, recognize, recall	Comprehension: ability to translate, explain, transform	Application: ability to apply solutions to real world predictable and unpredictable problems	Synthesis: ability to create, compare, design	Evaluation: ability to discriminate, appraise, consider
• Identify effective school systems and programs. • Know about the characteristics of individual schools including demographics, size, staff characteristics, culture, and educational programs.	• Understand effective systems and communicate that understanding to other colleagues. • Understand the unique characteristics of each school site and constructively dialogue about the school including its	• Apply knowledge of a school's specific characteristics and assessment data to make determinations about appropriate program goals or refinements to support and improve the school program. • Apply knowledge of a school's culture	• Design goal-setting activities that incorporate the characteristics of each school, the school's assessment data, the goals of the district, and the federal and state mandates that each school must address.	• Discriminate among various academic programs and school systems to make recommendations for schools that are research based and reflective of district goals. • Assist schools in their internal assessment of skills and culture to

Figure 3.6. *(Continued)*

Level 1 (Beginning)	Level 2 (Developing)	Level 3 (Maturing)	Level 4 (Strong)	Level 5 (Exemplary)
• Know about strategies for effective program implementation, including staff development activities. • Know about strategies and models for effective program evaluation.	strengths, needs, and internal dynamics. • Understand the dynamics of school change and program implementation. Have specific suggestions and strategies for implementing new programs. • Understand efficient and effective program evaluation and match evaluation strategies with the systems and programs being evaluated.	and dynamics to plan and implement effective strategies for goal implementation. • Support among schools networking efforts related to program implementation and assessment. • Support the goal-setting process by effectively working through key school groups including administrators, instructional staff, key parents, and site councils.	• Design implementation strategies that address the identified needs and goals of the school and that reflect the dynamics of the school's unique culture. • Design networking strategies that optimize the efforts of school and district staff in implementing and refining school programs. • Design strategies and activities that coordinate the efforts of the various participants of school program implementation, including school staff, parents, and district staff.	ensure that they have the capacity to implement desired programs and activities. • Discriminate among effective evaluation strategies to assist schools in their collection of useful and appropriate data. • Evaluate the effectiveness of coordinated district and school efforts and be able to pinpoint where intervention strategies would be most beneficial in program refinement.

Figure 3.6. (Continued)

LEADERSHIP PROFICIENCY #9	Efficacy
District Leadership Team members demonstrate personal and professional efficacy in impacting the quality of education for students.	DLT members who are proficient in this area have the courage to take charge and make things happen. They facilitate the work of individuals and groups. They understand the power of delegation and working through others. They show initiative and are willing to take risks to impact student success. They have a high level of productivity and engender significant levels of trust and credibility through personal integrity.

Proficiency Level Indicators:

Level 1 (Beginning)	Level 2 (Developing)	Level 3 (Maturing)	Level 4 (Strong)	Level 5 (Exemplary)
Knowledge: ability to identify, recognize, recall	Comprehension: ability to translate, explain, transform	Application: ability to apply solutions to real-world predictable and unpredictable problems	Synthesis: ability to create, compare, design	Evaluation: ability to discriminate, appraise, consider
• Identify when a situation requires facilitation or redirection. • Identify tasks that can be delegated. • Recognize the importance of risk taking.	• Explain the need for and power of good facilitation. • Explain tasks and expected outcomes to delegees. • Translate intentions into actions.	• Have the courage to facilitate groups of any size to reach intended outcomes. • Delegate appropriate tasks. • Take risks that impact student success.	• Create facilitation techniques based on analyzing what works in particular situations. • Design workplace systems to foster delegation.	• Consider the effects of facilitation on the ultimate outcomes of district goals. • Appraise specifically how productivity in your area of responsibility increases when you delegate.

Figure 3.6. (*Continued*)

Level 1 (Beginning)	Level 2 (Developing)	Level 3 (Maturing)	Level 4 (Strong)	Level 5 (Exemplary)
• Identify that trust is essential to the success of the district.	• Explain the importance of integrity and predictability in building trust.	• Engender trust by modeling integrity in all situations. • Demonstrate the courage to take charge of situations and be accountable for results.	• Create environments that encourage and support those who take risks. • Create activities that build trust.	• Consider the systemic effects of fostering risk taking. • Appraise the differences that trust building has on the organization and its employees.

Figure 3.6. *(Continued)*

LEADERSHIP PROFICIENCY #10	Effective Instructional Systems
District Leadership Team members design effective instructional systems that meet academic standards.	DLT members who are proficient in this area design and implement systems that help students meet academic standards. They help others understand the importance of a curriculum that matches the state standards and progresses logically K–12. They have the ability to set expectations through participatory processes and design assessments to identify what programs are working for students. Finally, DLT members organize the work of their area of responsibility to directly support academic standards and to model research-based educational practices.

Proficiency Level Indicators:

Level 1 (Beginning)	Level 2 (Developing)	Level 3 (Maturing)	Level 4 (Strong)	Level 5 (Exemplary)
Knowledge: ability to identify, recognize, recall	Comprehension: ability to translate, explain, transform	Application: ability to apply solutions to real-world predictable and unpredictable problems	Synthesis: ability to create, compare, design	Evaluation: ability to discriminate, appraise, consider
• Identify systems that help students meet academic standards. • Recognize the impact that district-level articulation and alignment work can have on student achievement. • Identify the importance of goal	• Explain the importance of focusing on systems in the district that can affect student performance. • Explain the necessary balance between classroom and building choice and need for district articulation.	• Organize systems that help students meet academic standards. • Build an articulated K–12 academic system and support school plans and actions that support its success (including uniform reporting systems, planned	• Compare program outcomes that most directly impact student learning. • Analyze the extent to which schools participate in the coordinated academic program. • Design assessment methods that are valid and reliable and	• Evaluate systems to discriminate which systems, processes, and programs benefit student learning. • Evaluate and revise the district's coordinated K–12 academic program based on data. • Discriminate among systems which are

Figure 3.6. *(Continued)*

Level 1 (Beginning)	Level 2 (Developing)	Level 3 (Maturing)	Level 4 (Strong)	Level 5 (Exemplary)
setting and assessment as a means to identify successful programs. • Identify how personal and professional expertise relates to helping students meet academic standards.	• Explain how expectations can be set through participatory processes, and how accountability can be shared. • Explain the benefits district office leaders and departments can bring to students.	course statements, and coordination with post-secondary institutions.) • Facilitate the construction of improvement plans with defined academic goals and measurable outcomes. • Apply knowledge in area of expertise to service and support schools and students.	always use data to inform decision making. • Revise area of responsibility to better impact academic standards.	research based and data driven versus those which are not. • Appraise and revise own area of responsibility in reference to student learning.

Figure 3.6. (*Continued*)

1. If the morale of your principals and district leaders is at an all-time low and beginning to affect the way they respond to children in need, what step would you take to address the issue of low staff morale?
   A. Meet individually with each staff person to praise his or her work.
   B. Become much more visible in the schools so individuals will have informal access to you.
   C. Strengthen your relationship with each individual by spending time with him or her.
   D. Pressure policymakers to provide a salary increase or some other incentive.

2. A varsity athlete is suspended from play for breaking training rules. A legitimate question emerges as to how long the suspension should last. The principal recommends the maximize length possible, while the student's parents appeal the decision to you, favoring the shortest suspension possible. What course of action would you take?
   A. Elect to support the student because students should always come first.
   B. Support the principal to affirm that high behavioral standards are important.
   C. Support the staff, but make restitution available to shorten the time served.
   D. Support the parents because community support is critically important to the success of the school.

3. You have just been appointed the superintendent of the Hard Castle School District. Your predecessor recommends that you articulate your beliefs to the staff at your first back-to-school rally. What would you do?
   A. Reject his advice, not wanting to appear too pushy.
   B. Ask the staff to articulate their expectations of you instead.
   C. Accept his advice and present your core beliefs about education in a concise statement, asking for feedback.
   D. Communicate to him that you would prefer to allow the beliefs to unfold naturally over time.

4. The principals recommend that you support a staff request for a "flexible Friday," meaning they could leave for home immediately after they finish their work for the day, to beat the weekend traffic. You allow the request, and it is quickly brought to your attention that the

staff have been leaving before their work is done, so as to get an early tee time at the country club. What would you do?

A. Tell the principals what you have been told, and when they admit it is true, eliminate flexible Friday to protect the professional image of the district.

B. Confront the offenders and withhold the appropriate pay.

C. Maintain flexible Friday but monitor it more carefully.

D. Publicly reprimand the violator.

5. A principal stops in to see you late one Friday night and indicates that he is seeing another woman behind his wife's back. What would be your reaction?

A. Listen at first, then try to get the staff member to see his minister.

B. Listen for feelings, expressing concern.

C. Try to reason with the staff member.

D. Ask the staff member to stop by when you both have more time.

6. The principals ask you to redo the annual meeting schedule because it seems unfair and conflicts with other duties. What would your reaction be?

A. Not agree to make any changes.

B. Agree to consider all requests over again and publish a new meeting schedule to model flexibility.

C. Ask the staff to get their preference in earlier next year so conflicts can be avoided.

D. Invite the staff to make a new schedule and submit to you for approval.

7. The elementary principals have already exceeded their annual allocation for instructional materials. They recognize that fact and still ask you if they can go to the PTSA with a request to purchase new science materials, even though the PTSA has made it clear that they want their resources to go for a new "big toy" for the playground. What would you do?

A. Not support the request from the PTSA because you know it will be rejected.

B. Ask the principals wanting science materials if they would like to convert their fund balance to instructional materials.

C. Ask the principals to try to plan a bit more carefully in the future.

D. Agree to give their request a high priority if the school receives additional resources.

8. The parents' organization asks you if you would be willing to allow the union to evaluate you. The board inadvertently hears about the request and opposes it because they say that administrators and teachers will be next. What would your reaction be?

A. Support the concern of the board and deny the request.

B. Agree to the evaluation because you believe in accountability.

C. Feel that staff are not really qualified to evaluate you so you deny the request.

D. Feel that union members are not objective enough so you deny the request.

9. The district staff objects to having a written school improvement plan for each school, arguing that principals say it takes more staff time than it is worth. What would your response be?

A. Understand the frustration of the staff and agree that the school improvement plan could easily become a multiyear document.

B. Express your understanding of the frustration but communicate that the annual plan is vitally important because the standards are still in constant flux.

C. Ask the staff to develop a proposal of their idea leaving the door open for an alternative to their annual plan.

D. Agree to make a request to the board to waive the annual requirement because of the frustration your staff is feeling.

10. You have just been hired as superintendent for the Hard Castle School District. Your predecessor was terminated because he had an affair with a custodian. The staff is extremely upset because she was a much-loved person, and they feel the process was unfair. It has significantly widened the gap between the district office, the school board, and the staff. Morale is so low it is beginning to impact students in a negative way. What would you do?

A. Establish a meeting with the district leaders to discuss the matter.

B. Have a meeting with the officials of all of the unions to address the matter.

C. Attempt to spend as much personal time with principals and district leaders as possible.

D. Provide a process for principals to provide input on policies and procedures leading to termination.

Directions   Transfer all of your answers to the data table. Total all of your responses in each column. Be sure to put all of your *C* responses in column C. Similarly place all of the *B* responses in column B. Now plug you totals into the formula where *B* equals *R*, and *C* equals *P*. Plot your *R* and *P* factors. Based on the illustration in figure 3.7, how does the actual result compare to your perceived outcome?

THE EDUCATIONAL REVOLUTION: A NEW WAY OF LOOKING AT WORK AND LEADERSHIP

The educational culture is evolving into a new way of looking at work and leadership. The shifts I have generated below describe the changing perceptions that are commonly held by America's educators (a highly educated and compassionate workforce). In my experience, it is not uncommon for 100 percent of the staff to have graduate degrees (all masters degrees and some Ph.D.s). Never has it been more ludicrous to say that "those who can do, and those who can't teach." Of the twelve hundred or so teachers I have worked with over the last eleven years where I was either the superintendent or deputy superintendent, that workforce could, in my view, outthink, "outtough," outwork, and "outcare" (empathy and compassion) any workforce anywhere. The point is, the rapidly changing world, coupled with the challenge of SBM, suggests that we need to approach educational leadership with fresh thinking. As schools move from the traditional model of schooling to the standards-based model, some of the basic assumptions about leadership and the schoolhouse need to be challenged. In the traditional system, management meant running a smooth but stable (unchanging) school. That is no longer the case. Schools are at the center of a volatile debate, and public rebuke and rebuff are bad and likely to get worse. It is not easy to argue that leadership in public schools has been overwhelmingly successful. In fact 93 percent of the principals in Chicago (the nation's third largest district) have either been asked to leave or have voluntarily stepped down. School leaders and teams are now expected to create something that never existed before and often with fewer resources,

	A	B	C	D
1				
2				
3				
4				
5				
6				
7				
8				
9				
10				
Relational Axis				
Productivity Axis				

Productivity Domain—What central office leaders know and do.

Relational Domain—What leaders believe and value

To reflect the heretofore differences the formula is as follows:

The formula is $R^2 \times P - Pc$.

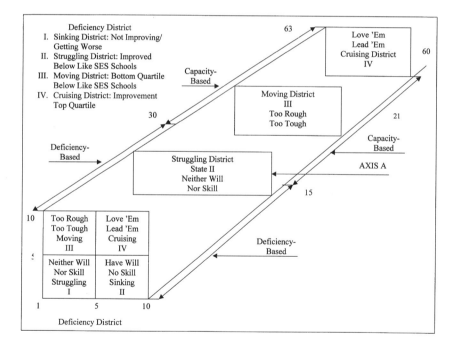

Directions:
Using the numbers on the quiz—plug them into the formula $R^2 \times P = PC$ Complete the equation and determine your Peak Capacity on the table above. R is the total of column B and P is the total of column C. Now plot your PC. Are you satisfied?

Figure 3.7. Scoring Data Table for District Office Proficiencies

which has proven to be something beyond the skills of most leaders and leadership teams.

To illustrate, let me say that *manager* is defined by the phrase "doing the thing right," while *leader* is defined by the phrase "doing the right thing." Leaders create a learning community where every adult is committed to personal and professional growth and aligns each to the vision. In my experience, there is a dearth of leadership for the key positions in education. Unfortunately, that has happened at a time when people want to be led.

The Eight Pillars of Emerging Capacity-Based Leadership

As schools move from the traditional model to the standards-based model, it is important to recognize that there has been a dearth of educational leaders. Therefore, we have largely failed to provide the kind of leadership necessary to insure a successful transformational change. We lack models from which to draw our leadership lessons. I have frequently used the word framework to describe the leadership structure we have been discussing. I am told that when carpenters build a building they also begin by building a framework. The framework then in turn supports the rest of the structure. For the framework to be strong enough to provide the needed support, the carpenters build weight-bearing walls into the structure. For our purposes here, I will call them pillars. The eight pillars are a critically important part of the structure because they not only support the framework they also support the remainder of the structure. The design of an SBS is very different from a traditional school so the design of the framework and the bearing walls (pillars) has also changed. What follows are eight bearing walls, or pillars, that support capacity-based leadership.

Table 3.3. The Eight Pillars of Leadership

From	To	To
1. Manager	Leader	
2. Centralized	Decentralized	Integrated
3. Strategic planning and delegation	Visioning and alignment	
4. Deficiency-based	Capacity-based	
5. Mistakes mean failure	Mistakes mean success	
6. Critical feedback support	Assistance in building on strengths	
7. I can't do it	I will find or make a way	
8. Aloof and independent	Connected and caring	

FROM MANAGER TO LEADER

A school needs to run smoothly before transformational change can take place. It is difficult to sustain meaningful change in a chaotic environment. The shift I am describing suggests that running a well-organized school was the expectation prior to the standards-based movement. The current expectation is that a high-performance school should be developed on top of a school that is well run. The point is that both are necessary. The school should not only be run well, but also be continually improving. The dictionary definition of manager is "one who is in charge of training and performance." The definition implies being in control of something through training and supervision. Lead, on the other hand, is defined "to guide or escort." The definition of leader implies accompaniment or companionship. People are reaching out for leadership because they want to be led. Managers would say they hope the people have faith in the leader, leaders would say they hope the leader has faith in the people. The following poem is an excellent summary of the point I would like to underscore.

Let's Get Rid of Management
People
Don't want
To be
Managed
They want to be led.
Who ever heard of
World manager
World leader, yes
Educational leader.
Political leader.
Religious leader.
Business leader.
Scout leader.
Community leader.
Labor leader. They lead.
They don't manage.
The carrot
Always wins over the stick.
Ask your horse.

You can lead your horse to water,
But you can't manager him to drink.
If you want to manage somebody Manage yourself.
Do that well
And you'll
Be ready to
Stop managing
And start leading.[24]

FROM CENTRALIZED TO
DECENTRALIZED TO INTEGRATED

From centralized to decentralized to integrated, schools are both centralized and decentralized at the same time. In most states, academic standards
are developed centrally within the district or within the state. The standards
are then superimposed (centralized) on the schools and teachers with the
expectation that the curriculum would be designed down from the academic standards. Further, as functions of school improvement history, most
schools have already moved from centralized to some type of site-based
decision-making structure (decentralized). It has been my experience that
the standards-based movement tends to gravitate toward more centralized
coordination. The primary challenge is in the area of equity of opportunity.
On the other hand, decentralized decision making errs on the side of too little uniformity. It also creates an expensive duplication of effort. As was
said earlier in this chapter, neither centralized nor decentralized decision
making works well in the SBS. That is true because ideas must be incor-
porated into the decision-making structure from a variety of locations and
decisions need to be made at the point closest to implementation. This concept will be discussed in much more detail in the next chapter.

FROM STRATEGIC PLANNING AND
DELEGATION TO VISIONING AND ALIGNMENT

Strategic planning assumes that someone can predict what action will
need to be taken in a complex environment that is perpetually changing.

Margaret Wheatly makes the general point in her book *Leadership and the New Science* that strategic planning is the first sign of a death rattle.[25] Clear direction is important but the visioning strategies create a more pragmatic "loose-tight" coupling, that allows for clear direction while still adjusting to a myriad of unforeseen changes in the environment. I believe an SBS must have a clear focus on academic standards. The most important resource we have is not technology but people. One must allow people to participate if one is interested in using human capital as a resource. Using human capital as a resource is a precondition for success. Deep ownership comes from being involved in the vision-building process and from realizing that the vision is an extension of the core beliefs of the individual. The vision helps to create that clear sense of direction. When a clear purpose exists, then educators can spontaneously align their program strengths and beliefs with the vision. When the adults are aligning their work to the vision, then a powerful precondition for success has been met. This is another significant difference between leaders and managers. Leaders establish a compelling, collective vision, then step back and let the power of the human spirit move the school forward. On the other hand, managers decide what to do, build a strategic plan, establish committees, and delegate responsibilities.

FROM DEFICIENCY-BASED TO CAPACITY-BASED

Capacity-based leaders focus on strengths rather than on weaknesses. It is much more motivating and productive to focus on strengths. Leaders work to insure that high-performance adults set the standard because it is much more efficient than working on the weaknesses of the mediocre performers. The distance between the high-performance individual and the average performer is constant. Leaders raise the level of performance of the strongest performer and that standard can affect the performance of the whole group. This notion is based on the principal of "leadership density" which suggests that capacity-based approaches work best when:

- Expectations are clear and realistic; and
- Staffs are recognized and rewarded (specifically and abundantly) when the expectations are met.

As was pointed out earlier, weaknesses cannot be converted into strengths. They can be removed, but they cannot be transformed. Remember, the goal is to manage the weakness so the strengths can be free to develop and become so strong that they make weaknesses irrelevant.

FROM I CAN'T DO IT TO I WILL EITHER FIND A WAY OR MAKE ONE

Persistence is important beyond measure; there can be no giving up. Only restarting the engine is acceptable. You must simply begin and adjust the course as you go. The direction is not as important as just getting under way. Getting to the destination is not as important as finding joy and fulfillment in the journey. Calvin Coolidge once observed,

> Nothing in the world can take the place of persistence.
> Talent will not; nothing is more common than
> Unsuccessful men with great talent.
> Genius will not; unrewarded genius is almost a proverb.
> Education will not; the world is full of educated derelicts.
> Persistence, determination alone are omnipotent.[26]

FROM MISTAKES MEAN FAILURE TO MISTAKES MEAN SUCCESS

At least in part because children are delicate and precious, educators have been reluctant to take risks. We cannot learn and grow if we do not step out a bit. As Ken Blanchard one observed, "Why go out on a limb? Because that is where the fruit is!" To say it another way, I would say, "The real key to success, is to fail more often." These comments assume that leaders have developed a learning community and therefore learn from their mistakes. Winston Churchill also noted that "success is a function of maintaining undaunted enthusiasm, while moving from failure to failure!" Leaders in this period of rapid change, coupled with fewer resources and higher standards, must be "strong in the broken places" (coined by Ernest Hemingway in *For Whom the Bell Tolls*) and willing to extend themselves and the school and to take some risks.

FROM ALOOF, STOIC, AND
INDEPENDENT TO CONNECTED AND CARING

Some have viewed successful leaders as strong, independent, and judgmental. There is no power in position, but in relationship; therefore, one must chose to be close to the people and exhibit a genuine care and concern for them as individuals. Earlier in this chapter, I talked about Douglas McGreggor's theory x and theory y. Theory x was monocratic and bureaucratic. Theory y was pluralistic and collegial. Then, we went on to say that an integrated theory of leadership was the most appropriate in an SBS. The aim was to balance productivity and relationships. Relationships are about people, and since education is a people-intensive structure, productivity occurs by working through people. To increase effectiveness, it is important to be caring and close to people. If we err, we should err on the side of the human dimension. Trust is the emotional glue holding the vision together, and trust is a direct by-product of closeness. The only way to develop trust is to earn it. A key to earning trust is to demonstrate that you genuinely like the people. Leaders show that they care by spending time with the people. Trust and closeness are in the same powerful relationship as vision and focus.

> Fail to honor people,
> They will fail to honor you
> But be a good leader, who talks a little,
> When his work is done, his aim fulfilled,
> They will say, "We did this ourselves."
>
> —Lao Tsu[27]

SUMMARY

The recent literature on leadership has fallen into three schools of thinking:

- School 1: Characteristics of leaders
- School 2: Behavioral patterns of leaders
- School 3: Beliefs of leaders

The contemporary school of thinking on leadership is still evolving, and that has given rise to what I call the integrated model of leadership, which represents approaches that grow out of capacity-based beliefs, rather than deficiency-based beliefs. This is one of the critical differences between leaders and managers. Managers focus on deficiencies or weaknesses and use critical feedback approaches to push mediocre staff to higher levels.

Capacity-based leaders are results oriented, yet sensitive to the needs of the people. This model is intended to establish a relationship between the leadership elements of productivity and relationships. While leaders build on the capacities of high-performance people by letting them set the performance standard, pulling others along as if the quality of their work were a kind of performance magnet. The study of strengths leads to the understanding of the difference between good and great. There is no alchemy for weaknesses—they can be removed but they can never be transformed into strengths.

The many forces previously noted have created complex circumstances requiring new thinking about the most productive leadership strategies that addresses the shifts of the eight pillars of leadership (see table 3.3).

NOTES

1. Carl Rogers, "The Psychology of the Classroom" (paper presented at the annual meeting of The Montana Association for Curriculum Development, Missoula, Mont., April 1969).

2. John Goodlad, *A Place Called School* (New York: McGraw-Hill, 1984), 17.

3. Peter Drucker, *The Effective Executive* (New York: Harper and Row, 1969), 99.

4. Marcus Buckingham, *First, Break All of the Rules* (New York: Simon and Schuster, 1999), 53.

5. Douglas McGreggor, *The Professional Manager* (New York: McGraw-Hill, 1960), 61–80.

6. William G. Ouchi, *Theory Z: How American Business Can Meet the Japanese Challenge* (New York: William Morrow, 1992).

7. Thomas Sergiovanni, *Moral Leadership* (San Francisco: Jossey-Bass Publishers, 1992), 37.

8. Stephen Covey, *The Principle Centered Leader* (New York: Simon and Schuster, 1990).

9. Stephen Covey, *The Seven Habits of Highly Effective People* (New York: Simon and Schuster, 1989).

10. Daniel McGinn and Keith Naughton, "How Safe Is Your Job?" *Time*, February 5, 2001.

11. McGinn and Naughton, "How Safe Is Your Job?"

12. Donald O. Clifton and Paula Nelson, *Soar with Your Strengths* (New York: Dell Publishing, 1992), 44–73.

13. Clifton and Nelson, *Soar with Your Strengths*, 45–54.

14. Clifton and Nelson, *Soar with Your Strengths*, 19.

15. Warren Bennis and Bert Nanus, *Leaders: The Strategies for Taking Charge* (New York: Harper and Row, 1985), 15.

16. P. R. Blake and T. S. Mouton, *The Managerial Grid* (Houston: Gulf, 1964).

17. Ken Blanchard and Paul Hersey, "Leadership Effectiveness and Adaptability Index," *The 1976 Handbook for Group Facilitators* (La Jolla, Calif.: University Associates, 1973), 89–99.

18. A. W. Halpin, *The Leadership of Superintendents* (Chicago: Midwest Administration Center, University of Chicago, 1959).

19. Blanchard and Hersey, "Leadership Effectiveness."

20. Blanchard and Hersey, "Leadership Effectiveness."

21. Sara Lawrence Lightfoot, *The Good High School: Portraits of Character and Culture* (New York: Basic Books, 1983), 23-25.

22. Daniel Goldman, Richard Boyatzis, and Annie McKee, *Primal Leadership* (Boston, Mass.: Harvard Business School Press, 2002), 3.

23. Charlotte Danielson, *Enhancing Professional Practice: A Framework for Teaching* (Alexandria, Va.: Association for Supervision and Curriculum, 1966).

24. Bennis and Nanus, *Leaders*, 22.

25. Margaret Wheatly, *Leadership and the New Science: Learning about Organizations from an Orderly Universe* (San Francisco: Berrett-Koehler Publishers, 1992).

26. Bennis and Bert Nanus, *Leaders*, 45.

27. From *Tao Te Ching* by Lao Tsu, translated by Gia-Fu Feng and Jane English, copyright © 1997 by Jane English. Copyright © 1972 by Gia-Fu Feng and Jane English. Used by permission of Alfred A. Knopf, a division of Random House, Inc.

Chapter Four

Building Community and Teamwork Comes First

Coming together is a beginning. Keeping together is progress. Working together is success.

—Henry Ford

ASSUMPTIONS

This chapter on building community and teamwork is written with the following assumptions as parameters:

- The SBS will need parental and community understanding and support to be successful.
- SBS and school improvement will respond to a rapidly changing environment.
- People will more readily support something they understand.

Involvement by working together builds trust. Trust is important because it is the lubrication that powers positive change; furthermore, it is the emotional glue that holds the organization together.

Trust must be earned and it does accumulate, but in paltry amounts. Participation tends to develop support and understanding while contributing to trust building.

As has been noted earlier, since about 1970 most schools have moved from centralized to decentralized decision making. I believe that education and other organizations went through a period of time when policymakers supported site-based decision making at the expense of centralized decision-making processes. In Oregon House Bill 2991, the statute requiring standards-based systems, also required site-based decision making (decentralized). The law requires each school to have a site council.

The SBS Generates a Pressure toward Uniformity and Centralization

The standards-based school system generates pressure toward uniformity and centralization. Site councils, by law in Oregon, are composed of teachers and nonteaching employees, and parents who are elected to the council by parents. The duties, which are very clearly articulated, include in general:

- School improvement planning, staff development planning, and grants applications
- Improvement of the buildings instructional program
- Development and coordination of the Oregon Educational Act for the Twenty-First Century.
- Administration of grants-in-aid for the professional development of the school

Every school and district in Oregon should have been completely decentralized by the early 1990s. Before the SBM, I was a strong proponent of site-based decision making. While I still believe that bottom-up strategies are much more effective, the advantages of centralized decision making in an SBS environment became increasingly clearer as we moved deeper into the SBS. We quickly learned that as soon as the public understood that the expectations were the same for every school, it became quite clear that the public expected equity of opportunity. This pressure was not necessarily new. It was different, however, from the equity pressures of the past in one significant way. The accountability factors of the state test and the pressure of annual school grades made the equity question much more visible (which is probably good). The key point is that this issue (i.e., equity of opportunity) created a policy-level interest in having more uniformity. Because the standards are uniform for all schools, some policymakers reasoned that there should be a uniform reporting system and a uniform school improvement process. I fully recognize that this point is not necessarily a logical position in many schools and communities; nonetheless, schools under the new system compete head-to-head for annual ranking and community support and recognition. For that reason, there was a mounting policy-level pressure toward more uniformity to insure equity of opportunity in all schools and grade levels. In my view, this is one of the more intricate challenges that district staff and school boards must resolve.

Neither Centralization nor Decentralization Works

The traditional argument about whether centralization or decentralization is a better method of governance is no longer germane. It is a perplexing dilemma because centralized decision making errs on the side of over-control. Specifically, we have learned that top-down strategies do not work because they do not honor the expertise of the school community. Given the unique character of each school, centralized decisions are frequently less effective than site-based decisions.

At the same time, I have also learned that decentralized decision making errs on the side of too little uniformity, and it frequently creates an expensive duplication of effort. A friend of mine frequently addresses this phenomena with the comment, "We need to develop a school system rather than a system of schools." Policymakers in my region were fearful that decentralized decision making would lead to inequity, chaos, and a poor use of public funds. Both centralized and decentralized decision making have strengths and weaknesses. However, one should tend towards decentralized decision making for the following reasons. One, resources are and will continue to be scarce. In an era of scarcity, our most valuable resource is people, not advanced technology or even improved pedagogy. People are human capital, if you will.[1] If we expect to use this important asset, we must involve people in decisions that affect them. That is why trust is so important! Whereas a deficiency-based leader might say, "I hope the people believe in the leader," as a capacity-based leader, I would say, "I hope the leader believes in the people." Two, creativity and innovation are especially important. Decentralized decision making, by its nature, goes hand in hand with creativity and innovation, which in turn increases exponentially as solutions are being determined.

The aforementioned arguments are the traditional arguments regarding which system is best, but they both really miss the mark. What is true is that "Neither centralization nor decentralization works, both top-down and bottom-up strategies are necessary."[2] Therefore, I have developed a decision-making model which exploits the advantages of both strategies. The integrated decision-making system, which is both top-down and bottom-up, is defined below.

Integrated Decision Making: Both Bottom-Up and Top-Down

I believe the current public skepticism about the quality of education, along with a rapidly changing environment and the pressure to change, creates the conditions whereby a strategic effort should be made to enhance trust and community support through participatory decision making. The two central assumptions that serve as parameters for this integrated model are as follows:

- Everyone who is affected by a decision should be involved in the decision-making process.
- The best decisions are made at the point closest to implementation.
- By its nature, decentralized decision making generates more innovation and creativity.

The integrated model, therefore, takes advantage of both bottom-up and top-down approaches. For an illustration of the integrated decision-making model, see figure 4.1.

DEFINITIONS OF THE MODEL

The most important component of the model is the go, no-go regeneration loop because the immediate sharing and collection of information creates understanding and support within the school community. Each decision-making group has one or more members who serve in a dual capacity on two parallel committees; therefore, a natural and uncomplicated structure for sharing and collecting information and making decisions literally falls out of the design. The dual membership quality helps to expedite information sharing.

Go, no-go decision making: A cybernetic feedback loop included to insure that timely decisions are made at the closest point to implementation.

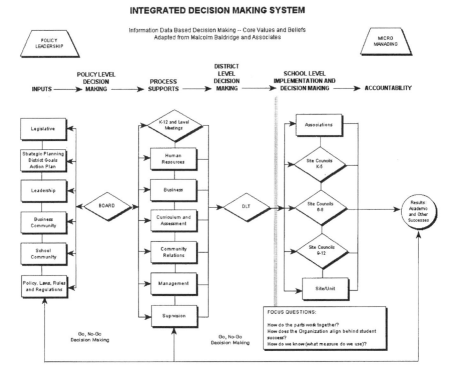

Figure 4.1. Integrated Decision-Making System Model

The system also relies upon dual committee membership to enhance communication and understanding.

Inputs: The expectations or requirements that set the direction for the school or district (i.e., statute or community beliefs). Expectations would include such things as district policy and administrative rule, federal and state statute, and funding levels.

Accountability: The degree to which students experience success, measured academically and by other measures, as determined by the site councils.

Results: Measure of student success including both academic and other types of success in school.

Diamonds: Where key decisions are made. This is neither a centralized nor a decentralized system, but rather an integrated system where people who will be affected by a decision will be involved in the decision-making process. The intent is to make the decision at a point closest to implementation.

Evaluation of the model: Three questions that can be used to evaluate the utility of the model:

- How do the parts work together?
- How does the organization align behind student success?
- How do you know (what measure did you use?)

Note: the emphasis is on alignment rather than deficiencies.

Liaison support through dual committee membership: Two feedback loops between inputs and accountability. The sharing and collecting of information occurs because there are liaison supports between each decision-making group each way. For instance, the superintendent provides liaison support to both the board and K–12 groups. Two rotating members of the board meet with the superintendent two times a month. Furthermore, one principal from each level (i.e., elementary, middle, and high school) serves on the district leadership team (DLT), providing liaison support to the principals.

Policy leadership: All decisions under and left of the shaded vertical line, falling under the jurisdiction of three different groups with the help of inputs and supports. The board has the primary responsibility for policy decisions with feedback from community groups and other entities. The principals (i.e., K–12 and levels) use district supports to create program-specific modifications for policies (if necessary). The DLT then uses feedback from the board and principals to finalize a workable proposal before sending it to the site councils for school-level implementation and decision making. Anything to the right of the shaded vertical line is considered site specific and therefore within the jurisdiction of the schools with feedback and guidance from the district leadership team.

No hierarchy: No visual display of hierarchy. The integrated model does not include any display of a hierarchy from top to bottom (i.e., a pyramid or a line and staff chart), and again the emphasis is not on who is on the top making all of the decisions and taking control. The issue is quality not power or prestige.

The Advantages of Integrated Decision Making

The four critical challenges or questions that must be addressed are:

1. How can the system collect and share the appropriate information in a timely way and in a meaningful form?

Essentially, that question is addressed through the use of feedback. I will use the term cybernetics as the systematic control of feedback data. In simpler terms, cybernetics is the formal process where the appropriate data reaches the right people (i.e., decision makers) in a timely way and in a usable form. While the model presented herein may appear stiff and formal, cybernetics must remain informal enough to be carried out in an ongoing basis.

In many ways, feedback allows a system to change and adjust to an environment that is fluid (like schools with unique cultures in change). While discussing the black box approach to systems, Stanley Young suggested that the feedback loop increases the capacity of a system to maintain itself and adapt to its changing environment.[3] The feedback loop provides a kind of sensitivity that is crucial in developing an SBS. More than that, however, cybernetics is the process that cements the system together. Without a continual spiral of feedback data, movement toward a high-performance SBS would remain static and unchanging.

The cybernetic effect of the model can be viewed in two separate modules. Data control and feedback has been addressed within both the policy and school decision-making cycles (see figure 4.1).

2. How can quality decisions be made in a timely way and still avoid a perceived change of direction at the very last moment?

The response is to utilize diverse participation and the go, no-go decision-making processes. The following three elements of the model control quality while still allowing for timely decision making:

• The decision-making quality of the committee system
• The go, no-go decision loop between the policy levels
• The school-level cycles, as well as the liaison support between each group, which provide a realistic and workable feedback loop

Each decision will get careful review from the perspective of many people, thereby reducing any last minute surprises. In addition, the fact that at least one member of each committee sits as a formal member on the next committee, spiraling either way, insures meaningful feedback. It also breaks up the formal hierarchy of the system, which enhances trust.

3. How does a school board know when its actions may be perceived as micromanaging?

Some boards and specific board members have been accused of micromanaging the school system. Webster's dictionary defines micromanaging as measuring minute differences. According to Chait, Holland, and Taylor, one of the six major competencies of an effective board is to have an active sphere of influence in strategic or policy-level direction.[4] The key point is that the board should not be involved in the sphere of the day-to-day operation of the school; rather, the board has legitimate authority in the area of policy (strategic) level decisions and fiduciary activities. This is a very troublesome area for many boards and an engrossed source of conflict between some boards and their school leaders. Therefore this decision-making model clearly delineates the two spheres of influence with the shaded line (see figure 4.1). Everything to the left of the shaded line is the purview of the board. Everything to the right of the shaded line is the responsibility of the administration or some other entity.

The board makes policy with inputs from the key stakeholders. The site councils are responsible for decision making and implementation at the school level. The board clearly sees and understands that its sphere of influence is at the policy level and that an effort to take a formal role in site-based decision making and implementation is not appropriate and termed micromanaging.

4. How can quality control be assured when citizens do not usually have the training to be involved in some of the more technical decisions (i.e., curriculum design and instructional delivery)?

The answer is that the community provides input to the board at the policy level only. The general policies are then detailed (made into administrative rules) and made operational by district administrators and site councils. The policy-level direction, therefore, is fine-tuned by educators as policy approaches implementation.

Capacity-Based Success Strategy 15: Alignment Steps

Begin to align the organization by asking the following three focus questions about the organizational components:

- How do the parts work together?
- What activities will you undertake to support the district goals?

- What data will you collect to demonstrate your alignment with the district goals?

PROPOSED TIME LINE WITH RECOMMENDED GROUPS

- All administrators—late summer
- District administrators (cabinet)—fall
- Community—fall
- Students (proposed groups who will respond to the focus question)—fall
- Schools (focus on only one goal: rigorous academics)—fall
- Units (food service, operations, maintenance, and transportation)—late fall
- Budget committee—late fall
- Parent clubs—late summer
- Teachers (through the OEA)—before the end of late fall
- Classified employees (through the OEA)—before the end of late fall
- School board—last, as a culminating activity

SUMMARY

The SBS requires the use of a participatory decision-making process because parental support and understanding are critically important. Parental support is paramount, and working together builds trust and understanding. The changes will take place in a rapidly changing environment. Uniform standards create pressures to centralize that must be resisted. Neither centralization nor decentralization works. Both top-down and bottom-up strategies are necessary in an SBS. The integrated decision making presented herein meets the following parameters:

- Every one who is affected by a decision is involved in the decision-making process.
- Effective decisions need to be made in a timely way and at the closest point to implementation.
- A cybernetic feedback loop creates a kind of sensitivity to the wants and needs of the audience.

The model provides a planned response to the micromanaging by board members that is hard on the morale of the leaders in the district.

NOTES

1. Eli Broad, "Preparing Leaders for the New Economy," *The School Administrator* (March 2001), 46–49.
2. Michael Fullen, *Change Forces* (New York: Falmer Press, 1993), 37.
3. K. Feyereisen and John Fiorino, eds., *Supervision and Curriculum Renewal: A Systems Approach* (New York: Meredith, 1977), 47–55.
4. Richard P. Chait, Thomas P. Holland, & Barbara E. Taylor, *Improving the Performance of Governing Boards* (Phoenix, Ariz: Oryx Press, 1996), 8.

Chapter Five

Education as a Moral Purpose

Education is not suffering from a lack of efficiency, It is suffering from a lack of humanity.

— Arthur Combs "The Concept of Human Potential and School" (paper)

As I have articulated how the adults must be nurtured and cared for in the SBS and I have also voiced strong support for balancing productivity with humanity, I am more deeply convinced than ever that the model is correct for standards-based educational institutions. It is critically important that teachers and instructional assistants create a safe and wholesome classroom atmosphere for students, just as leaders are compelled to do for the adults in the school. Why do we need to balance challenge and threat? As I began to look at the literature on SBS, I found very little that addressed the humanity of the child. Actually, children were frequently overlooked (or studied only anecdotally) in the SBS literature. In my review, it appeared as if the focus has largely been on how adults would be affected, rather than students. In fact, to do any justice at all to this consideration, I found myself looking into the educational psychology of learning theory for direction. In light of what has been said in chapter 1 about the power of positive discrimination (change axiom 6), I am not going to idle away from the tough and acrimonious question. The focus question I would like to consider is: How do high standards and performance-based assessments affect students and what can and should educators do to ameliorate the consequences and accentuate the strengths?

EDUCATIONAL PSYCHOLOGY AS A FORMULATION

Children should come first. Everything that is done should be done with children in mind. Unfortunately, adults often dominate the decision-making process for their own convenience or well-being. It is important to note that SBS was not initiated out of a concern for the well-being of students, but rather for the well-being of adults. Adult-related concerns tended to focus on the economics of international competition, taxpayer value, and politics; far in the rear were the concerns about students. For the most part, the impact of such a system on the student is not given serious attention in literature. On the other hand, it is the single most common focus of teachers and other educators. You will remember that in chapter 1 students often come last when adults consider the high-priority educational issues (i.e., positive discrimination for students). I will narrow my response by establishing limits or parameters. In that regard, the use of Abraham Maslow's conceptualization of the field of psychology will be helpful. He suggested that psychology could be divided into three schools of thought:

- Maslow labels the first school of thought "classical" psychology largely because of the classical conditioning components, as portrayed by Thorndike and Skinner in relation to behaviorism.
- Maslow labels the second school of thought "depth" psychology. He suggests that this Freudian construct has historically dominated the whole construct of clinical psychology.
- Maslow labels the third school of thought "third force" psychology" and argues that it was a response to the gross inadequacies of the other two.[1]

My comments will spring from Maslow's third force concept.

I would like to use another concept that Maslow has developed to place an additional springboard under this analysis. In general, Maslow believes that learning is either *intrinsic* or *extrinsic*. Extrinsic learning, according to Maslow, revolves around the traditional instructional conceptualization: "The teacher is the active one who teaches a passive person who gets shaped and taught and is given something which he then accumulates and which he may lose or retain." On the other hand, intrinsic learning grows out of those "experiences in which we learn who we are, what we love, what we hate, what we value, and what we are committed to."[2]

Maslow concludes his analysis by suggesting that "if you are willing to accept this conception of the two kinds of learning, with learning to be a person being more central and more basic than the impersonal learning of skills, then you must have a definition of a good teacher and his or her function."[3]

The conceptualization of intrinsic and extrinsic learning is very useful in assisting us to consider the emotional impact of instruction in the standards-based classroom, even though intrinsic and extrinsic learning occur simultaneously and cannot be separated. The thinking here proposes that the concept of education revolves around Maslow's intrinsic factorial. What is the real purpose of education, or what is the goal behind the goal, so to speak? The educational process, especially in a democracy, needs to be not only the mastery of basic academic skills, but also the mastery of social development. Education must also engender intelligent and ethical behavior so that the constituent will foster attributes that are adequate and functional. As Combs has asserted, the goal of education is to produce "adequate personalities, people who can be counted upon to behave effectively and efficiently and to contribute freely to the welfare of all."[4] In a democracy, students must understand that each individual is connected to every other individual—if one loses one's rights, so do the rest.

The point is made through the poetic power of friend Kim Safford: "The opposite of a microscope is not a telescope, but an education—a lens of mind and heart that reveals the dynamic interconnection of things, however small or seemingly far away."[5]

If intelligent and ethical behavior is the goal of the educational process, then what psychological theory can be applied to assist educators in the pursuit of goal attainment? In my judgment, a framework that provides a viable conceptualization of the complex nature of human psychology can be extrapolated from perceptual psychology.

Perceptual Psychology: A Definition

"Perceptual psychology is grounded in a view of behavior that suggests that all behaviors, without exception, are a function of the student's perceptual field at the time of behaving."[6] To say it another way, "I am not who you think I am, I am who you think I think I am." In other words, a student's behavior is not a response to a stimulus, but is a response to how he sees the events around him. The behavior of the student is seen as proactive rather

than reactive. This expression is a significant deviation from classical stimulus–response theory. I have, therefore, chosen to look at behavior from the
point of view of the student. The key consideration is not what is real in a
student's environment, but what he perceives to be real. As Combs has eloquently noted, "People do not behave according to the facts as others see
them. They behave according to the facts as they see them."[7]

The Self-Concept

When a child sees himself, it is considered a perceptual phenomenon. The
result of that perception is self-image. Obviously, this perception is composed of a vast number of exchanges that any student has with the environment. The self-concept, then, is the result of a countless number of
judgments a child makes about himself in relationship to the environment.
As has been pointed out earlier, a child's behavior depends on how he perceives his surroundings in relation to how he perceives himself.

If these assumptions are true, then the implications for SBS are almost
never ending. First, a child's image is not static, but changing and fluctuating. It is both a process and a product. While the self-concept is a result
of past experiences, it is also continually adjusting to an interaction with
the phenomenal field. The poor self-image, then, contributes much to the
continual lack of success a child might experience. It is crucial for educators to understand that the self-concept is a learned consequence of experience and therefore must be given a central priority in educational planning. Each student must be placed in an environment where he can
experience success. Anything less is destructive.

Educators must continue to seek ways of allowing students to successfully take more responsibility for their own education. Dale Parnell has
demonstrated that "applied academics" can be very useful, in assisting students to find meaning in the teaching–learning process.[8] Others have found
that individualizing a course offering can be helpful in providing students
with a framework for success. In my judgment, however, the specific
method utilized is significantly less important than the conceptualization
that positive self-image is a direct outgrowth of successful experience. To
experience success in life, it is critically important for students to experience
success in meeting high academic standards. I have met those who with
good intention believe that attempting to create a safe and wholesome learn-

ing environment for students is to dilute the real-world experience, making students soft and unprepared for the realities of life in a brutally competitive world. Honorable people can and will disagree on this issue. However, when children experience success, they learn how to become successful; conversely, when children learn to fail, they also learn how to become failures. Even the eminent football coach Vince Lombardi, who was noted for his fiercely competitive spirit and demanding coaching style, became almost infamous when one of his players said that Lombardi "Treated us all equal—like dogs!" During the Super Bowl years, even the illustrious Lombardi refused to show his players any game film with mistakes. He always carefully edited the film to show only the successful plays.

Beyond just academic success, students also need to be technologically literate. And thereby, I believe, there are intangibles as important as academic skills. For instance, students who graduate in the rapidly changing age of information must be able to traverse the digital divide. Graduates also need to be creative risk takers who have a sense of confidence and possess a can-do attitude. Simply said, the SBS is developed so that students are provided the opportunity to break the vicious cycle of failure. Combs related a vivid portrayal when he commented that, "Thousands of people in our society are trapped, prisoners of their own perception, believing they can only do X-much. Then the rest of us see them only doing X-much, so we say, 'that is an X-much person'—which only proves what he thought in the first place."[9] The point I am making is that the adults in the SBS must not allow students to perpetuate a self-concept that is self-limiting and therefore self-destructive. That balance between a healthy challenge and a hostile threat is delicate and can be managed by only the very best of the best people (teachers). Please know that when I use the word teacher, I am including every adult employee in the school setting.

SELF-CONCEPT AND SELF-FULFILLMENT

According to some psychologists, people continually seek to enhance their self-concept by drawing from the environment what is positive and blocking what is negative. Abraham Maslow's "hierarchy of needs theory" suggests that students seek to satisfy basic needs (i.e., physiological, security, social, esteem) in an attempt to self-actualize—that is, to fulfill their potential.[10] If students are continually seeking self-actualization, then it certainly has a direct bearing on the proverbial problem of motivating students. In Combs's book, Donald Snygg is quoted as describing the problems of American education the following way: "We are madly providing children with answers to problems they ain't got yet."[11] On occasion, we seem unable to fulfill student needs and then suggest that the problem is a lack of student motivation. If self-actualization is a driving force, then students are always motivated. The human species has been motivated enough to survive some of the most ferocious environmental conditions since human life began. The lack of motivation is not the issue. The challenge that educators face is to develop an SBS that meets the needs of the child. That is why it is so important to get the support of the community and parents.

The Educational Climate

As has been suggested, the educational climate must be accepting and rewarding for all educational participants, both students and adults alike. In chapter 2, we said that high-performance schools are simultaneously results-oriented and sensitive to the human element. The leader in an SBS must be accepting and tolerant of mistakes. The SBS must place an emphasis on human dimension while not losing sight of productivity. Therein is the magic of this environment! Leaders attempt to generate the same environment for adults as we all want for students. Leaders need to create an environment for the instructional staff that the staff should replicate for students. Positive relationships with students need to precede academic success rather than emerge from it. In chapter 2, we said that relationship building on the human dimension was the foundation for productivity. That is no less true for the students than it is for the adults. The leader, therefore, should be held to the same standards of human nurturing and sensitivity in his or her interactions with the adults as adults have in their interaction with students.

Students and adults must be provided the luxury of making errors without the implication of personal failure. In other words, a student must be challenged and given responsibilities to grow in self-esteem. Combs has made it clear that in his judgment "self-worth comes from accepting responsibility for bringing tasks to a successful conclusion."[12]

Students must be given the opportunity to try and fail without loss of self-esteem. Obviously, making mistakes is an essential part of learning, as well as teaching, in a system with high-stakes testing like an SBS. On the other hand, a very clear distinction must be made between challenge and threat. If an environment is threatening, it will be viewed as hostile and potentially destructive of self-image. In a threatening environment, people's perceptions are narrowed to the object of the threat. Little that is positive can occur if students see the school as hostile. One of the goals of education ought to be to broaden perception, which is incompatible with threat. According to Combs, "When people are threatened, they are also forced to defend their existing position. The hotter the argument gets, the more a person sticks to the position that they had in the first place. Again, this is directly antithetical to everything we are seeking to accomplish in helping a person (child or adult) use his world effectively."[13]

Carl Rogers captured my point when he eloquently noted that schools "should remove threat so a psychological greenhouse of creativity can blossom."[14] It cannot be stated too strongly that a nurturing environment that is nonthreatening, yet challenging, is crucial to an individual's pursuit of self-fulfillment. It is a delicate balance.

There are two dilemmas I have experienced in generating this thinking: (1) the apparent contradiction between the learning theory in this chapter and my support of SBS, and (2) the SBS seems to fall short of educating the whole child. Let me address the initial dilemma first.

Toward a Learning Theory That Works in an SBS

Is there an inherent conflict between learning theory and the SBS? In March 1978, I heard Arthur Combs say to a group of teachers at the University of Montana, "Education is not suffering from a lack of efficiency, it is suffering from a lack of humanity."[15] It simply does not follow that because a school is well organized and efficient, it is necessarily inhumane and cruel. Quite the opposite, efficiency does not have to negate humanity. Actually, the contention presented here is that the reverse is true. Self-esteem and self-actualization can actually be enhanced in a school that is well organized with clear academic standards. Specifically, the intent of the systems approach discussed in chapter 4 is to create a more "humane use of human beings."[16] The father of cybernetics, Norbert Weiner, suggested, "The ultimate goal of the designer of man systems is to increase human welfare."[17]

We need to understand that all children (no matter who they are) have untapped resources and unimagined potential. We now know that children who come to school from poverty are no less capable than those children who come to school ready to learn. I can almost feel the school people roll their eyes and sigh, feeling quite misunderstood. Please let me say more! "Today we know that intelligence can be created. If you doubt this, let me recommend J. McVicker Hunt's book, *Intelligence and Experience*, which reviews the evidence of how we know this is true. We now know, for example, that the longer a child has been in an institution, the lower his IQ; when you put him in a rich environment, his I.Q. rises. We know that between World War I and World War II, the intelligence levels of men taken into the armed forces rose significantly."[18]

The idea that intelligence is not fixed is tremendously exciting for those of us who are working with children. It means that schools are not the victims of less intelligent children. We must learn to see possibilities because teachers and leaders are dealers in hope. Instead of trying to create places where gifted children will be challenged, we need to figure out what happened to create their giftedness. Then, we need to ensure that all students are given those same advantages. The failure of a child must be recognized as an anguished scream for help, while the child is thrashing up against a barrier of poor self-image and instinctively searching to discover his or her true potential. A child can discover an expanded life with our support and help. Human capacities are only confined by the lack of opportunities. We need to eliminate the limiting constraint of what is possible for "those children." We create contrived limits based on how we perceive children, which is a narrow-minded kind of bigotry that we must eradicate with Herculean haste to ensure all students equity of opportunity.

A child's potential is only limited by opportunity. In chapters 1 and 2, we made the point that the schoolyard bullies refuse to concede that it takes more time and resources to educate some students than others. The necessary resources and time that were mentioned should be used to provide opportunities to children who have not received them in any other way. It is recognized that creating those opportunities is not the sole responsibility of the school. Nonetheless, the SBS needs to be partners with parents and extended families because when we treat perceived low achievers differently than we treat perceived high achievers, we condemn the low achievers to a life with less intelligence, less richness, and less fulfillment, leading to a rubicon that we will all revile.

Even if these points were not true, the reality is that the public is demanding educational accountability. In many ways, I believe that the public is entitled to productive measurable results. James Popham has made a strong case when he asserted that the educational community has little choice but to "produce results and become accountable."[19] Under these conditions, then, a proper balance between academic performance and compassion will need to be maintained.

The key concern in this matter is that the notion of accountability will be translated into, and correspondingly be perceived as, threat. The intended goal for the leader, therefore, is to create an environment that is challenging, yet as threat free as possible, for all the members of the school community, including staff, parents, and students. There is probably no culture that is totally threat free and a bit of natural tension is probably healthy. The point is to develop a school culture that systemically mitigates threat and anxiety, thereby generating tolerance and empathy, rather than generating tenacious performance-based pressures. The motivation for academic achievement should be intrinsic and natural, rather than extrinsic and artificial. Maslow maintains that artificial pressure will simply accentuate threat and ultimately decrease productivity (i.e., academic success). To address this issue, the education community needs to define a framework for teaching that defines the proficiencies for teachers who teach in standards-based classrooms (i.e., addresses the human dimensions). I have made a start with the proficiencies for school leaders, but teacher proficiencies are beyond the scope of my purpose here. Happily, that work is already off to a flying start with the advent of a visionary book by Charlotte Danielson entitled *Enhancing Professional Practice: A Framework for Teaching*. In her work, she identifies and defines four "components of professional practice," along with sixty-four subcomponents, that serve to define the four larger components.[20] From my reading, it does not appear that she created a framework specifically for a standards-based classroom, but there is a framework within which to work. Nevertheless, one of Danielson's four components addresses the relational domain (i.e., the classroom environment), and twenty-three of the subcomponents also appear to be aligned with the relational domain.

Success Strategy 16
The Power of Hiring for Talent Match

- When adding new staff, make selection decisions consistent with the needs of the students in an SBS.
- Work with the staff to create a framework for teaching in an SBS as defined by your school or district.
- Use the framework for teaching in your SBS as a basis for staff development, which includes peer coaching (peer support).
- I would not recommend making the leap to use the framework as an evaluation instrument without considering all of the success axioms.
- Apply the success axioms that are appropriate for your school or district.
- Systematically involve parents and students in the curriculum process (as defined in chapter 7), so they will understand the expectations.
- Assemble and meet monthly for a meal with a student advisory committee of student school leaders who are as representative as possible of the student body. Request that they advise you as to other techniques that might be used in your school or district to recognize academic achievement (i.e., academic pep assemblies and academic letters, etc.). More mature students may also be used for other input, depending on the skill of the facilitator.
- Rotate the high school students as ex officio (nonvoting) advisors to the school board. This is a successful technique to always keep the focus on students (positive discrimination), even if it is only symbolic. A by-product is that the behavior of the adults at board meetings improves.
- Involve students and parents in the development of a scope and sequence for each course. As elements of the SBS become clear over time, students will proceed through the program with less fear and anxiety about the unexpected. Clearly articulated expectations will enhance school pride and student self-confidence and self-esteem.

CHARACTER EDUCATION AS A
RESPONSE TO EDUCATING THE WHOLE CHILD

I have often heard teachers communicate that the standards are so demanding that there is little time for anything else. Then the claim is made that there is not enough time to develop character, and besides, isn't that a family responsibility? With all due respect, that is just not the case!

Do high academic standards mean that a school will not be able to educate the whole child? Actually, high academic standards can be the impetus for developing a character education program. When I am discussing character development programs, the focus should be on traits that are universally acceptable. In fact, providing instruction toward character education in our children will contribute to their studies and learning, as family members and contributing citizens. When I began to develop the foundation for an SBS, we identified a community-based committee and asked the members to identify and define character traits that would help students in their studies and as citizens. The identified traits and definitions follow:

Success Strategy 17: The Power of Character Education Personal responsibility: Being responsible for one's own actions and future. Having ownership and being accountable for the outcomes of decisions, and learning from mistakes.

Courage: Having the internal strength to follow through on what one believes to be right. Taking action on personal commitments.

Honesty and integrity: Honesty—truthfulness, genuineness, being true to one's beliefs, attaining goals in a fair manner. Integrity—being true to one's ethical beliefs and taking action based on those beliefs.

Self-discipline: Being able to control or improve one's pattern of behavior in moral, mental, and physical wellness.

Social responsibility: Being willing to participate in, or develop community through, volunteerism, voting, community service, and showing respect for country.

Justice: Upholding what one believes to be fair. Being fair-minded in the treatment of others.

Kindness: Thinking and caring about the welfare of others, the considerate personal interaction that enriches the lives of others.

Respect: Recognizing the worth and the rights of self and others, and the value of property and the environment. Valuing authority and being courteous to others.

WHY CHARACTER EDUCATION IS
NECESSARY FOR STUDENTS

Accountability pressures in an SBS tend to reduce or eliminate any instruction that is not aimed directly at meeting the standards. I do believe that it is possible for a school to become so single-minded (i.e., standards based) that it fails to teach children the larger lessons of life. While eliminating enrichment activities or lessons that have nonmeasurable objectives sounds like a positive efficiency adjustment, that is not always the case. To underscore that point, I would like to share an article that first appeared in the *Winnipeg Associations Bulletin:*

CAN EFFICIENCY BE TAKEN TOO FAR? ABSOLUTELY

A company president had been given a ticket for the local symphony performance of Schubert's *Unfinished Symphony*. He couldn't go that evening so he gave the ticket to his management consultant who was an efficiency expert. The next morning he asked his efficiency expert how he enjoyed the performance. Instead of getting a few plausible observations, he was handed the following memorandum:

Dear Sir:

For considerable periods of time the four oboe players had nothing to do. The numbers should be reduced and their work spread over the whole orchestra, thus eliminating peaks of activity.

All twelve violins were playing identical notes. This seems an unnecessary duplication, and the staff of this section should be drastically cut. If a large volume of sound is required, it could be obtained through an electronic amplifier.

Much effort was absorbed in the playing of semiquavers or eighth notes. This seems an excessive refinement, and it is recommended that all notes be rounded up to the nearest quaver. If this were done, it should be possible to use trainees and lower grade operators.

No useful purpose is served by repeating with horns the same passage that has already been handled by the strings. If all such redundant passages were eliminated, the concert could be reduced from two hours to twenty minutes. In fact, if Schubert had attended to these matters, he probably would have been able to finish the Symphony after all.

— Author unknown

With that bit of levity in mind, let me provide you with two practical examples of the negative implications of being overzealous. In one of our high schools, the site council decided to eliminate Latin because the course was no longer a part of the standards at that time. Unfortunately, the community saw the course as a symbol of academic rigor and therefore had a very hard time understanding the repeated explanations. After several years of refusing to offer Latin, the parents became so concerned about the perceived lack of academic rigor, they petitioned to start an academic booster club.

The second example is even more extreme. In Oregon, we have a reading program (SMART) in which community volunteers come to school one day each week to read to a child who is experiencing reading difficulty. Many of these children have limited adult role models, so the weekly visit became a very important highlight for the child each week. You can imagine that because many of the citizens recognized the needs of the children, they went out of their way to help and consequently became quite proud of, and attached to, their "Smart Reader"! In two elementary schools, the volunteers could only come to school in the morning, creating the unacceptable consequence of having to pull the children from the classroom during the daily reading and math lessons. As important as this program was to the children, teachers, and volunteers, two schools (prompted by me) elected to drop the program so they could concentrate more instructional time on the academic standards. The point is that in an SBS, any program that does not directly address the academic standards is often dropped or reduced. What can be even more of a worry is when district leaders applaud such decisions. Moderation and balance in all things is wise, and character education can help maintain that balance.

Character education, therefore, should be considered a formal program in any SBS because it helps to blunt the aforementioned pressures. Additionally, character education is a legitimate option for at least two reasons:

- Students who are studying and participating in character education will usually do better in school. For example, students who exercise personal responsibility, courage, and self-discipline will do better academically.
- Educators have an important moral responsibility to prepare students for life; therefore, instruction toward developing character in our children and youth will contribute to their lives as family members, workers, and citizens.

OTHER BENEFITS OF CHARACTER EDUCATION

Some type of character education will probably be taught in most class-rooms anyway. If character education is not taught directly, it will proba-bly be taught inferentially. Students will come to know the values and be-liefs of the teacher and usually try to emulate them. Character traits like honesty, integrity, kindness, respect, and social responsibility are just a few character traits common in most classroom management plans. If some form of character education will be taught informally in any case, why not pull together and team up schoolwide? The community can sup-port the effort when students are on break and involved in community ac-tivities as well.

Soon, children begin to expect adults with whom they come in contact to exhibit the character traits as well. That reminds me of a powerful story I heard when I was visiting a school and happened to visit a class meeting at the primary level. In this particular room, the teacher would post the character trait of the week on the board and then ask the children, during their weekly class meeting, to cite how they had exhibited that trait dur-ing the week. At one point a child reported that his family had had a spat the previous evening, so he took it upon himself to teach the family mem-bers the importance of kindness and respect.

In addition, police officials reported at a community meeting that juve-nile crime had decreased. When the community asked why, I was de-lighted and surprised to hear the police chief credit the character educa-tion program. Frankly, there was no hard data to substantiate the claim, but the perception was helpful anyway. I have always believed that the character education program really took off when the adults modeled the traits and pointed it out to the children. I also believe very firmly that the behavior of the adults also improved over time.

CHARACTER EDUCATION AS
INTEGRATED CURRICULUM

Character education is the type of curriculum that ought to be integrated into the academic curriculum. In other words, the curriculum should be in-tegrated rather than taught as a stand-alone. For example, an experienced teacher can teach reading using the character trait self-discipline as the context through which reading, at home, is monitored. We created a curriculum guide for character education by asking teachers from every grade level and subject area to work with a common lesson format. The teachers created dozens of character education lessons that met the academic standards and could also be taught in any subject or any grade level.

A SCHOOL-BASED EXAMPLE: AN ACT OF KINDNESS

An elementary school staff created a schoolwide, character education kickoff program that was so successful it deserves to be mentioned here. They called it the Act of Kindness program. Students in every classroom studied kindness and then were challenged to make an effort to be kind in some way each day. When a student did something kind that was also very special, the teacher made a paper link to a chain with the student's name and the act of kindness. The goal was to see how long it would take to extend the paper chain the entire length of the hallways. The student then went to the office to get a treat from the principal and to insure that his or her link was added to the paper act of kindness chain. When both chain halves were linked together near the office (like the transcontinental railroad), completing the chain, there were celebrities on hand and treats for everyone. As I observed the celebration, I observed that all of the students were actively involved. I could not open a door for myself, pick up a piece of paper, ask students to walk, or ask students to please be polite, because the students were taking care of it.

Success Strategy 18   The following steps can be used to create a character education program that is supported by the community:

Step 1:   Set up a character education development committee. Attempt to recruit the most credible person possible to represent each group that could be affected by the program (suggestions follow):

- Parent club leader
- Youth group leader
- Two religious leaders

- Local law enforcement official
- Area business representative
- Juvenile office representative
- Teachers
- Administrators
- Students
- Union members
- Charity representatives
- Others who represent your community

Step 2:   Begin with a needs assessment by collecting the appropriate research and finding a district or school that has a program. Either visit the program or invite the program members to meet with your committee.

Step 3:   Begin to identify character traits. This is an important time to get the community involved, the more, the better.

Step 4:   Work to get reaction on the traits from the school community.

Step 5:   Make any adjustments necessary and report them to the school community.

Step 6:   Ask teachers representing all grade levels and subject material to meet to design exemplary lessons. Formalize the results and plan a staff development program in which those teachers would present their best lessons.

Step 7:   Hold an education summit to explain the program. Ask the participants to write down what they would be willing to do to support the effort. Organize the offers of support into groups of similar offers. Ask those who contributed to meet with the staff you have selected to facilitate each group. Have them meet and create a time line of activities to undertake.

Final step: Plan a big kickoff. This is a great activity around which to plan a back-to-school event. Use that same day to complete the staff development activity described in Step 5.

Success Strategy 19: How to Hire Teachers Who Are a Good Match for SBS To create the environment necessary to insure student success, leaders must:

- Make selection decisions (i.e., hire staff) that are consistent with the needs of students who are being educated in the SBS.
- Work with the staff to create a framework for teaching that clarifies the proficiencies necessary of all the adults who work in the school to nurture student success.
- Use the framework for successful teaching in an SBS to design the staff development program for everyone.

SUMMARY

Just as adults must be nurtured and cared for in the SBS, it is even more imperative for students. The key question to consider is: How do high standards and performance-based assessments affect students, and what can and should educators do to ameliorate the consequences and accentuate the strengths?

The impact of such a system is not given much attention in literature, so I turned to educational psychology (i.e., *Third Force Psychology*) for a working framework. Extrinsic motivation revolves around the traditional instructional construct. On the other hand, "intrinsic learning grows out of those experiences in which we learn who we are, what we love, what we hate, what we value, and what we are committed to."[21]

While intrinsic and extrinsic learning occur simultaneously and cannot be separated, they are still a valuable tool to consider the implications of the SBS on children. Perceptual psychology holds that a student's behavior is seen not as a response to a stimulus, but rather, a response to how the student sees surrounding events. The self-concept, then, is the result of countless judgments a child makes about himself in relationship to his environment. A child's image is not static, but changing and fluctuating. The poor self-image contributes much to the continual lack of success a child might experience. Conversely, school success is a direct result of a positive self-image.

Adults must be cared for and nurtured in an SBS, meaning productivity and humanity must be balanced to attain a high-performance school or district. The lesson that educational psychology teaches use is that educators must strike that same balance in working with students as well. It is very powerful to emphasize that leaders need to model for the staff the exact behavior that is needed in working successfully with students. Students seek to satisfy basic needs in order to self-actualize, which has proven difficult in the traditional educational system. The SBS, therefore, is the kind of school where students are provided the opportunity to break the vicious cycle of failure. This can occur if students are given the opportunity to fail without loss of self-esteem and if the culture of the school is as threat free as possible. The efficiency of the SBS does not necessarily have to negate humanity. Actually, the theory presented here is that the reverse is true. Self-esteem can be enhanced more easily in a school that is well organized with clear academic standards, rather than in a traditional school where academic achievement is less important than social acceptance as defined by superficial things like designer clothes, physical appearance, friends, and some loosely articulated behaviors.

NOTES

1. Abraham H. Maslow, "Some Educational Implications of the Humanistic Psychologies," *Four Psychologies Applied to Education*, ed. T. Roberts (New York: Schenkman, 1975), 305–313.
2. Maslow, "Some Educational Implications of the Humanistic."
3. Maslow, "Some Educational Implications of the Humanistic."
4. Arthur W. Combs and Donald Snygg, *Individual Behavior* (New York: Harper and Row, 1959), 365.
5. Kim Safford, "Education as an Opportunity" (paper presented at the Northwest Writing Institute, Lewis and Clark College, Portland, Ore., June, 1989).
6. Arthur W. Combs, "New Concepts of Human Potentials: New Challenges for Teachers," *Four Psychologies Applied to Education*, ed. T. Roberts. (New York: Schenkman, 1975), 296–303.
7. Combs, "New Concepts."
8. Dale Parnell, *Logolearning, Searching for Meaning in Education* (Waco, Tex.: Center for Occupational Research and Development, 1993), 6–9.
9. Combs, "New Concepts," 300.
10. Maslow, "Some Educational Implications," 309.
11. Combs, "New Concepts," 299.
12. Combs, "New Concepts," 296–303.
13. Combs, "New Concepts," 301.

14. Arthur W. Combs, *Curriculum and Instruction in the Elementary School*, (New York: MacMillan, 1975), 341.

15. Arthur W. Combs, "The Concept of Human Potential and the School" (paper presented at the annual meeting of Montana Supervision and Curriculum and Development, Missoula, Mont., March 1978).

16. K. Feyereisen and John Fiorino, eds., *Supervision and Curriculum Development: A Systems Approach* (New York: Meredith, 1970), 44.

17. Combs, "The Concept of Human Potential and the School."

18. Marcus Buckingham and Curt Coffman, *First, Break All of the Rules*. (New York: Simon and Schuster, 1999), 297.

19. James W. Popham, "The New World of Accountability: In the Classroom," *Four Psychologies Applied to Education*, ed. T. Roberts (New York: Schenkman, 1975), 209–14.

20. Charlotte Danielson, *Enhancing Professional Practice: A Framework for Teaching* (Alexandria,Va.: Association for Supervision and Curriculum, 1996), 43.

21. Maslow, "Some Educational Implications," 298.

Chapter Six

Nuts and Bolts: Efficiency Must Precede Effectiveness

Destiny is not a matter of chance; It is a matter of choice. It is not something to be waited for; but, Rather something to be achieved.

—William Jennings Bryan

The nuts-and-bolts concept includes the basic structures that help to keep the standards-based system or school running smoothly. In my experience if a school is not running smoothly, then major changes, even for the positive, usually flounder. The trains must be running on time, so to speak, before one lays new track to expand the railroad. In other words, a school that is on the edge of chaos or organizational vertigo is not likely to effectively embrace meaningful change. The first objective is to nurture an environment that is gratifying and rewarding for the adults and wholesome and challenging for students. There are a number of structures, in my opinion, that are universally applicable and should be developed to serve as a foundation for schools and districts that want to pursue the standards-based system or school. Those basic structures (that I affectionately call nuts and bolts) are as follows:

NUTS AND BOLTS

Basic Strategies of School Improvement

- Vision
- Communication
- Recognition density

- Written school improvement plans
- Data-based decision making
- Participatory governance
- Curriculum alignment

I will take each of these structures and define what they are and how they work together interactively to create a solid foundation on which to develop an SBS.

Basic Strategy 1: Vision as a Powerful Precondition for Success

A vision statement is a clear, compelling statement of the best that can be imagined for a school or district in five years. A vision statement is important because it helps to clarify the purpose of the school. In today's fast-paced world, there is much to obscure the priorities of a school. More importantly, when a school does not focus on academic standards, its students fail to meet standards as frequently as schools whose students do focus on academic standards do meet the standards. To be effective, a school has to have a clear sense of purpose. Because the vision must be based on the core beliefs of the people in the school, the people need to be involved in the vision-making process. If there is a sense of purpose in a school, then the adults can naturally align their programs and academic goals with the vision that serves as a kind of improvement magnet, pulling their school or district together to form a more efficacious school community. When the adults in the school own the vision, a powerful precondition for success has been met. Leaders establish a compelling vision, then step aside and let the power of the human spirit move the school toward the vision. Those who cannot, or do not, develop a compelling vision are forced to manage the power of the human will. If the vision is not owned and understood by the people, the vision can feel superimposed. The vision is, therefore, an unnatural and unwelcome activity that becomes layered on top of the strongly held pre-existing activities. Schools without a clear vision are forced to react to every pressure or educational fad that comes their way. The steps outlined below are provided to enable you to begin planning a vision building process.

Basic Strategy 2: Vision Building and Leading the Emotional Soul

Step 1:   Employ the vision building techniques discussed in chapter 2 to identify the core belief of the community.

Step 2:   Work with the board (district) or site council (school) and the core beliefs to develop a vision and goals that stretch the strengths of the school or district.

Step 3:   Design solid communication strategies to create a deep understanding of, and support for, the vision and the goals.

Basic Strategy 3: Building Community and Teamwork through Communication

Most communities have a well-developed rumor mill (i.e., informal communication network) that becomes active around critical issues in the community. In many communities, education is one of the more prominent issues for discussion. In our community, there was a well-developed informal network, so we decided to put it to work for us.

We started to develop our group (rumor mill) by identifying people we called key communicators. To identify the group, we asked school office managers and school administrators to nominate adults for this recognition by naming people who met three important criteria that follow. Name an adult who resides in your service area who:

• Frequently talks with other adults
• About schools, and
• Is believed.

Individuals who were nominated two or more times were given the honorary designation of being a school district key communicator. We developed a packet of materials for each nominee that was personalized as much as possible. In each packet we included a plastic key card (i.e., looked like a credit card) with the superintendent's home phone number and e-mail address and invited these key communicators to contact the superintendent if they ever needed some information to help clarify some confusion, or if they had some important information the superintendent should know about. They were all told that if they said that they were key communicators, then the superintendent would be in touch with them within twenty-four hours. We invited key communicators to have lunch with the superintendent where they were honored. Initially, we had a long, formal agenda, but quickly found that the key communicators simply wanted time to ask questions. At that time, we told key communicators that they had a standing invitation to get in touch with the superintendent whenever, or however, appropriate. Initially, I was concerned about how the privilege might be abused by a few. To my pleasant surprise, the key communicators were very respectful of my time and honored their role. I believe that without information, the community will frequently do much to obstruct a new idea or direction. With information, however, they quickly become ambassadors for a new idea. The insider knowledge made them a kind of disciple for the district or school, and the designation was viewed as an honor.

For example, I was asked to introduce a rather important businessman to the Rotary for a presentation about his business, so I asked the individual to provide me with a vita that I might use to prepare his introduction. To my surprise, the individual listed the key communicator designation as an important honor to be referenced during his introduction.

The fast fax process (described below) helped us to solidify and to build on our relationship with the community. Each week we created an information update that went to the school board, administrators, and site council members, so we agreed to simply fax or mail a copy to the key communicators if they wanted to be kept up to date. That weekly update (called *Inside Our Schools*) made key communicators feel valuable (and they were), and it solidified our relationship. As time went on, the fast fax process fell out of favor with the group. When individuals expressed a preference for e-mail, we happily made the transition because it was easier and less time dependent. We used that process to share and collect information about our schools almost overnight. I keep saying we, but I should point out that we had a wonderful communications specialist who put all of this together.

After the first year and cycle of luncheons, we discovered that many of the people who had been nominated to be key communicators were business people with no children in school. While we were pleased with that outcome, we realized that we also could benefit from a network of parents as well. So we used the same criteria to create a second group that we called school ambassadors. So we again asked school office managers and school administrators to nominate parents who frequently spoke with other parents about school and were believed. We used the same process with the packet of information, but elected to meet in larger groups at a time between the end of the workday and before dinner. This was a time more convenient for most parents, because the meeting would easily fit the time slot between work and dinner with the family. We had also learned that this group might not respond well to the free lunch idea, so we served cookies and fruit. We added the fast fax option as soon as possible. Between both the key communicators and the school ambassadors, we had about seven hundred to eight hundred people helping us to use the rumor mill process to advance positions that were good for children. Over time, they became friends of the district and were invited to help in a variety of ways.

I will provide you with one example of how the groups helped. During the 1997 legislative session, the legislature in Oregon passed a statute that allowed a school district to levy a tax to supplement the money that was provided by the state. Our community continually asked for programs that exceeded the allocation received from the state, so we felt we had a responsibility to ask if a local levy (tax) would be supported. We established two focus groups, one with the key communicators and another with the school ambassadors. We asked just two questions of both groups:

- Do you think the community would support a local tax increase for schools? And do you agree with what the community might want?
- If we did place a tax increase on the ballot, how should the money be used?

Before we impaneled the two focus groups, I was quite convinced that the community would support a tax increase, especially since I had come to view many as my friends. Therefore, I was very gratified that we used the process. Both groups said the community would not support a tax increase and each group agreed with (what I thought was) the negative perception. Interestingly, the groups differed how the money should be used. The key communicators (business) said the money should be used for deferred maintenance, while the school ambassadors (parents) favored using the money to enhance programs for students. Some of the board members had attended the focus group meetings as observers and listeners, and with this information from people whom we viewed as our friends, they unanimously agreed that a school tax would be unsuccessful and elected not to put one on the ballot.

Basic Strategy 4: The Power of Recognition

> Emotion is the track; knowledge is the train; enduring understanding the destination.
>
> —Gary Phillips "Sited-Based Decision Making
> and School Improvement" (paper)

High-performance schools and districts work at being successful primarily by moving consistently step-by-step, over time. Of course we are short of needed resources, but the real antagonist is not money but time. The point was strongly underscored when Epictetus once said, "no great thing is created suddenly, any more than a bunch of grapes or a fig. If you tell me you desire a fig, I answer you that there must be real time, let it first blossom, then bear fruit, then ripen."[1] Once the direction has been set, policymakers need to stay the course. In my eleven years of working with principals, superintendents, and leadership teams, the most common request of policymakers (when times were serious) was "stay the course!" Given a little time and solid incentives, both the teachers and the students will quickly become more wily (a good word that I borrowed from an elementary principal describing his teachers) about how to achieve the standards. People are motivated by any number of incentives including money, fame, power, and recognition to name just a few. High-performance schools and districts have people who are self-starters, taking the initiative without being asked or directed. In chapter 5, we determined that Maslow's hierarchy of needs made intrinsic motivation very powerful. Recognition is a powerful motivator, as well, because it is intrinsic in nature. More than that, it is especially powerful in schools because educators come to their life's work for reasons of the heart.

Use the vision techniques described in chapter 2 to identify the core beliefs in the community. Then set goals to achieve those beliefs. Design powerful communication techniques to create an understanding of, and support for, academic achievement as measured by the goals. Whenever possible, publicly recognize students, parents, and staff for the academic achievement of the standards.

The kind of recognition being discussed here is intrinsic in nature. This three-step strategy is consequential and a key capacity-based leadership strategy in developing a high-performance system. The effectiveness of this strategy cannot be overstated. As has been mentioned previously, I call it the student, staff, and parent all-star program:

Step 1: Publicly identify the community beliefs as academic goals.
Step 2: Measure progress toward the goals annually, and report the results to the teachers, students, and parents.
Step 3: Recognize the students and staff who are successful in aligning to and achieving district academic goals. Attempt to make the recognition a celebration of excellence by having the ceremony at board meetings, school assemblies, or any other public format that works for your organization.
Step 4: Invite family members to attend and to be honored (recognized) as well.
Step 5: Allow the community to exert pressure on the system to become more effective in reaching the academic standards.

Basic Strategy 5: Written School Improvement Plans Are the Road Map

Each school should be invited to create a written school improvement plan (SIP). A written SIP provides a means of accountability for academic performance and improvement. Equally importantly, the written SIP establishes the focus for the year and simultaneously makes a strong statement about what is valued. There is always some coercive pressure to change the focus. The well-meaning Parent Teacher Student Association (PTSA) or booster club seems to have a myriad of things to pressure a school to undertake. What is true is, it is never a matter of having a good idea, but rather which good idea. Those requests can be more easily managed if there is a written plan, because if done properly, the SIP and vision represent the shared core beliefs of the staff and community. Then, the caring educational forces can readily see how their ideas might fit into the SIP in subsequent years. SIP becomes the road map, which allows the principal and site council (i.e., parents, staff, and students) to construct a plan used to monitor progress and inform work on the next year's SIP. Following are several components important to the plan.

Component 1

It is valuable to have each site council present its written SIP as well as progress that has been made during the last academic year. This is a time for annual celebration, which allows the policy leaders and parents, business leaders, and others an opportunity to affirm the team for their strengths and successes (i.e., stretches).

Component 2

The goals should be written in measurable terms; for example, 90 percent of the students will meet or exceed the tenth-grade math standards. It is my recommendation that site councils keep this parameter in perspective. This is a difficult challenge for school people because school leaders do not feel in control of all the important variables like available resources and socioeconomic status (SES). In addition, some of the more important areas of improvement can be difficult to measure using the traditional quantifiable strategies. That reality should not be allowed to dissuade a team from pursuing some of the more complex measures. I understand that there is a school of thinking that supports only mathematically quantifiable approaches. I understand the need for science, but that statistical mindset is discouraging for parents and staff who are eager to challenge some of the more difficult areas to measure. For example, a site council may want to focus on student respect for self and others. While some objective data may be collected to demonstrate progress, the constraints of pure, statistical analysis are challenging, indeed. For that reason, I support a solid subjective approach such as professional judgment. To initiate such a process, one simply needs to ask the school community the question, "In the area of student achievement (or any area of interest or concern at school), what is better today, than a year ago?" The results are truly amazing. What is true is that the leadership team is able to ascertain the relative level of satisfaction of the key constituents.

Component 3

The written time line and master plan should include the following components: A list of activities designed to attain the goal; who is responsible for completing the activity; what resources will be used; the anticipated time line, including the year and quarter; and how the activity will be evaluated. I have included three examples from schools that will remain unnamed. These examples are not perfect, but at the time they were an excellent work in progress. Please notice how the SIP is organized for action and evaluation. Also, look for the school profile data that was used to support the identification of the goal. That is an excellent sign that the team is using data-based decision making (see the next nut and bolt for more). I would always press for measurable goals where possible, allowing for the use of nonparametric statistics, of course. The purpose of these examples allows your team to study the design and then to modify it to meet your specific needs.

Instructional Goal 1

Increase learning opportunities that move students toward meeting the Certificate of Initial Mastery (CIM). Profile data that supports the implementation of this goal. See figure 6.1 for middle school improvement plan example.

Instructional Goal 2

Identify skills which will be essential to student success with integrated applied learning, leading to the attainment of the CIM. Profile data that supports the implementation of this goal, adding comments. Our students regularly score ten to twenty points above the national average on the nationally normed test of basic skills, while our state assessment scores tend to be at or below the state average on applied learning. Our school vision, which is strongly supported by staff and students, focuses on the balance between basic skills and applied learning. See figure 6.2 for an example of a high school improvement plan.

Instructional Goal 3

Ninety percent of students will meet or exceed standards in math, writing, and reading on the state assessments. Math domains from 1995 state data of numeration, computation, problem solving, geometry, measurement, probability and statistics, mathematical relationships, and estimation. Reading domains from 1995 state data of word meaning,

Activity	Assigned to	Resources	Time Lines Projected Year	Quarter F	Quarter W	Quarter Sp	Quarter Su	Evaluation
Strategy 1: Expand the development and use of integrated units/projects with opportunities for community involvement.								
1.1 Teacher in-service on the writing of integrated units.	Site council integrated units.	Time for in-service and planning. Money for substitutes, speaker with expertise on writing	1995	X				Attendance roster
1.2 Release time to investigate others integrated units.	Principal	Time, substitutes, other experts.	1995–97	X	X	X		Attendance rosterusing summaries.
1.3 Planning time for teachers to develop units.	Site council	Time and funding.	1995–97	X	X	X		Written units to share.
1.4 Staff in-service to share developed units.	Site council	Time	1996	X	X	X		Summary presentations.

Figure 6.1. Middle School Improvement Plan

1.5 Investigation of assessment practices (also see strategy 2)	All staff	Time	1995–97	X	X	X	Develop a menu of assessment tools.
1.6 Implementation of units into classroom instruction.	All staff	Written units	1995–97	X	X		Staff sharing and sample work.
1.7 Display of student projects showing thematic units carried out by staff work teams.	Staff, parents club, and community volunteers	Student projects at various locations	1995–96	X	X		Survey from students and participants.

Person with Overall Responsibility for Goal #1: _____

Figure 6.1. (*Continued*)

Activity	Assigned to	Resources	Time Lines Projected Year	Quarter F	W	Sp	Su	Evaluation
1. Align basic skills by grade level with the building and district CIM skills plan.	Site council	District CIM skill plan and building CIM skill plan	1995–96	X				Completed building plan in chart or booklet form.
2. Retain high scores on CTBS test—grades 2–4	Classroom teachers	ESD testing service	Ongoing				→	October 1995 test scores Comparison of '95 test scores to prior years
3. Select teaching strategies which teach basic skills in relation to and/or in conjuction with applied learning.	Classroom teachers	Building staff development money/district staff	1995–97	X	X	X	X	Teacher goals-evaluation portfolios which show growth in this area.

Figure 6.2. High School Improvement Plan

| 4. Teachers will align demonstration tasks for CIM skill attainment with classroom instruction. One component of each demonstration task will focus on basic skill mastery | Certified staff | Summer institute team planning | 1995–97 | X | X | X | Parent communication of each unit will list major learnings, required activities, projects, presentations, demonstrations, and scoring guidelines, including basic skills focus. |

Person with Overall Responsibility for Goal #1: _____

Figure 6.2. (*Continued*)

literal comprehension, locating information, inferred comprehension, mass media, and evaluative comprehension. See figure 6.3 for an example of an elementary school improvement plan.

Basic Strategy 6: Data-Based Decision Making Is Essential

If the site council is expected to use data to design and evaluate the SIP, then it will need student data to analyze. Therefore each school should be provided with a school profile. The school profile is a published document and should include:

- At least three years of data (if possible); plus
- Student achievement data compared to self, the state average, and other schools that are similar demographically; and
- Other data, including demographic data (i.e., percent of students on free and reduced lunch), school's mobility rate, and attendance. In Oregon, those are the three categories used to measure socioeconomic status (SES), along with the educational attainment level of the highest educated parent. It is helpful to compare the results to state district data.

There are at least three data techniques that are grounded in capacity-based (versus deficiency-based) leadership beliefs:

- It is most advisable to compare the school's results to a school that is similar demographically. The concern was raised in chapter 1 that the schoolyard bullies refuse to recognize that it takes more time and money to educate some students than it does others. Comparing the school's results to schools that are most like the school in question addresses that legitimate concern relatively fairly.
- Each school should establish a baseline and demonstrate improvement every year. Each school needs to be committed to the concept of continual improvement until the standards are met. From a capacity-based leadership perspective, the most successful way to approach the concept of continual improvement is to obtain the commitment of each individual. This point is an important precondition of success because either people improve or programs won't. Personal improvement always precedes program improvement.

Activity	Assigned to	Resources	Time Lines					Evaluation
			Projected Year	Quarter				
				F	W	Sp	Su	

Strategy 1: Staff will understand the following documents: the district's curriculm and assessment framework as aligned with the state content standards and scoring guides; and understand the following processes: performance tasks and collection of evidence.

Activity	Assigned to	Resources	Projected Year	F	W	Sp	Su	Evaluation
1. In-service on: ✓ Alignment of curriculm and assessment ✓ State testing ✓ Collection of evidence, performance tasks, scoring guides. 2. Make faculty aware of ✓ Time lines ✓ Expectations for our students	Name of individual	List resources or individual(s)	August 1996 district in-service				X	Follow-up August 29 Short staff evaluation synthesized by RP + C²

Figure 6.3. Elementary School Improvement Plan

	Assigned to	Resources	Time Lines		Quarter			Evaluation
				Projected Year	F	W	Sp	Su	

Strategy II: Staff will examine and analyze state assessment test.

	Assigned to	Resources	Projected Year	F	W	Sp	Su	Evaluation
1. Take state assessment tests in math and reading to determine what skillsand knowledge need to be taught to be successful on state tests. 2. Discuss what we currently teach that matches with the tests. 3. Identify teaching strategies to be used in all classes to reinforce assessed skills and knowledge.	Name of individual(s)	List resources or individual(s)	August 1996				X	Test Results

Person with Overall Responsibility for Goal #1: _____

Figure 6.3. *(Continued)*

- Each school should be encouraged to broaden the criteria of measuring success to areas like attendance and dropout rates, percentage of teachers certified to teach in their assigned content area, parental involvement, and student discipline including defiance, fighting, and drug possession or trafficking. I believe the best measure of a school or a district is customer satisfaction. For example, even if a school is strong academically, but has a four-year dropout rate of about 25 percent (6 percent per year), it would be unlikely that the community would view the program as successful. If the community voices strong support for academic achievement and assumes that most of the students will graduate, only to find out that most do not graduate, the community will be disappointed. If that anomaly occurs in a community that has communicated core beliefs about the importance of graduation, even though the school was doing well academically (as measured by the standards), the satisfaction level would still be understandably low for parents, students, and probably staff because academic success was viewed as less important than school graduation. A satisfaction measure of the type described above is a good way to surface that kind of information.

When I use the term data-based decision making, I mean that student data is used in two ways:

- The site council at the school uses student data as the basis for making decisions about the goals, objectives, activities, and community involvement that make up the SIP.
- The site council uses student data to assess the progress of the school in meeting the goals stated in the SIP (school effectiveness).

How to Use Student Data to Design the SIP

The school-based councils need to be trained so they possess the skill to use data drawn from the school profile to support the implementation of each goal in the SIP. For example, goal 2 is supported by such profile data as:

- Number of students in alternative learning environments
- GPAs

- Credits toward graduation
- Earned proficiencies
- Enrollment in school-to-work opportunities
- Graduation rates

How to Use Student Achievement Data to Assess Progress on the SIP

Either student achievement or demographic data should be used to assess progress on each SIP goal annually. The site councils should create a summative report of their progress and mail it out to all parents in their service area. Resources should be provided for this task. Note that one high school determined that it would use state assessment tests in reading and math to determine what skills and knowledge needed to be taught and mastered for students to be successful on state tests. In other words, if the goal was to have 90 percent of the students achieve the state math standard or if the goal was to improve by ten percentage points, the site council would simply compare the assessment outcomes to the goal as a way of measuring the relative success rates.

Basic Strategy 7: Participatory Governance

School improvement is a cyclical process of community involvement and shared decision making. A basic precept of the capacity-based leader is that those people who will be affected by decisions need to be involved in the decision-making process. This is another difference between a leader and a manager. Leaders move toward the vision by working through others (by using their ideas), while managers recruit support for their vision and manipulate and align movement. When I was working on my first school improvement program in the early 1970s, a good friend and mentor said to me during a basketball game, "School improvement is a cyclical process of shared decision making through community involvement."[2]

Basic Strategy 8: Attention to Alignment

The improvement of schools that set academic goals and measure and report their progress on the goals, accelerates. Therefore, each site council should be invited (annually) to report its progress to the community (school board) on how its school improvement plan (SIP) supports the goals and vision of the district. It is equally important for the board and district office staff to demonstrate how their work supports the vision and goals of each school. The idea is for each component in the district to demonstrate how they align behind student achievement. (See integrated decision-making model, page 145.) Curriculum alignment is the second precondition for a successful transformation. For students and teachers to succeed, it is critically important that teachers become very clear on what students should know, or be able to do, and what they should be (character education). If students and their parents know what the academic expectations are, they are more likely to meet them. I have always believed in the old school improvement proverb that says, "The prescription for improvement is process."

Learner Outcome Construction

Developing a written curriculum and aligning it to the standards is such a critical component of a high-performance school that I have expanded the nuts-and-bolts chapter to spend an additional chapter to focus exclusively on the skills of curriculum alignment. While this process is not terribly complex, few principals or superintendents have the background they need in the area of curriculum alignment. These comments do not mean that principals and superintendents must do the curriculum alignment personally, but they do need to insure that the appropriate tasks are carried out. Doing so, they closely observe the process and provide the necessary support, encouragement, and recognition on an as-needed basis.

SUMMARY

The nuts and bolts described in this chapter are a universally applicable basic framework that all standards-based schools need to consider. Efficiency (doing things right) must precede effectiveness (doing the right things). The basic structures are as follows:

Vision

Vision is a powerful precondition for success. There is much to distract schools from their basic mission. When there is a shared sense of purpose in school, then the adults can align their programs and goals with the vision of the school. If the people own the vision, then it serves to pull people voluntarily in a common direction.

Community Involvement in Decision Making

Information is power. Without it, people will often resist change. With information, they will often become leading ambassadors for the change. We developed two groups designed to help the district communicate. In each case, we invited principals and school office managers to nominate people who met the following criteria: frequently talks with other adults, about school, and is believed. We called the final group that represented parents school ambassadors, and the group representing business people key communicators.

Recognition

High-performance districts work at being successful primarily by setting the course and by staying the course. This basic structure is the third step of a three-step process so it should work in conjunction with the first two. The three steps are as follows:

1. Create a vision that captures the beliefs of the school community, and is therefore owned by them.
2. Set and publicize goals designed to meet community beliefs or expectations.
3. Publicly recognize students, staff, and community (simultaneously) who help to pursue the vision.

Written School Improvement Plans

Written school improvement plans (SIP) help provide the school with direction, while also addressing issues of accountability. Each year, the school should present its plan to the school board, along with a description of how the school did in meeting the goals of the SIP. In addition to presenting improvements to the board, each site council should be invited to create a summary of progress and send it out to parents, along with tips the parents could execute to help their children perform at higher levels. Also, it is a good idea to ask for their suggestions at the same time.

Goals should be written in measurable terms. It is my recommendation that this parameter be kept in perspective, because all viable goals are not as easily measured with traditional quantifiable strategies. It would not be positive to avoid difficult to measure goals (i.e., affective or abstract) just because they could not be measured with traditional techniques. Some of the most noble and important of goals easily fall into this category. With a little help, you will find that almost every serious goal can be measured in some technically respectable way. Surveys and professional judgment are two avenues that are worth exploration. There are parameters, of course, but the desired approach simply needs to make sense in an intellectually honest way. Technically, that approach is called "face validity."

Data-Based Decision Making

Site councils need to be given the training and resources to use data to develop and evaluate the SIP. Each school should be provided with a profile which should, under optimum circumstances, include (1) three years of student achievement data, (2) comparison to self, the state average, and other schools with similar demographic data, and (3) other demographic data which reflects the core beliefs of the school community.

Attention to Organizational Alignment

Schools or organizations that set community-based goals, and annually measure and report their progress, improve at accelerated rates. Each site council, therefore, should be invited to report on how its SIP aligns to the vision and goals of the district. The central notion here is threefold:

- How do the parts of the organization work together?
- How does the organization align behind student achievement?
- How do we know or what measure did we use? (See the integrated decision-making system in chapter 4).

The curriculum alignment issues are quite technical. They are also a critical precondition for success. For that reason the rest of this basic structure is addressed in the next chapter.

NOTES

1. Epictetus, *The Best of Success*, ed. Wynn Davis (Lombard, Ill.: Celebrating Excellence, 1992), 70.

2. Gary Phillips, "Site-Based Decision Making and School Improvement" (paper presented at IDEA School Improvement Program, Battleground, Wash., July 1994).

Chapter Seven

Curriculum Alignment Is a Precondition for Success

Be out and about, enjoy the process, crave the goal.

—Ken Blanchard, *Words to Lead By* (videotape)

Clear academic goals are a precondition for success in a high-performance school. Students can and will meet the academic standards if teachers, students, and their parents are clear on what students should know and be able to do as a result of instruction. With clear, written academic goals, exit and entrance academic requirements of the curriculum can be strengthened if gaps or overlaps occur. When the goals of the academic content are so clear that entrance and exit requirements exist between grade levels and subject areas, then the conditions have been developed where more teamwork is a natural by-product. By teamwork, I mean teamwork between teachers, between home and school, and between work and school. Having clear curriculum goals is critically important because it takes the mystery out of school success and encourages partnerships and school support. It is critically important for a high-performance school to develop clear academic goals. The first step in that process is to design and implement a broad-based participatory process to align the curriculum to the content standards. Once that is achieved, every student (and adult) in every classroom should be able to learn one thing each day worth remembering for a lifetime. The planning process described herein can be used to achieve that goal.

WRITTEN CURRICULUM IS THE
PRESCRIPTION FOR SCHOOL IMPROVEMENT:
CAPACITY-BASED LEADERSHIP IS THE PROCESS

Curriculum Alignment: What Is It?

In an SBS, the curriculum should be performance based and standards driven. When I speak about curriculum alignment to the community, they will often dismiss its importance by saying, "That is just teaching to the test!" That concern usually comes from people who are referring to a traditional school, prior SBM. Please let me explain why teachers cannot teach directly to the test in an SBS. The nature of the questions on tests that are used in an SBS make it difficult to teach to specific test questions. Students on a performance-based test are frequently expected to use simple recall (level 2 comprehension) in a complex, multistep operation.

In a simple knowledge-level test (traditional school), the student can recite the mathematical formulas (level 1 knowledge) that can be used to translate verbal material into mathematical formulas. In a more sophisticated multilevel comprehension test, the student is able to translate verbal material into mathematical formulas (level 2 comprehension). In an even more sophisticated test, the student will successfully judge the value of a work (i.e., art, music, writing) through the use of internal math standards.

The six levels of the cognitive domain, according to Benjamin Bloom, from the simplest to the most complex, are listed below.[1] For a more complex explanation of the cognitive, affective, and psychomotor domains, see http://education.nebrwesleyan.edu.

- Knowledge
- Comprehension
- Application
- Analysis
- Synthesis
- Evaluation

The Power of a Living Curriculum

Developing a written curriculum that defines the instructional goals has inherent value in any school, but most especially in an SBS. One cannot begin to pursue becoming a high-performance SBS without a written curriculum. A written curriculum is a valuable road map for many reasons. While the following iteration supports the need to have a written curriculum, it is not intended to be all inclusive.

The following is a rationale for having a written curriculum:

- A written curriculum establishes a base upon which the processes of evaluation and revision are more effectively carried out.
- A written curriculum provides a common curriculum offering across all grade levels.
- A written curriculum insures a commitment to a common understanding of student academic expectations.
- A written curriculum defines some important professional growth activities.
- A written curriculum helps in the development of future budget needs.
- A written curriculum provides a basis on which the curriculum is effective in meeting the academic standards.
- A written curriculum makes use of the best of the best curriculum in a school.
- A written curriculum makes the academic expectations completely clear to all, thereby demystifying the connection between schoolwork and school success.

If the curriculum is valued and used by teachers, I call the curriculum a living curriculum, because it creates the instructional framework through which the appropriate curriculum adjustments can be made. It is extremely important for teachers to agree on the instructional program. When I visited classrooms prior to the SBS reform, it was completely apparent that the teachers were hardworking and caring. At that time in the evolution of schooling, I did not frequently see a group of closely connected professionals working together to match entrance and exit requirements. Instead, what I saw reminded me of a proud and dedicated group of all-American basketball players playing one-on-one. In other words, teachers taught content in relative isolation of each other. It just seemed to me that they had not been asked to work together or to pass the ball to the appropriate player, so to speak.

The most challenging and noble vocation in the history of modern America is made doubly difficult when people are not given the chance to work together. It is not uncommon for some teachers to remain isolated from those across the hall or grade or department. Often, a school does not hold shared academic expectations. For example, is an *A* in Mr. Smith's class the same as an *A* in Mrs. Jones's class? Of course, we all know that it is not! Those of us who work closely with today's youth recognize that today's kids are the most talented and hardest working in our history. The point is that this is a systems issue, not a student or teacher issue. Simply said, curriculum planning and clear academic goals have not been expectations until most recently. In fact, until just recently, cooperation has not been a major systemwide emphasis. The structure of school is so isolating it is almost as if there has been a sinister plot to isolate caring and capable teachers from each other. This common phenomenon in American schools is the fundamental challenge that faces public school education in America.

It is of paramount importance that we as a school community get clear on what students know and are able to do as a result of instruction. It is important because one cannot strengthen an unwritten curriculum that has no identifiable, definite direction, and whose connectedness exists only in the memory of some teachers. One cannot make systemwide changes that make a difference if there is no consistency from classroom to classroom, or school to school. For example, if students do not do well in horizontal math (i.e., $14 - 12 = 2$) in the third grade and there is no written curriculum, it will be more difficult to remedy the problem. But if there is a written curriculum that does not introduce that concept until the fourth grade or teachers spend just one lesson teaching horizontal math in the third grade, then one could examine the scope and sequence of the pertinent data. It might then be appropriate to ask teachers to consider the possibility of lengthening or moving the unit on horizontal math to grade three instead of grade four. If teachers felt that it was not in the best interests of their students to move the math unit, then they would know the consequences of that decision with purposeful intent. No more mystery.

Success Strategy 20: Developing Written Curriculum as a Precondition for Success It is important for principals and superintendents to understand the process of curriculum development because academic achievement is the highest priority in an SBS. With that knowledge base, the formal leader can provide the necessary support and recognition (recognition density) to develop such a curriculum and align it to the standards. To that end, the following four-step process can be used:

- Phase 1: Needs assessment
- Phase 2: Learner outcome construction
- Phase 3: Implementation and data collection
- Phase 4: Regeneration and renewal.

Did we reach gap closure?

PHASE 1: NEEDS ASSESSMENT

Process to Be Used: Definition

For the purpose of this work, a needs assessment will be defined as a formal process designed to surface the gaps between what is and what is preferred in precise, explicit terms. In a more general sense, the needs assessment is the systematic process by which curriculum needs are identified. In this case, a discrepancy is defined as a discrepancy or gap between what is (i.e., the current curriculum) and what is preferred (i.e., the desired curriculum including the assessment specifications). See figure 7.1.

Needs Assessment

What is (current):		What is preferred (desired):
Result A _____	No Gap _____	Result A
Result C _____	Gap _____	Result A

Figure 7.1.   Needs Assessment

As a point of clarification, the needs assessment should not become a solutions assessment. To be specific, it is important to identify discrepancy gaps in outcomes rather than procedures (ends not means).[2] This issue is being raised here because it seems that this is a common type of perceptual error, especially at the secondary level. The needs assessment that

will be defined herein contains the following components that are crucial
to a living curriculum (i.e., valued and used by teachers):

- The needs assessment should be teacher based.
- The needs assessment should result in the production of specific learner
  outcomes (i.e., what students should know or do).
- The model includes a formal process for evaluation, data collection, and
  regeneration.
- The model provides for continual renewal with an ongoing cybernetic
  feedback loop.

The Systems Approach to Curriculum

Some of the reasons that support the systems approach to curriculum revision are as follows:

- The process model is primarily teacher based.
- The system provides for continual curriculum evaluation and renewal.
- The committee system provides for specific points of interim decision
  making.
- The model is grounded on capacity-based leadership.
- The model allows for teachers to emerge as curriculum leaders.
- The process articulates a district-level commitment to curricular devel-
  opment.
- Procedures provide for involvement from every person impacted by
  curriculum decisions.
- Procedures provide for community and student input.
- Budgeted amounts for curriculum and instruction are allocated as part
  of a broad-based five-year plan.
- The model will produce a scope and sequence that is articulated in
  learner outcome terms.

Teacher-Based Decision-Making Model

All curriculum generation, implementation, evaluation, and renewal
should grow out of a committee structure that allows for a maximum contribution by the classroom teacher. Leadership on each committee should

be democratically determined. Principals should assume the role of grade and department level facilitators, while elected teacher leaders will chair all building level committees.

Committee Structure (Building Level)

Note that in this model the working committee structure at the building level functions at two levels. Model components 1.1, 1.2, and 1.3 of phase 1 represent grade- and department-level working committees. All staff are members of these building-level committees. The chairperson is elected, and a building administrator functions as facilitator. See figure 7.2.

	Committee		Membership		Leadership
1.1	Elementary grade-level curriculum committee by building	1.1	All building grade-level teachers	1.1	Chairperson: elected facilitator: principal
1.2	Intermediate grade-level curriculum committee by building (selected or elected)	1.2	All building grade-level teachers	1.2	Chairperson: elected facilitator: principal
1.3	High school department curriculum committee by building (selected or elected)	1.3	All department members	1.3	Chairperson: elected facilitator: principal
1.4	Building curriculum committee (selected or elected)	1.4	All grade-level team leadership (building)	1.4	Chairperson: elected facilitator: principal
1.5	Curriculum development commission (selected or elected)	1.5	All districtwide grade-level team leaders	1.5	Chairperson: elected facilitator: principal
1.6	Curriculum commission	1.6	All principals, directors, superintendent, curriculum director	1.6	Chairperson: elected facilitator: curriculum director

Figure 7.2.   Building a Curriculum Committee

In an effort to create curriculum continuity, there will at times be districtwide grade and department level meetings. Grade and department-level meetings will be held to establish consensus on a K–12 basis. The teacher who represents a particular grade level on the district curriculum committee will preside as chairperson during those working grade-level sessions. A principal will be available at the meeting as a communications link (facilitator) to the curriculum council.

In addition to grade and department-level committees, a building curriculum committee should be convened on an as-needed basis to insure curriculum continuity within that building. All grade and department-level leaders should be members. The chairperson is elected by the members of the grade level. In addition, the building principal is the facilitator. See figure 7.3.

Committee Structure (District Level)

Each curricular study area will be directed by a curriculum development commission (see step 1.5 of figure 7.2.). As an example, in the area of social studies alignment, the committee will be called the social studies curriculum committee. All grade-level and department leaders are members. The chairperson is elected. A building principal, with content and process expertise, will be assigned the role of facilitator by the curriculum commission. In that way, the curriculum commission will ensure a total districtwide curriculum continuity.

The curriculum commission is comprised of the superintendent, all directors and principals, and the curriculum director. The chairperson of the commission is elected, and the curriculum director is the facilitator. It is the role of the curriculum commission to orchestrate all curricular activity in the school district. See step 1.6 of figure 7.2.

It is important to note that the committee structure allows for both vertical and horizontal articulation. Constant feedback will enable obstacles to be surfaced and defused before the development of significant barriers to change.

Identify Sources of Input and Activate Data Collection

After the organizational structure has been established and the corresponding responsibilities defined, the partners who will be invited to

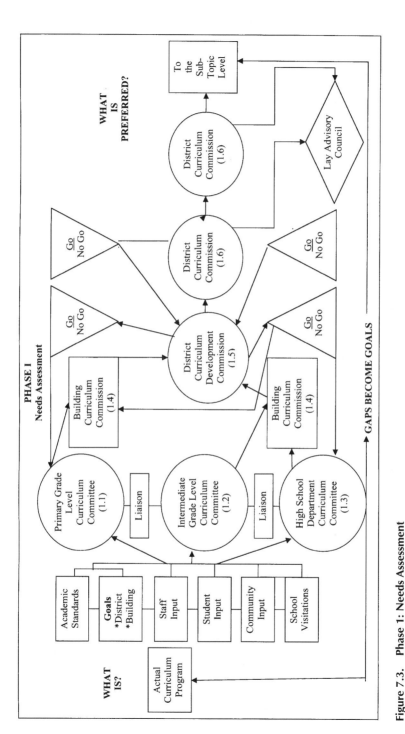

Figure 7.3.   Phase 1: Needs Assessment

participate in the needs assessment should be identified. Kaufman suggests that a viable needs assessment should include input from three sources: the community, the educators, and the learners.[3] In a standards-based system, one additional data point is necessary and that is the academic standards. As has already been suggested, the teachers need to play a sizable role—the specifics of which will be discussed later. While I believe that the involvement of learners is paramount, the specifics of their involvement should be coordinated at the building and curriculum committee levels. Community input provides an area of greater potential complexity. It is for that reason that the district curriculum cadre will, in their needs assessment work, orchestrate the process by which the community will be involved. Kaufman suggests that town hall meetings, mailers, and questionnaires have all been used successfully.[4] Whatever the choice, statistical considerations should be taken into account. What type of sampling technique should be utilized (i.e., simple random, systematic random, proportional stratified random, or purposeful sampling). My recommendation is to use stratified random sampling. When using that technique, one should take great care to invite a credible group that adequately represents the diversity in your community. How can the instruments be field tested and what statistic, if any, is appropriate? These kinds of considerations should be analyzed at the central office level. In my judgment, however, the school district should not go to the community with great rapidity. In addition, a purposive stratified random group of community members should be selected early and then invited to attend a planning session. This very diverse, small, carefully selected citizens group would then assist in developing a model for community input. I have come to believe that community input should be an honest source of input. To seek community validation of a decision that has already been made is not only dangerous, but in some ways deceitfully manipulative, and it could lead to the loss of credibility or trust over time.

Techniques of Data Collection

The four primary sources of input should be from teachers, parents, students, and the assessment specifications (i.e., standards). There is a variety of ways to collect student data. Useful student-centered data generally falls into one of three categories: student achievement data, demographic data, and student satisfaction data. In an SBS, the most important types of data are student achievement data and satisfaction data. In my view, the weakest kind of achievement data one can use is the Normed Referenced Test (NRT). Generally, the academic content for an NRT is drawn from the most widely used textbooks nationally. The academic standard or cut score (score needed to pass) is established by students who are as demographically and academically typical (average) as possible. In addition, the NRT is designed to create a range of scores (to spread scores as widely as possible) generating the infamous bell-shaped curve, where approximately 50 percent of the students score within the second and third quartiles (around the fiftieth percentile). The issue with the NRT is that if your students are demographically unlike the students used to create the NRT, or, if your school does not use the same instructional materials on which the NRT is based, then the NRT will not measure your program for effectiveness and efficiency (defined below).

Weaknesses of the NRT

- Definition of effectiveness: How well your students do compared to other students across the county, state, or region. NRT will measure effectiveness.
- Efficiency: How well your students do compared to your own academic goals. NRT will not measure efficiency.

Standardized tests are used in some places because valid and reliable tests are very difficult and expensive to create. The great strength of the NRT is that it readily allows one to compare the school or district with schools and districts across the country. The real issue behind the issue, however, is unrelated to the aforementioned points. The central liability of the NRT is that it discourages students and teachers. It is very difficult for the school to have much of an impact on how the NRT is developed or used. Frankly, as early as 1964, a congressionally commissioned study demonstrated that the school had less to do with how well students performed on a normed referenced test than the SES of the family and the educational attainment level of the mother.

For that reason, I feel that the criterion-referenced test (CRT) is the most useful assessment instrument available for an SBS because the curriculum being taught is the same content that is being tested, and usually there is a way to control for the effects of poverty. In Oregon, we have been fortunate in that the state had the vision to develop a CRT. The downside is that it has been expensive and difficult to design. Therefore, the test lagged behind the development of the academic standards. In honesty, while that reality is perfectly understandable, the perceived slow progress has not been well understood by the entire school community, and therefore it has caused rather serious credibility problems from time to time.

In addition, I would encourage the creation of student advisory curriculum committees, especially in the basic skill areas like reading and math. This model will provide for their organization at the building or departmental levels. These committees could be working groups with the specific purpose of constructing a process to collect the general student feelings about the standards. Suggestion boxes, student interviews reported in the school newspaper, and program evaluations are just some of the viable possibilities. While the data collection process is being initiated with the community, the students should begin the simultaneous collection of data from teachers. Obviously, in-service training is necessary to teach how to complete a curriculum mapping experience. Teachers should be asked to flow out (map) their curriculum at the building, departmental, and grade levels. This process is designed to involve all teachers and instructional assistants working initially in large groups. In my judgment, it is advisable to identify grade-level topics and specific course offerings in large groups, and then break the large groups into triads by area specialty for a continuation to at least the subtopic level. The facilitator for this project should be the principal who will therefore require in-service training in flowcharting (mapping) curriculum. In my judgment it is crucial to allow for release time to do this work especially in the early stages.

By the end of the needs assessment phase, each teacher will be involved in mapping "what is" by grade level and course offering, including the standards at the topic and subtopic level as appropriate. In each case, the "what is" component is compared to the "what is preferred" component in an attempt to surface a discrepancy gap between the current curriculum and the academic standards. If it is determined that there is a gap and if the state standard makes sense for your students, then it should be identified as a need and the gap closed. This process will readily generate a curriculum for each subject or course over a twenty-four-month period (it could be faster, but maintaining a sense of balance is important for staff morale). In addition to collecting data from students, teachers, the public, and the academic standards, I suggest visitations to other schools that have a successful standards-based curriculum. This component not only assists in gathering useful information, it also helps to broaden the question to include instructional approaches. I would also recommend the use of professional consultant teachers. Obviously, in-service training is necessary to teach teachers how to map curriculum. As I displayed in phase 1, input will be provided for in eight areas: state curriculum, academic standards, student input, community input, teacher input, professional consultants, school visitations, and test and research data.

All of these activities will be going on simultaneously in an attempt to determine if discrepancy gaps (i.e., needs) exist in the curriculum. Notice that there are go, no-go points at each level. This is the same element that is described in the integrated decision making first described in chapter 4. The notion in both places is to orchestrate conflict resolution by working hard at creating consensus. In an attempt to avoid dislocation and promote harmony, votes are not taken as a means of resolving conflict. If the SBS is going to acquire support from the stakeholders, then time must be taken to pursue divergent approaches and attitudes. All of the data that is surfaced as a result of the data collection phase is sorted and paired in an attempt to determine "matches and mismatches."[5] At this point, the gaps or needs that all partners agree on will be listed and set aside. When gaps are identified that suggest a disagreement, then consensus will be sought. If agreement is reached, then obviously another match has been exposed. If consensus cannot be reached, then it will be necessary to collect more data. Once the gaps or needs have been identified, they will be placed in priority order. Now, consensus should be reached on those gaps that will be selected for closure. At each level, go, no-go decisions are made until the district curriculum cadre is given the authority to approve the standards-based curriculum. These discrepancy gaps are then converted into goals, and the learner outcome construction is initiated.

PHASE 2: LEARNER OUTCOME CONSTRUCTION

In that regard, it should be noted here that the model will employ the same decision-making structure described during the needs assessment phase in integrated decision making (figure 4.1). Phase 2 demonstrates the use of grade-level and course-level teams to construct the specific learner outcomes. Again in-service training is crucial and teacher release time paramount. As is pointed out in phase 1, the principals will facilitate the process by which the learner outcomes are developed at the building and department level. It should also be pointed out that the building curriculum committees are not involved as part of the formal decision-making process in phase 2. Ultimately, a scope and sequence will be developed during this phase for each grade level and for each course offered through the various departments, and grades K through 8 and grades 9 through 12. See figure 7.4.

The Power of Scope and Sequence

Because the leadership responsibilities of a school or district leader are vast and complex, it is less than realistic to expect a principal or superintendent to personally provide the leadership for the curriculum alignment process. Since academic achievement is central to the success of an SBS, however, the school and district leader must have the technical expertise to provide support and recognition for curriculum work. This is another difference between a leader and a manager. A leader sets the standard for staff by having the technical expertise to support and recognize good curriculum alignment work. A manager does not necessarily have the technical expertise and might therefore be forced to remain isolated from the effort. A school leader's mission is to have a positive impact on the academic success of each student by working through adults, primarily teachers and parents. The mission of a district office leader is to have a positive impact on the academic success of each student by working through other adults, primarily principals and community leaders. To provide support and recognition, then, school leaders must know what a scope and sequence is and how to recognize a good one.

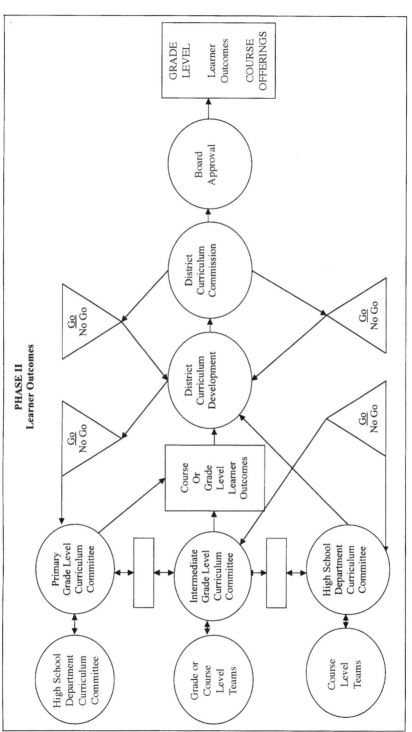

Figure 7.4. Phase 2: Learner Outcomes

SCOPE AND SEQUENCE: WHAT TO LOOK FOR

I define scope and sequence as the total range of the curriculum. Other acceptable and commonly used synonyms are breadth and width. For our purposes here, scope will be defined as the specific swath the curriculum effort has cut through the larger body of a given subject area. Sequence, on the other hand, refers to the when, or the chronology, of subject matter within the scope of the curriculum.[6] The development of a viable scope and sequence that aligns the curriculum of an SBS with the academic standards is one of the primary purposes of the needs assessment process. In that regard, I would like to discuss the role of the principal or superintendent in relationship to specific questions that might arise regarding the course content and learner readiness. Judgments about the specifics of the scope and sequence must remain with the developers (i.e., teachers). The role of the principal is to effectively orchestrate the process. Personal experiences are useful and certainly shared, but generally teachers must be regarded as professionals and encouraged to have confidence in their own perceptions and experience. In other words, teachers must be freely given top-down trust.

To establish any other role would be a dangerous precedent to set, because the specifics of each scope and sequence of the curriculum are now a near impossible task for any leader to realistically manage with any precision at all. As Rogers has pointed out, "The difficulty seems to stem from the administrator's inability to decipher new knowledge and to reformulate it for . . . higher level abstractions."[7] While teachers are encouraged to have confidence in their ability to develop a viable scope and sequence, a principal must be prepared to evaluate each curriculum effort with the following criteria in mind.

Criteria 1: Stated Learner Outcomes

One of the primary goals of flowing out the existing curriculum during the needs assessment phase is to allow teachers to reach the appropriate instructional level (i.e., usually the subtopic level) of conceptualization. This assists the instructor in creating learner outcomes that are both logical and meaningful. In many ways, a careful analysis of the stated learner outcomes is the best way to start the scope and sequence analysis. This following information provides leaders with the knowledge to surface gaps or overlaps in the curriculum. If you do find gaps or overlaps in the written curriculum, begin to ask clarifying questions. Never criticize— simply objectively communicate your observation and conclude with the question, "Is that what you intended?" Each scope and sequence should include the most recently revised edition of the respective flowchart, as well as stated learner outcomes (see figure 7.5).

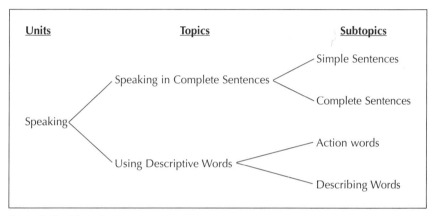

Figure 7.5. Flowchart

Generally, learner outcomes tend to spring naturally from the subtopic level, but may reflect a synthesis of more than one level of the flowchart. By definition, a learner outcome simply specifies some content to be learned and something the student is expected to be able to do. In one of the first-grade classrooms at one of our elementary schools in Battleground, Washington, the following belief remained on a bulletin board for all to see.

Tell me, I forget,
Show me, I remember,
Involve me, I understand.

—Author unknown

By using action verbs with intent, one can write learner outcomes that require students to go beyond simple recall to the application level, and beyond the application level to synthesis or evaluation. Other designers can write outcomes that require higher-order reasoning.

Each learner outcome involves an appropriate operation (which I call an action verb) as well as a corresponding content element. In the example below, the action verb is *apply* (operation) and the content element is the pronoun.

The student will be able to: Apply the correct pronoun I, me, she, he, her, and him.

Criteria 2: Learner Outcomes Should Be Designated as Mastery or Developmental

Developmental outcomes allow for the development of higher-order curriculum instructional goals. For our purposes here, a developmental outcome is defined as a learner outcome that is so complex that students are not expected to master the outcome immediately, but will evolve to a level of mastery over time. When the designer anticipates that the student will at some time complete all of the prerequisites and complete the development of a skill or a concept, the outcome is labeled mastery. (For a more detailed explanation of the cognitive, affective, and psychomotor domains and a list of action verbs that can be used to write learner outcomes that address domain balance and taxonomy complexity, access the website http://education.nebrwesleyan.edu.) This aspect of the curriculum allows the designer to create hands-on, or applied, academic outcome on an as-needed basis. The outcome has also been designated as mastery with the bold *M* noted beside the number one. An examination of the outcome, then, tells us that the designer expected the student to master a higher-order (i.e., level 2 application) outcome. If the outcome had been labeled developmental, then one would also know that the designer did not intend to measure that particular outcome in the short term.

In that regard, this model allows the scope and sequence designer to designate each learner outcome as either mastery (*M*) or developmental (*D*) and therefore measurable or nonmeasurable. With the advent of the computer and computer games, students tend to have well-developed visual and tactile skills so the outcomes can be customized to the needs of the learner.

The Demonstration
The theory I got right away,

But on the demonstration I would like a replay.
Thank you, I see it much better right now
If you will show me again, I'm sure I'll know how.
That was very good—but there's one little part
I'd like to see again before I start.
I hate to be slow, but what the heck
If I could see it once more just to check,
I'm sure I'd be ready to go
Into the class to tell and to show,
And the practice I really don't need to do—
I've already been teaching for a year or two
And the nature of the difference is such
That actually, well—here just isn't much
Well, if you insist I'll show it to you but you see I am one of those rare few
who can get it just by seeing it done?
So could you show me again, just for fun?

—Author Unknown

The articulation of a written curriculum is a critically important and useful process. As Robert Gagne has pointed out, "Objectives allow for communication . . . among and between the designers of instructional material, the planners of courses and programs, the teachers, the students, and the parents."[8] Beyond just communication, learner outcomes provide a basis for curriculum spiral, vertical articulation, program integration, and most importantly, evaluation, program regeneration (renewal), and materials selection. One of the problems with the current curriculum model is that there is no planned evaluation of the program. Once a program has been implemented, it automatically remains in place with very few generalized improvements, without regard for how students do academically.

Criteria 3: Spiral

In addition to a review of the stated learner outcomes, school and district leaders should have the technical skills to review a curriculum to determine if the curriculum has adequate spiral. In an SBS, spiral should exist not only from level to level and from course to course, but also within each specific grade level and course. It appears logical that structure, organization, and continuity in curriculum design can only aid learners in their intellectual and social growth. As Jerome S. Bruner has asserted, "Every subject has a structure, a rightness, a beauty, it is this structure that provides the underlying simplicity of things, and it is by learning its nature that we come to appreciate the intrinsic meaning of a subject."[9] Part of the purpose of this curriculum model, then, is to provide a contextual spiral that helps to accent the underlying simplicity of the study of core academic subjects. The clarity will allow the learners to be more responsible for their own learning. The starkness of the subject matter could easily support the perceived low achievers as they suffer through all of the mystical pretentiousness of the curriculum.

Criteria 4: Vertical Articulation

For our purposes here, vertical articulation is defined as the process of designing and teaching curriculum that naturally extends a previous learning. In other words, each new concept is presented so as to build on a previous concept. Vertical articulation is a curriculum component that is crucial to teachers, students, administrators, and parents. The mapping process and learner outcome identification provides a system whereby gaps can be easily surfaced and discussed. Skills and content components can be readily displayed on a matrix allowing for analysis at a glance. See figure 7.6.

Reading	A	B	C	D	E			
Math	A			D	E	G	H	I
Writing	A		C	D	E	G	H	
Science	A		C	D	E	G	H	
Social Studies		B	C				H	

Figure 7.6.   Skills Components Matrix

Skills or Content Components Matrix

The matrix depicted in figure 7.6 helps teachers to see gaps and overlaps within the curriculum. It is of particular note that one should also use this matrix to ascertain if the curriculum is aligned with the academic standards. In addition, it helps to initiate teacher discussion of how the curriculum addresses the content standards. These kinds of judgments should be allowed to surface naturally. All children can learn, but not in the same way or at the same rate! All children do not come to school with the same advantages; therefore, the sequential nature of the curriculum spiral will be more concrete and therefore helpful to students. A curriculum that is vertically articulated builds on itself and creates more order for students. Jerome Bruner once argued, "Anything can be taught in some intellectually honest form to any child at any stage of development."[10] Clearly it is features like spiral and vertical articulation that help to create an organizational framework where students are aided by the framework, connections, and context of a well-designed curriculum. Concrete lessons are more attainable than abstractions that appear disconnected and isolated. An orderly well-organized curriculum helps to address the perplexing problem of inequity of opportunity.

I indicated in chapter 5 that standards should not be allowed to create a threatening, hostile, and inhumane environment for students. Curriculum goals that are vague, disconnected, and obscure have proven to be cruel and inhumane. The lucidity of clear curriculum, however, that is well organized and connected moderates the hostility and uncertainty of vague, poorly organized curriculum. Clear academic expectations are heartening for students. Finally, clear expectations moderate the hostility of vague curriculum goals that few understand. Therefore, it is my contention that clear standards create confident, motivated students. Furthermore, clear standards may well insure a level of confidence for both the student and the teacher to be sure that there are no gaps in vertical articulation and spiral of the content standards. Actually, the clarity presented herein can be used to create a secure and safe environment for students. It is significant to note that self-esteem can be more easily enhanced in a school that is well organized with clear academic and social behavioral standards. Academic standards can be positive as long as the standards do not create a hostile learning environment for students and teachers alike. I have made that argument to underscore the point that it is important that each standard be reviewed regarding the fit or the appropriateness for a given group of students in a school or district. I have always maintained that schools should change only those things that make sense for their particular students (i.e., discrimination axiom). If for example, a particular standard simply does not make sense for your students, then it should be set aside until consensus has been reached as to the viability of a given standard for specific students.

Criteria 5: Measurable and Nonmeasurable Outcomes

While discussing stated and unstated outcomes in instructional planning, Carl Rogers suggests that some outcomes should not be listed "because tangible products are not readily available for examination."[11] Quite contrary to Rogers's view, we need to encourage teachers to use nonmeasurable objectives. This quality of the scope and sequence can be a freeing experience for both teachers and students. Curriculum designed around nonmeasurable objectives should not be reserved just for the gifted student who has already met the academic standards. The inclusion of nonmeasurable objectives as a scope and sequence component will encourage teachers to include instructional periods that are less rigid and where students experience a higher success rate. In addition, nonmeasurable criteria can motivate the teacher to formally identify and plan for those less-structured moments that allow the class to focus on higher-order reasoning skills, or outcomes, that address the affective (i.e., feelings) domain. Those moments can be designed to intently meet the needs of the whole child (i.e., character education) and correspondingly create a wholesome and nurturing environment that is absent of threat for students and staff.

Criteria 6: Domain Balance

It is not necessarily correct to assume that if a school or district is well organized and efficient, it will necessarily be cruel and inhumane. One important way to strike a balance between efficiency and humanity is not only to create nonmeasurable outcomes, but also to systematically create balance between the cognitive and affective domains. The challenge educators face seems obvious—provide structural learning patterns that assist students in experiencing success and balance, rather than failure.

A brain-compatible classroom suggests that teachers talk a lot, usually at the recall level in the cognitive domain.[12] Therefore, thinking skills should be taught as an overt (teacher directed) activity. Continuing with that thought, no one has taught until someone has learned. Educators have understandably become so hyperconscious of standards that in some classrooms, teachers are so busy covering the content of the standards, they fail to uncover it for students. More is not always better. Teaching can be like asking students to get a drink out of a fireman's hose. Some water may get to the stomach but more will be spilled. "When we read or listen to a lecture or observe or experience life, no new learning occurs unless the mind creates imagery or metaphors of related life experience." "Emotion is the track, knowledge the train, enduring understanding the destination." Research suggests that if teachers teach a cognition (cognitive domain), and then use some type of activity (demonstration) to thoughtfully connect the content to an image, an emotion, or a feeling, enduring understanding will be the destination.[13] I have made these points to suggest that a balanced higher-order curriculum can be developed with some careful forethought. Therefore, curriculum designers (i.e., teachers) need to be encouraged to design a natural balance in stated learner outcomes that are not only intended for the cognitive domain, but also the affective and psychomotor domains as well. It is easy to have teachers check the overall domain balance and taxonomy balance of their own work by visually displaying the pattern of the learner outcomes as they relate to domain balance (see figure 7.7).

Domain and Taxonomy Balance			
	Cognitive	Affective	Psychomotor
Mastery	10	10	5
Developmental	10	10	5
Learner outcome Total	20	20	10

Figure 7.7.   Domain and Taxonomy Balance

In a further attempt to address designer awareness regarding the taxonomy of the learner outcomes within each domain, teachers should be asked to keep a running measure of the level to which the learner outcomes have been designed. See figure 7.8.

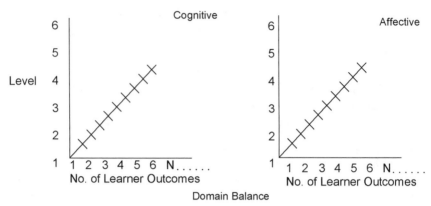

Figure 7.8.   **Domain Balance**

These visual tools have not been designed to pressure designers into any hidden outcome, but rather to address issues with good information. It is certainly possible that some units must be designed to produce a preponderance of cognitive outcomes.

PHASE 3: IMPLEMENTATION
AND DATA COLLECTION

The particular structure of this systems model allows for a natural, ongoing discrepancy analysis. The ideal–actual construct quickly becomes a pattern of thinking and acting. In the preferred–actual needs assessment model, the learner outcome phase and the data collection phase are cyclically repeated until the gaps are closed. Once the systemic design of the process is understood, it becomes a pattern of acting at all levels.

This conceptualization is a useful by-product of the needs assessment phase of the model. Once the discrepancies have been identified, prioritized, and conceptualized, a systematic process for gap closure has been designed and initiated. In this model, gap closure is initiated when outcomes are developed and the scope and sequence formalized (see figure 7.9).

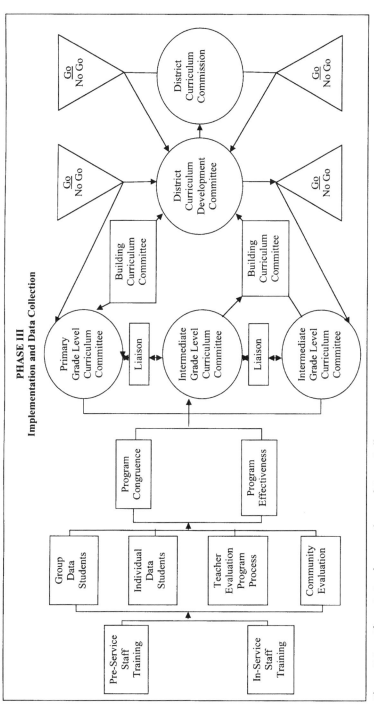

Figure 7.9.   Phase 3: Implementation and Data Collecton

The curriculum cadre then develops a scope and sequence implementation strategy. The "what is preferred" standards-based curriculum is then implemented with the intention of establishing gap closure. This model will allow for data collection to begin immediately. As it becomes obvious that some discrepancies remain, or that others have appeared, steps should be taken to eliminate the problem areas by consensus. Typically, these kinds of decisions should be encouraged at the course and grade levels. These minor adjustments in the scope and sequence will demonstrate that the natural urge to close gaps has been harnessed and systematically put to work in improving the standards-based curriculum. The keystone in this model is process. In a high-performance, standards-based school, school improvement is not a program or an event, but a cyclical process of shared decision making. Therefore, the prescription for school improvement is process.

As soon as teachers have gained an adequate conceptualization of discrepancy analysis, the structure of the model allows for those curriculum adjustments to be made and coordinated.

Ultimately, of course, the data collection phase reveals the extent to which the discrepancies that were surfaced during the needs assessment have been closed. Very subtly, then, the "what is preferred" has become the "what is," and the process begins anew. A simplified model of the process is presented in figure 7.10. The purpose of figure 7.10 is simplified to demonstrate that the process is cyclic in nature. Once the formalized scope and sequence (with indicators) has been approved by consensus, then the implementation and data collection phase can begin.

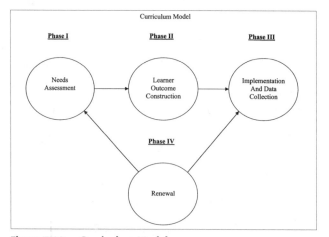

Figure 7.10.   Curriculum Model

PHASE 4: DATA COLLECTION
AND REGENERATION

This curriculum alignment model has been designed so the first two phases will be completed by June of the following year. In other words, partners should be selected, data collected, discrepancy gaps surfaced, needs selected for closure, and learner outcomes developed. The goal is to have scope and sequence available for analysis at the end of the first academic year. It is at that point, then, that judgments will need to be made that will allow for full or partial (pilot) implementation. In each specific instance, however, data collection should be initiated with program implementation. If a partial or pilot adoption was made, then the full program would be implemented the following year after data collection, analysis, and refinement. If the full program is adopted, then the first year evaluation cycle will allow for modification in the spring and summer following implementation.

At the second year of implementation, there will be a formal evaluation of the curriculum project. At its conclusion, the curriculum cadre will recommend either revision or discontinuation. If the system is revised and continued, then the curriculum project in question will undergo regeneration the following year. (Refer to phase 4 in figure 7.11.) In addition, the model would be applied to other basic academic areas.

Schools or districts cannot become standards-based overnight because each core academic area takes two years to align and that is only if phases 1, 2, and 3 have gone so well that the curriculum achieves full implementation in phase 4. The most important variable is time. Each four-phase curriculum cycle can easily take three years if everything stays on schedule. If, for example, the school wanted to align and improve math, reading, writing, and science, and if this work went on simultaneously, the entire process could be expected to take much longer. Please be reminded that after the curriculum is aligned, the pedagogical issues will need to be addressed. After the what to teach (alignment) issue has reached consensus, then critical questions remain regarding what is the most effective instructional strategy. This model is designed to produce optimum results in as short a time as possible. The systems approach is not a quick-fix approach, but it works. If these kinds of outcomes are considered realistic, then policymakers must be willing to make a *multiyear* commitment and fund the development, purchase, and training associated with the effective use of quality instructional materials. An SBS cannot be developed in the

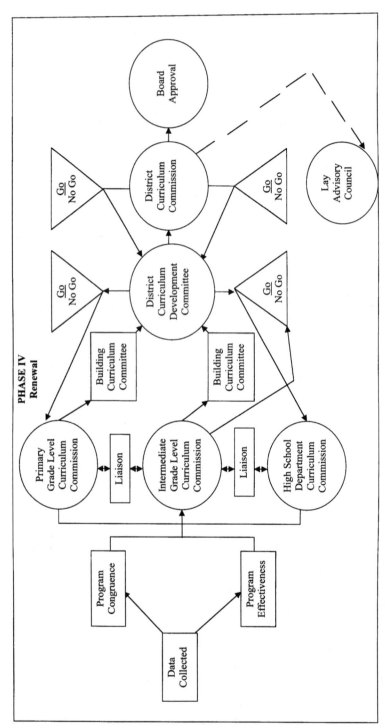

Figure 7.11.   Phase 4: Renewal

short term, because curriculum alignment simply takes time. There is no shortcut to anyplace worth going!

Cost

The cost of materials is based on a variety of variables. It would be realistic to budget approximately fifty dollars per student for reading or math book purchase. It has been my strong experience that parents want every child to have his or her own book on loan (at least in the core academic) from the school, so children have the materials necessary to adequately complete homework assignments. While it is not popular, it is sometimes possible to buy just classroom sets if an adequate supply is kept in the media center (i.e., library) for checkout. In the core academic areas, I recommend a book for every child. I realize that the cost is prohibitive, but so are the social costs of having people who do not possess entry-level job skills to provide for their family. If there are eight thousand students in a district and the district purchases a book for each student, the expenditure could easily cost as much as $400,000. That should include solid supplementary instructional materials, as well as teacher training. The point is that if these types of changes are important, the policymakers need to plan for adequate lead time and resources. If policymakers were deeply aware of the prerequisites, I wonder how many SBSs would have made their way into law. Nevertheless, this direction is necessary and appropriate.

FINAL THOUGHTS

I have heard it said that education is the key to maintaining a competitive economy in the new world order. Children should not be educated just so our economy will remain competitive. The Carnegie Foundation has given a deep and penetrating look at American education, not for reasons of corporate profit, but for national development. As one looks at history, it becomes completely apparent that wealthy nations win wars, and enlightened nations sustain development of civilization. Over time, nations have been allowed to borrow billions for war. Never has a nation borrowed so much for education. There has never been a nation wealthy enough to adequately fund war and civilization simultaneously. The thought reminds me of a line from an old script: "D'ye think th' colleges has much to do with the progress of the world?" asked Mr. Hennessy. "D'ye think," said Mr. Dooley, "tis th' mill that makes th' water run?"[14] Economic power is primarily responsible for exporting America's economy. Magnanimous education is how our civilization has been sustained and shared.

At the highest level, education should be the vehicle through which we perpetuate our belief in equity, civility, honesty, and generosity. I believe that unless people are educated and enlightened, it is idle to expect the continuance of civil liberty or the capacity for self-government. Further, Henry Ward Beecher was miraculously prophetic when he said, "The ignorant classes are the dangerous classes. Ignorance is the womb of monsters."[15]

SUMMARY

Curriculum alignment is a critical precondition for success. In an SBS, curriculum should be performance based and standards driven. Curriculum alignment is the process whereby one designs curriculum down from the academic standards—it is not a process of teaching to the test. Developing a written curriculum is critical to the success of an SBS because the process clarifies the academic expectations for staff, students, and parents. For a school to be successful academically, it is of paramount importance that the school community gets clear on what students should know and be able to do as a result of instruction. To develop and align a curriculum in an SBS, a four-phase process can be used:

Phase 1:   Needs assessment is the formal process designed to surface the gaps between what is and what is preferred.

Phase 2:   Learner outcome construction is the process in which content standards are clearly articulated for staff and students.

Phase 3:   Implementation and data collection is the process whereby the preferred curriculum is implemented, and data is used to determine if the perceived gaps were closed.

Phase 4:   Regeneration and renewal is an ongoing process of determining if the preferred curriculum is in place.

The process is teacher based; therefore, teachers emerge as curriculum leaders, and building administrators facilitate the process. There are two ways to measure the effectiveness of the curriculum: (1) effectiveness which means how well your students do compared to other students, and (2) efficiency which means how well your students do measured by your own academic goals (the standards). In that regard, criterion-referenced tests are the most appropriate instruments to measure student academic success.

The criteria that can be used by leaders to evaluate the effectiveness of the curriculum of a high-performance school:

- Learner outcomes are stated.
- Learner outcomes are mastery or developmental.
- The curriculum has spiral.
- The curriculum is vertically articulated.
- Learner outcomes are both measurable and nonmeasurable.
- The academic expectations have domain balance.
- The curriculum process is cyclical and ongoing.
- Teachers emerge as curriculum leaders.
- The school community is involved in developing the curriculum framework.

NOTES

1. Benjamin Bloom, *Taxonomy of Educational Objectives* (New York: Longmans, Green, 1956).

2. Roger Kaufman, *Needs Assessment* (Englewood Cliffs, N.J.: Educational Technology Publications, 1979), 187.

3. Kaufman, *Needs Assessment*, 55–59.

4. Kaufman, *Needs Assessment*, 68–69.

5. Kaufman, *Needs Assessment*, 75.

6. Morton Alpern, *The Subject Curriculum: Grades K–12* (Columbus, Ohio: Charles E. Merrill, 1967), 3.

7. Carl R. Rogers, *Freedom to Learn* (Columbus, Ohio: Charles E. Merrill, 1971), 151.

8. G. Hass, ed., *Curriculum Planning: A New Approach* (New York: Schenkman, 1975), 205–8.

9. Jerome S. Bruner, *The Process of Education* (Cambridge, Mass.: Harvard University Press, 1977), 7.

10. Bruner, *The Process of Education*, 210.

11. Rogers, *Freedom to Learn*, 164.

12. Robert Marzanno, *Tactics: A Strategy for Teaching Thinking* (Aurora, Colo.: Mid Continent Regional Educational Laboratory (MCREL), 1986), 1.

13. Marzanno, *Tactics*, 13.

14. Raymond V. Hand, ed., *American Quotations* (New York: Random House, 1989), 74.

15. Hand, *American Quotations*, 73.

Chapter Eight

Lead 'Em and Laugh

What you do speaks so loudly that I cannot hear what you say.

—Ralph Waldo Emerson

Some things you can't learn from others, you must feel the fire.

—Norman Douglas

As I was leaving the house early one rainy Friday morning in February 1998, my wife and best friend said to me, "You can't keep burning the candle at both ends," referring to the long days and busy schedule I had been keeping. I remember thinking how much I disliked that overused phrase as I turned and said, "I guess you will never understand that I am not going to work, I am going out to play." I really did not think about her candle burning comment too much until the next day, when she visited me in the hospital. After a warm greeting, she gently reminded me of the comment that she had made the day before, trying to warn her prodigal husband to stay home, slow down, and rest.

Unfortunately, I did not listen and consequently sustained a serious injury while attending an Oregon State Board of Education meeting as an advisor representing superintendents. About midday on Friday, February 20, 1998, I suddenly felt a bit dizzy and took a brief respite in the restroom. In short order, I found myself lying on the floor in a public restroom with strangers asking me if I was feeling okay. I said, "of course," I was feeling fine. Happily, a friend of mine knew better and had the presence of mind to make a call to 911. I soon discovered that I had experienced a stroke. The fact that I had a stroke astonished everyone I knew, including me. Most people saw me as this energetic person with a zest for life. At least in part, because I had never been bashful about preaching health and balance. In fact, I made it a point to frequently mention that I jogged about five miles every morning and tried to maintain a low-fat diet.

I did not look out of shape. In fact, I was a fifty-two-year-old male with about 12 percent body fat. The point is that I certainly did not meet the profile of a stroke victim. I was working hard, experiencing success, and feeling very strong, if not a bit infallible. I was confident of my health because I had been getting annual physicals and even took a stress test two years earlier; there simply was no warning.

I now realize that I was a victim of a near-death injury because I was ignorant of the deadly effect of chronic stress. For me, we need to rename chronic stress something more descriptive like the silent killer. It is still a mystery to me that after more than twenty years of formal education, I was so unrealistically and completely ignorant about the destructive power of chronic stress. Some very competent medical professionals put me through a complete battery of tests looking for the cause, and they were as amazed as I was that I had had a stroke (officially called a brain attack). I was eventually told that my cardiovascular system was like that of a male in his early twenties. Nevertheless, for some unknown reason, my blood was a little stickier than desirable, which ultimately caused the stroke. No one could say for sure why that was the case.

At any rate, I returned to work only days after the stroke and never really took the time to rest. At first, everyone was helpful and even a little forgiving, as I indelicately bumbled around a bit more than I was really aware of. I refused to admit that anything was really wrong with me, and ironically, I believe that is why I was able to come back at all. So I just rammed forward, until trusted friends began to complain that my performance was not up to the standard I had set for myself before the stroke. Feeling betrayed and deeply hurt by my beloved colleagues, I resigned, to escape an increasingly toxic work environment and to write the book you are reading. I have learned that balance and health are investments in the success of high-performance people. While my highly qualified wife (nurse with a Ph.D.) caringly advised me to slow down, I simply could not and would not comply. Although I trusted her judgment without question, for some reason I did not heed the warning. I could only say that stress is for sissies and I could take care of myself. Maybe that was the case here, or I simply believed that hard work was healthy and honorable (certainly not dangerous), a lesson that I had learned from my father at an early age. There are some things that we simply cannot easily learn in the formality of the classroom. For those things we need the hard reality of the "earth school," coined by Gary Zukav in *Soul Stories.*

HIGH-PERFORMANCE PEOPLE AND ORGANIZATIONS NEED TO PRACTICE BALANCE

Steven Covey articulates a vivid metaphor to emphasize that it is important for each individual to invest in his or her own well-being. Covey makes the point with the following tale. Covey imagines that "A person happened to walk leisurely up to a lumberjack in a forest cutting down a tree. The person immediately notices that the worker is sweating, hot, and obviously fatigued. She stops and asks the lumberjack what he is doing. He replies that he had started cutting down a tree at dawn, but it has been slow going. Then the visitor asks why it was so hard, and the lumberjack obtusely replies it was 'going slow' because his saw was dull. So the visitor asked the lumberjack why he didn't stop to sharpen his saw. So the lumberjack quickly replies that he simply didn't have the time." Covey concludes with the comment and lesson that "Habit 7 is taking time to sharpen the saw . . . because it is the habit that makes all of the others possible."[1]

Can you imagine an early pioneer with a family, winter quickly approaching, and the pioneer is focused so hard on finding and storing food for his family, that he collapses and nearly dies because he refuses to take the time to eat? For me, my job became like food collecting. I became so focused on my job that I had no regard for my bodily needs, so I almost died from a stroke.

The concept of balance is a remarkably simple, yet powerful one. If our lifestyle choices decrease our joy for living while having a negative impact on our level of performance in life and in work, then the question is not whether we should make the investment (to sharpen the saw), but rather when and how. As a teacher, I need to try to share what I have learned. This is a high-priority lesson for all leaders, even if you personally are doing fine. There will be those most assuredly who are working with you who are on the verge of a near-death experience, if they are lucky. One of the lessons of leadership (larger than life) is that if we care, we will step in with a gentle hand and a friendly reminder.

MANDATORY SUCCESS STRATEGY 1: BALANCE DEFINED

I have elected to conclude this book with what I consider to be the most important lesson (success strategy) of all, because most of us are left to learn this lesson on our own and if we do not learn it, success will be perverse. Unfortunately, it has been my experience that those of us who are the most at risk for a stress (work) related medical injury are also the least open to the subject. Further, most preparation programs do not include a unit of study on the importance of health and balance. As noted earlier, I did not learn the lesson of balance in my formal schooling; rather, I was forced to take this required course through the earth school (i.e., the hard way). Therefore, I really never survived my work (successfully). I would like to make the point that my concept of health and balance goes beyond just physical fitness. In my mind, the balance of health and wellness includes attention to mind, body, and soul. Physical fitness is certainly an important element of balance, but a complete effort must include the equal development of three entities. If we focus on the development of just one of the entities to the exclusion of the other two, then the imbalance is threatening. Therefore, when I think of balance, I refer to the equal development of the physical, emotional, and spiritual spheres. This is complex work that can take a lifetime. In my view, the effort is not only well spent, but critically important to me as a leader because of the values it models. It can also create a richness that is difficult to reach in any other way. Therefore, I believe that the work that leaders do here is an investment that continues to pay well beyond realistic expectations of any other successful, external change. Public schools need to change, and that is good so let it begin with me! Developing a wholesome, emotionally nurturing, balanced life is a powerful place to begin.

THE PARABLE OF INVESTING:
A LESSON FROM THE EARTH SCHOOL

My father was a railroad man, and our home was located within several hundred yards of the railroad track. Occasionally, hoboes would knock on the back door wanting a handout, so my father would slip them something to eat (even when we had little to spare). On one particularly cold and windy fall afternoon, my father and I took one gentleman (who knocked on our door) down to the Roosevelt Hotel, and retained a room for him. My father enjoyed talking with these men, so he visited with him for a few minutes, and then we walked back home together. I heard the man tell my father that just a short time earlier he had had a good job, a home, and car, along with a wonderful wife and two children. Then there was a sudden downturn in the economy, and he was laid off. Because he did not understand the value of saving money, he lost everything in just a matter of weeks. My father used that experience to teach me, as we walked home, that saving a portion of each paycheck was really a prudent investment in my future. After that he often told me that "A wise man always maintains a savings account to draw on in emergency situations." I was taught that a savings account was an investment in one's security. I believe that health and balance is also a kind of investment that one can draw on to insure a peak performance over time. The lesson I learned was that going to bed early, eating right, and daily exercise take a great deal of discipline. That investment is as important to success in life (either for the individual or the organization) as saving a percentage from each paycheck for the economic security of the individual or family. High-performance individuals must exercise such discipline to insure their own success, as well as the collective success of the organization as a whole.

As we learn more about our physiological world, we are learning that everything is connected. I believe that each person has a physical, emotional, and spiritual center. Further, I believe that we need to maintain a balance in those domains to perform at our peak capacity. Every great religion teaches moderation and balance at some level. "Philosopher Herb Shepard describes the healthy balanced life around four values: perspective (spiritual), autonomy (mental), connectedness (social) and tone (physical)."[2] When I say balance, I mean that each dimension should receive a relatively similar amount of development in the areas of time, exercise, and attention. If someone is unhealthy, poorly nourished, or emotionally distraught, he or she cannot perform at high levels for long periods. These conditions are all connected to each other. In 1998, Don Reid and Walt Stoll made an insightful comment when they said, "We are presently in the midst of perhaps the most radical paradigm shift in the history of the race—the shift from seeing our universe as separate pieces to seeing it as an invisible web of relationships. This is because this time it is about our basic nature of being human—humanity's capacity for health and its relationship to the rest of the cosmos."[3] I was recently discussing these concepts with a friend of mine and his wife, and he offered that he had created a model of his own. It is important to understand that this individual is very committed to community service. When I first met him, he was the chairman of our school board, and then he resigned to win a seat on the city council. I asked him to share his thinking with me, and he said that he visualized it as a diamond or fulcrum with the three corners being made of the following three dimensions: body, soul, and spirit. And balanced on that fulcrum was a plane with a continuum made up of spouse, family, friends, work, church, and community. He communicated that he had recently given values to each of the dimensions on the plane, and surprisingly they turned out generally balanced (level), but he needed to include sleep in the family category to make it work. I think it is simply amazing that this person has taken the time to invent a model that works for him, and then he even took the time to calculate balance. This activity should serve as an example for us all.[4] My ideas have come from these kinds of discussions, teaching, and Stephen Covey's brilliant book *The Seven Habits of Highly Effective People*, with significant input from Barbara May, Ph.D., RN, psych-mental health practitioner, and my wife. For me, the model for balance means three concepts that are physical, emotional, and spiritual. I do not see any of these three as a stand-alone because they are so tightly interrelated to such a strong degree that in some way they become synonymous. For that reason I will display my thinking as a diagram of intersecting circles. The components include physical, emotional, and spiritual. See figure 8.1.

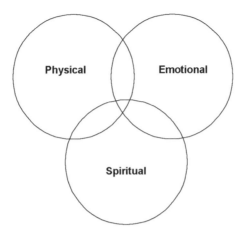

Figure 8.1. Holistic Balance

We define a school or district as a complex structure of dependent and interdependent elements whose properties are largely defined by how they function as a whole. Therefore, the whole of the school or district is more than the sum of its individual parts. In a similar way, the concept of balance unifies three powerful and discrete entities into one whole entity, with efficacy. For example, "when we see a beautiful picture on television, what we see is a vast array of dots called pixels, which form a pattern. If we were to focus on the individual dots (pixels), then we would see specks of color rather than the beautiful picture."[5] The same is true if we listen to a fine orchestra. One does not hear the individual notes or instruments, but rather the beautiful aural experience. The music selection as a whole and a beautiful picture on television are certainly more than the sum of the individual parts. The same is true with the concept of health and balance.

PHYSICAL FITNESS AND BALANCE

*Training gives us an outlet
for suppressed energies created
by stress and thus tones the spirit just as exercise
conditions the body.*

—Arnold Schwarzenegger[6]

When I think and work at my own physical fitness, I concentrate on three entities: cardiovascular training, resistance training, and diet. Cardiovascular training helps to develop the heart and blood vessels.

Cardiovascular Training

Different types of cardiovascular training (cardio) are running, biking, swimming, TaeBo, Jazzercise, climbing stairs, treadmill walking, and stationary biking to name a few. According to the training program through Gold's Gym, there are four variables to cardio training (FITT):

- Frequency of exercise: The frequency of exercise should be no less than three days a week, with no more than two days of rest between workouts.
- Intensity: Intensity is the speed or the workload of the workout. Intensity can be measured by breathing rate. The breathing-rate test means that at low to moderate intensity you should be able to talk and breathe comfortably throughout the workout. At high intensity, your breathing will be significantly more strenuous. While you should still be able to talk, you find it difficult to do so in complete sentences.
- Time of exercise: The time of exercise is how many minutes you exercise, not including warm-up and cool down. In order to obtain cardiovascular benefits, you should exercise from twenty to sixty minutes per session. You are considered minimally fit if you can raise your heart rate to 60 percent of your maximum pulse rate, the top speed your heart can beat and still pump blood through your body. Your maximum heart rate is generally considered to be 220 less your age times .6 (60 percent). In other words, if you are 30 years old, your maximum heart rate is 114: (220 − 30 = 190 x .6 = 114). The best training is generally considered to be between 2 percent and 87 percent of your personal maximum.
- Type of exercise: Type of exercise is the way you choose to do your cardio, for instance walking, running, or bicycling. Typically, people choose exercises that they can do conveniently at home and are also low impact enough so that repeated workouts do not lead to injury.

Resistance Training

Like cardio training, resistance training contributes to your physical fitness. Resistance training increases nervous system and muscle protein activity. This creates an after-burn that continues for hours, even days after exercising. Your body uses more calories (increased metabolism) during the after-burn than normal. One of the advantages of resistance training is that the increased metabolism helps you to burn calories and lose weight long after the activity is over. In addition to increased metabolism and weight control, you will experience improved work capacity, increased self-esteem, improved posture, and beneficial effects on depression.

In my own experience, resistance training has had a positive effect on my weight because my system had stabilized around a weight I considered to be about ten pounds too high. In addition, my stamina for work was increased, and I most assuredly experienced a positive effect on depression.

Diet

When I mention diet, I am not thinking about your need to reduce calories to lose weight. Rather, I am interested in eating reasonable amounts selected from all four food groups. I believe that people improve their quality of life and leadership by eating a balanced diet from the foods pyramid.[7] See figure 8.2.

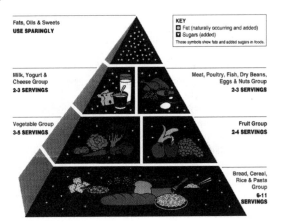

Figure 8.2. Food Pyramid. Courtesy of the Federal Food and Drug Administration

Emotional Development and Balance

Emotional balance is different for each individual, of course. Nevertheless, in each case the issue is harmony within a person. In general, are we living a life that is consistent with our purpose or core beliefs. For example, are your core beliefs in harmony with your actions as an educator? Do you provide the necessary support to family members, or do you shift just a little support of them to work? The following questions are designed to help you think about harmony at work and at home.

Are you in search for harmony between mind and body? Do you know what your core beliefs really are? If you do know what they are, take the time to address the following questions. Are your core beliefs about family in harmony with your lifestyle choices? If you believe that quality time with your family is important, do you create the necessary time? The following lifestyle and harmony quiz will help you analyze your consistency:

Table 8.1. Harmony with Family Questionnaire

1. Do you eat at least three meals a week with your entire family?	Yes	No
2. Do you take a cell phone with you when you are with your family and away from work?	Yes	No
3. Do you call the office at least twice a day when you are on vacation?	Yes	No
4. Do you usually think about work when you are with your family?	Yes	No
5. Do you attend events that involve members of your family once a month?	Yes	No
6. Do you complete one household chore each day?	Yes	No
7. Do you personally purchase presents for your children and spouse on special occasions?	Yes	No
8. Do you attend church and other special events with your family?	Yes	No
9. Do you attend parent conferences and other school-related academic activities for your child?	Yes	No
10. Are meals at home interrupted with calls from the office more than once a week?	Yes	No

If you answered yes to three or more questions, you should truly examine with input from your family the following question: "Do members of your family perceive you to be a caring and active part of their lives?"

Harmony and Education as Your Vocation and Avocation

Education is a very challenging career. Public-school education is maligned to such a degree that it is difficult for some educators to feel as if they are valued. Further, resources seem to be declining just as the highest academic standards in the history of public education have been set. Therefore, the question is as follows: "Are the rewards you receive from your career choice (education) in harmony with both intrinsic and extrinsic rewards?" The following questions are intended to help you think through the question of career harmony. Parents on leadership teams are invited to use these same questions by just substituting their specific vocation.

- Did you ever have a yearning to be an educator? And has the career met your needs and expectations?
- There are deficiencies with every vocation; nevertheless, are you generally happy with your career choice?
- Have you accomplished about what you set out to accomplish given the pragmatic realities of public-school education?
- If you had it to do over again, would you choose education, or substitute some other vocation?

On a scale of 1 to 10, how would you rate your satisfaction with education (or other career) as a career choice? A rating of 1 is low or very poor, and 10 means that the choice was perfect for you and as a result you are self-actualized. If your answer was 5 or below, please consider completing the following exercise:

Career Rating

Please rate the satisfaction level you have with your career choice. Please put an "x" on the continuum from 1 to 10 representing your satisfaction rating level as you assess it. Then please indicate why you feel that way.

1 (low) ＿＿＿＿＿＿＿＿＿＿＿＿＿＿＿＿＿＿＿＿＿ 10 (high)

Why?

＿＿＿＿＿＿＿＿＿＿＿＿＿＿＿＿＿＿＿＿＿＿＿＿＿＿＿

＿＿＿＿＿＿＿＿＿＿＿＿＿＿＿＿＿＿＿＿＿＿＿＿＿＿＿

＿＿＿＿＿＿＿＿＿＿＿＿＿＿＿＿＿＿＿＿＿＿＿＿＿＿＿

＿＿＿＿＿＿＿＿＿＿＿＿＿＿＿＿＿＿＿＿＿＿＿＿＿＿＿

Spiritual Development and Balance

The spiritual domain is a very personal entity. At a minimum, I believe it
is a belief system that sustains one during the most difficult of times. It
represents a way of behaving that is an expression of good. It also represents an existence beyond our earthly domain, a greater good, a universal
intelligence, the Creator. In my view, spirituality does not have to be religion, but it could be. Spirituality is a universal intelligence that is your
core essence, your core belief system, an element that is fundamental to
your existence, a place from which to draw strength when nothing else
will do, a greater good to serve as an example. The definition of spirituality is unique for every individual, but includes at least some of the following concepts: close, yet distant; mysterious, yet defined; magical, yet
concrete; always there, yet just out of reach; exasperatingly illusive and
beautiful, yet frightening.

The ability to explain the spirituality of anyone else is beyond my ability, so I will share what is true for me. These beliefs may or may not be
true for you. You must decide. My expectation is that the process itself
may be helpful in clarifying your beliefs.

I believe that all beings have a spiritual center. If that center is empty,
we try to fill it with work or some other type of busyness. And if the center hurts, we fill it with alcohol or other drugs to self-medicate the pain.
And if that center is lonely, we fill it with people, activities, parties, sex,
generosity, or anything else to achieve acceptance. We continue to fill the
hole with spurious chattels, until finally when nothing else works, we fill
that empty center with our universal good, the Creator. Once the hole in
our soul is sufficed with the universal intelligence, we become complete
as destined. Then and only then can we find a way to breathe and to stand
strong, facing unflinchingly into life's powerful uncertainties, with confidence and peace.

Therefore, spiritual renewal is a journey unique for each individual that
must be taken step-by-step, or one lesson at a time. As noted earlier, I believe that each of us has a spiritual gap or hole, which must be filled with
a universal intelligence, the Creator, your god, or some omnipotent being
or force, that will show us the way, the truth, and the light. When that happens, we know that we are accepted and worthy. Somehow, our blight has
been washed away, and we know that we are acceptable and something of

immense value. When I seek spiritual renewal, I turn to Christ the Lord through prayer or meditation because I am a Christian. I also turn to beautiful music and the written verse. The point is that each individual must find that way on his or her own. When I was recovering in the hospital from the stroke, Pam Skinner (a friend and fellow educator from my district) sent me a wonderful book by Arthur Gordon, which tells the story of a person whose life had gone flat, tedious, and seemed to lack meaning.

THE PARABLE OF SERENE LIVING

So the man whose life seemed to lack purpose went to his physician with his troubles and asked for his help. The doctor who had no psychiatric training looked for a long time at his patient through a tent he had made with his fingers. Finally he said, as he reached for his prescription pad, "Will you follow my directions?" The man said yes, as the physician wrote three prescriptions and numbered them, while he said, "Where was your favorite place to go as a kid?" The man said it was the ocean.

So the physician said, folding the numbered prescriptions, "go there tomorrow, and take these prescriptions in numerical order at nine, twelve, three and six." The man then said in disbelief, "Are you kidding?" Then the physician said, "you won't think this is a joke when you get my bill." After the shock wore off, the man decided to drive to the ocean the next day to complete the prescribed treatment. He arrived at the ocean just as a storm was rolling in, and in time to open the nine o'clock prescription.

He carefully unfolded it and gasped as he read two words: "just listen." He was exasperated and disturbed. "What does he want me to listen to anyway? There is nothing else out here." So he got out of the car determined to follow through on the commitment. He listened and heard the obvious sounds—the wind in the grass, the seagulls. Then he could not hear anything more except for the crashing sea, so as he tried harder to listen he began to hear subtle sounds that he had not noticed before. Then he began to hear the silence and to remember the lessons that the sea had taught him as a child. And as he listened now, more intently than before, he realized that in the silence he could hear himself listening to things other than himself. It was as if the silence was so loud that it covered the self-talk that had been focused on the man which allowed him to harbor thoughts, bigger than himself and he discovered that there was peace in that.

By noon the sky had cleared, and he carefully opened the second prescription and then he just sat there confused and bothered again, as he read just three words, "try reaching back." He thought, "Reaching back to what?" Obviously he was supposed to think about the past, but what about it, he thought?

He reasoned that he had selected the ocean because it was a happy place, so he began to think in rich and vivid detail about his happy childhood memories. Very gently and easily his problems just seemed to drift away as he experienced a calm and tranquility he had not felt for many years. By now the tide was out and it was time to open the next prescription. So he began to carefully unfold the third prescription, but he was unprepared for what he saw. He immediately became defensive as the prescription sounded like an order, as he read, "Reexamine your motives."

Defensively, the man thought "my motives are just fine! I like my motives! Sure I want to be successful, but who doesn't? Yes, I want to be secure and valued, but who doesn't?"

Then he unexpectedly began to think about his work and realized that his work had ceased to be spontaneous and fun. He suddenly realized that the job had somehow become just a job, and that he was working for the rewards rather than to help people. Then suddenly he realized that his motives had changed because he lost the gift of giving to others. He also realized that if the motives are wrong, nothing else could be right.

Then he listened to the tide turn as it began to come in again, and he tried to put it all together. First he was asked to listen carefully, and it calmed him. It somehow seemed to shift his focus from his own internal problems to something else bigger (outside), and it felt comforting. Then he was told to try to reach back, and he realized that he could block out his current problems with the positive memories of the past. Then the doctor ordered him to reexamine his motive and he realized one needed to bring one's conscience and capabilities into alignment with one's motives or nothing would be right. He realized how difficult it was to examine his motives but knew his mind had needed the quiet to successfully complete such a task.

And now he was ready for the six o'clock and last prescription. He opened it carefully and methodically. This time there were just six words, "Write your worries in the sand." He let the paper drop and the wind blew it away. He bent down and wrote his worries in the sand with a broken shell and walked away, knowing the tide would erase his written words.[9]

EMOTIONAL DEVELOPMENT AND BALANCE

When I communicate about emotional balance, I will focus my comments on stress management and cardiovascular disease.

Definitions

The cardiovascular system refers to the heart and blood vessels. In nonmedical terms, it is the human plumbing that gets oxygen to all of the cells of the body through the circulation of oxygen-rich blood. The heart pumps blood out into the body through the blood vessels and draws it back. The blood travels though a system of pipes (vessels) to various parts of the body and then returns to the heart to retrieve more oxygen. Chronic stress puts pressure on the cardiovascular system, causing injury and disease. Chronic stress is a force that strains the body and specifically the cardiovascular system, creating health-related problems including, but not limited to, chronic headaches, ulcers, heart disease, and job burnout. The rest of this chapter is intended to help you.

1. Understand what the stressors (pressure pushers) are in the significant parts of your life.
2. Get some indication of the amount of stress you are currently under.
3. Appreciate and identify the typical behaviors of people who are constantly under stress and those who are more relaxed about life.
4. Develop your profile for risk of cardiac and stress-related disease.
5. Then conclude with some ways to begin to manage stress to support a peak capacity performance in both your personal and professional lives.

Pressure Pushers

What are the pressure pushers in your life? Use the form below to list things, events, and situations that are pressuring you and causing stress. See figure 8.3.

	Personal	Classroom, Office, School	Society
1.			
2.			
3.			
4.			
5.			
6.			
7.			
8.			
9.			
10.			

Figure 8.3.   Stressors or Pressure Pushers

Stress Buildup

What kind of stress are you under? Excess stress is one of the biggest causes of burnout. It overloads your circuits and saps your energy. Since most people don't have circuit breakers, the indications of too much stress are chronic headaches, ulcers, heart disease, and job burnout.

The test in figure 8.4, "Social Readjustment Rating Scale," developed by two Seattle physicians, T. H. Holmes and R. H. Rahe, can give you an indication of the amount of stress you are under. Add up the points in parentheses for each of the questions that applies to you.

What are behaviors of people who are and are not under stress?

_____ Minor law violation (11)

_____ Christmas (13)

_____ Vacation (13)

_____ Change in eating habits (15)

Change in number of family
_____ get-togethers (15)

_____ Change in sleeping habits (16)

Loan or mortgage for less than $10,000
_____ (17)

_____ Change in social activities (18)

_____ Change in recreation (19)

_____ Change in church activities (19)

_____ Change in residence (20)

Change in work hours or conditions
_____ (20)

_____ Change in schools (20)

_____ Trouble with your boss (23)

_____ Change in living conditions (25)

_____ Change in appearance or habits (24)

_____ Spouse began or ceased work (26)

_____ Begun or quit formal schooling (26)

Outstanding personal achievement
_____ (28)

_____ Son or daughter leaving home (29)

_____ Change in work responsibilities (29)

_____ Trouble with in-laws (29)

_____ Foreclosure of a loan or mortgage (20)

_____ Mortgage over $10,000 (31)

Change in number of arguments with
_____ spouse (35)

_____ Change in line of work (36)

_____ Death of a close friend (37)

_____ Change in financial status (39)

_____ Sexual difficulties (39)

_____ New family member (39)

_____ Major business change (39)

_____ Pregnancy (40)

_____ Change in health of family member (44)

_____ Retirement (45)

_____ Marital reconciliation (45)

_____ Loss of job (47)

_____ Marriage (50)

_____ Major personal illness or injury (53)

Death of family member other than
_____ spouse (63)

_____ Jailed (63)

_____ Marital separation (65)

_____ Divorce (73)

_____ Death of spouse (100)

_____ Total

What does your score mean?	Total score 150–199	Mild Life Crisis
	Total score 200–299	Moderate Life Crisis
	Total score 300+	Major Life Crisis

Figure 8.4.   Stress Buildup Test. T. H. Holmes and R. H. Rahe, "Social Readjustment Rating Scale," *Journal of Psychosomatic Research* **2 (1967) (p. 216). Reprinted with permission of Elsevier Science.**

Type A People Constantly under Stress (Typical Behavior)

- Hurried speech
- Constant, rapid movement
- Open impatience with the rate things happen

- Several things performed at once
- Attempt to dominate the conversation
- Vague guilt during relaxation

Type B People More Relaxed about Life (Typical Behavior)

- Complete freedom from type A
- No sense of urgency
- No free-floating hostility
- No felt need to discuss achievements
- An ability to relax without guilt

Cardiac Risk Profile

Cardiovascular problems still head the list of deaths in this country. What is your risk of cardiac disease?[10] See figure 8.5 for a tool for assessing your risk of cardiac disease.

Managing Stress

How to Handle Stress

- Work it off.
- Talk out worries.
- Learn to accept what you cannot change.
- Be in peak condition.
- Balance work and recreation.
- Do something for others.
- Take one task at a time.

See figure 8.6.

Principles of Time Management

- List goals/set priorities.
- Make a daily "to do" list.
- Start with *A* items, not *C* items.
- Decide what is the best use of your time right now?

	Heredity	Blood Pressure	Diabetes	Smoking	Weight	Cholesterol	Exercise	Emotional Stress	Age	Sex and Build
6	Three or more relatives who had heart attacks before age 60 (parents and siblings only)	High blood pressure not controlled by medication	Diabetic with complications (circulation, kidneys, eyes)	More than 40 cigarettes daily	More than 50 lbs. overweight	Over 281	Complete lack of exercise	Intense problems, can't cope, see a psychiatrist	Over 60	Male, very stocky
5	Two relatives who had heart attacks before age 60	High blood pressure partly controlled by medication	Diabetic on insulin—no complications	21–39 cigarettes daily	30–50 lbs. overweight	256–280	Sedentary job, light recreational exercise	Constantly need pills or drink for stress	51–60	Male, fairly stocky
4	One relative who had a heart attack before age 60	Persistent mild high blood pressure, untreated	High sugar controlled by tablets	6–20 cigarettes daily	21–35 lbs. overweight	231–255	Sedentary job, moderately active recreation	Take pills or drink for stress on occasion	41–50	Male, average build

Figure 8.5. Cardiac Risk Profile. From *The Complete Book of Running* by Jim Fixx, copyright © 1977 by James F. Fixx. Used by permission of Random House, Inc.

3	Two or more relatives who had heart attacks after age 60	High blood pressure only when upset	High sugar controlled by diet	Fewer than 5 cigarettes daily	6–20 lbs. over-weight	206–230 (or don't know)	Sedentary job, very active in recreation	Moderate business or personal pressures	31–40	Female after menopause
2	One relative who had a heart attack after age 60	Normal blood pressure (or don't know)	Normal blood sugar (or don't know)	Cigars or pipe only	Up to 5 lbs. over-weight	181–205	Moderately active in job and recreation	Rare business or personal pressure	21–30	Male, thin build
1	No heart disease in family	Low blood pressure	Low blood sugar	Nonuser or stopped perma-nently	More than 5 lbs. under-weight	180 or below	Very active physically in job and recreation	No real business or personal pressures	10–20	Female still menstruating

My score

◇

Figure 8.5. (*Continued*)

	Professional	Personal
Comforter		
Clarifier		
Confronter		

Figure 8.6. Support System

- Handle each piece of paper only once.
- Do it now!

Executive functioning skills figure into a leader's life prominently. What is a typical day in the life of an administrator? See figure 8.7.

Stress is difficult in a leadership position as the above day reveals. Identifying strategies for dealing with it and making the practice of these strategies a habit, may be quicker and easier with the use of a things-to-do type of tool. See figure 8.8.

More on Managing Stress

A Change Process

- Self awareness
- Data collection
- Data interpretation and pattern identification
- Selection of alternatives
- Examination and implementation of alternatives
- Adoption, rejection, adaptation
- Recycling

Getting Things into Perspective

Part 1 Your lifetime goals
Part 2 What you would like to accomplish in the next five years
Part 3 How would you live if you learned you would die six months from now?

1.	Checked the daily calendar for appointments.		
2.	Returned three telephone calls from previous day.		
3.	Discussed emergency situation with personnel director.		
4.	Answered call from maintenance director and suggested action.		
5.	Went through daily mail.		
6.	Dictated answers to letters and inquiries.		
7.	Set up times for pending appointments.		
8.	Signed necessary forms for personnel and maintenance departments.		
9.	Attended administrative council meeting.		
10.	Scheduled meetings with architects.		
11.	Helped secretary call directors for an emergency meeting.		
12.	Returned calls that secretary had accepted.		
13.	Met with employee about salary discrepancy.		
14.	Talked to news reporter regarding legal problems.		
15.	Picked up board member to attend luncheon meeting.		
16.	Returned to office from lunch—returned several phone calls.		
17.	Interviewed future employee for personnel department.		
18.	Held a conference with a principal.		
19.	Placed call to director of transportation regarding traffic problem.		
20.	Attended conference with attorney on lawsuit.		
21.	Dictated letter to secretary as follow-up conference.		
22.	Signed several letters and memos.		
23.	Discussed emergency maintenance job with custodian.		
24.	Set up travel schedule for trip to Boston next week.		
25.	Telephoned assistant to come to office for conference.		

Key: A. Administrator only should do this. Cannot be delegated.
      B. Task should be delegated to other professional staff.
      C. Secretary should handle this task.

Figure 8.7. A Day in the Life of an Administrator

Things To Do Today Name: Priority A – High B – Medium C – Low Date	Only I Can Do	Delegated	Started	Completed
1.				
2.				
3.				
4.				
5.				
6.				
7.				
8.				
9.				
10.				
11.				
12.				
13.				
14.				
15.				

Special Attention

Figure 8.8. Managing Stress

SUMMARY

I did not listen to the warnings of those who cared about me and consequently experienced a stroke. I was in relatively good condition at the time and did not meet the profile of a stroke victim, so the stroke was unexpected and shocking, and it changed my life. I returned to work shortly after the stroke. At first, everyone was helpful, but eventually trusted friends complained to the board that my performance was not up to the standard I had set for myself before the stroke. Feeling hurt and betrayed by what I thought were my beloved friends, I resigned to escape an extremely toxic work environment. I learned that chronic stress is a killer! I further believe that highly motivated people need to maintain a balance in their emotional, physical, and spiritual worlds. All three domains are interrelated, so the approach needs to be unique for the individual and equitably distributed between the three domains. There are some general guidelines, however. Individuals must exercise discipline to insure they reach the goal of balance.

Physical fitness involves exercise and eating a balanced diet. Exercise should ideally involve both cardiovascular training and resistance training. Emotional development and balance involves maintaining consistency between core values and choices in life. Spiritual development and balance is a very personal experience. I believe that all beings are born with a spiritual center that remains empty until filled with the Creator. Each person seeks to fill the spiritual center with spurious things until they finally fill it with their universal good or intelligence or their god. Once that happens, we learn that our destiny is not a place or an event, but a plan to successfully understand and appreciate oneself.

NOTES

1. Steven Covey, *The Seven Habits of Highly Effective People* (New York: Simon and Schuster, 1989), 287.

2. Covey, *The Seven Habits*, 287.

3. Ron Freed, Ed.D. and Walt Stoll, M.D., "Healthy Behavior: The Implications of a Holistic Paradigm of Thinking through Body, Mind Research," *Electronic Journal of Health and Education* 1 (January 1, 1998): 2–18.

4. Jim Linhart and Garyann Linhart, conversation with the author and his wife (February 2001).

5. Peter Levine, *Walking the Tiger* (Berkeley, Calif.: North Atlantic Books, 1997), 67.

6. Apex Fitness Group, *Elements of Success: Fitness Handbook* (Middletown, N.Y.: Gold's Gym, 1999), 18.

7. Apex Fitness Group, *Elements of Success*.

8. Mary Stout Henning, "Organizational Culture and Professional Life" (paper presented at the Twentieth Annual Northwest Fire Service Management Seminar, Portland, Oregon, March 1, 1989).

9. Arthur Gordon, *A Touch of Wonder* (New York: Jove Books, 1978), 79.

10. T. H. Holmes and R. H. Rahe, "Social Readjustment Rating Scale," *Journal of Psychosomatic Research* 2 (1967): 216.

Epilogue

LOVE 'EM AND LEAD 'EM

If you want to succeed as a leader, you must possess the courage to fail more often. From my experiences, I have discovered that it is difficult to learn the important lessons in life from victories. In fact, when I was coaching, teaching, and working in administration in secondary schools, I always felt that the student athletes could learn more from a defeat than from a victory. I certainly have learned more about leadership from my leadership failures than from my successes. Every success strategy included in this book has been utilized successfully. Some of the thoughts that went into writing the book were prompted by a leadership experience that I consider to be unsuccessful. Therefore, this book was not written by someone who has all of the answers. My only claim here is that I worked as a leader, I have taught leadership, and I have studied leadership for thirty-two years. I have made new finds every day as I circle back over familiar territory. The following poem by T. S. Eliot underscores this point beautifully:

> We shall not cease from exploration
> And the end of all our exploration
> Will be to arrive where we started
> And know the place for the first time.[1]

In 1995, I was named superintendent of a well-regarded Oregon district. I was at the peak of my career with ten years until retirement. The state of Oregon had just enacted a top-down standards-driven system that had mixed support (fiscal and political). The magnitude of the job in this community was enormous! Academic achievement was deplorable, the school roofs were in disastrous disrepair, there were no student computers, and all of the wiring was outdated. The local tax proposal had just been soundly defeated. And finally there were two secondary schools and a major athletic program that were perceived to be failing. The community was proud of the schools and of their local history. Therefore, I pushed hard to make improvements, ultimately bungling and stumbling around to do so. It was then that I realized that other communities faced the same general challenges. Yet in each school and district, we were working in isolation, not only of each other, but more importantly, in isolation of what we were learning about providing leadership in a standards-driven system. In each case, a successful direction and improvement process needed to be developed simply because there was no blueprint or model. I would have to characterize the leadership wisdom of the day by saying that there was a pervasive, common belief that each community or school was so unique that it was simply a waste of time attempting to follow anyone else's lead. To some degree, I believe that is somewhat still true. Therefore, in this work, I have attempted to define some universal principles that would be cosmically applicable in school cultures by serving as a framework or a general planning guide.

On a more mundane note, I truly believed that having high academic standards for students, parents, and staff—even with all of the inherent challenges—I wanted to be part of a district that could make it happen. In fact, I was not bashful about saying, "If we cannot build an SBS here, it can't be done anywhere." While I was realistic enough to recognize the challenges, I threw myself into the fray, with all of the enthusiasm of a young boy with his first baseball glove. On our first try and by using the key communicator process described in chapter 3, we passed the local tax for fifteen million dollars, which allowed us to fix our roofs, plan for growth, build a state-of-the-art technology program, and begin to bridge the digital divide. I also cleaned up the two secondary schools and the athletic program. While I thought my work was unfolding with good regard, I made enough mistakes along the way to become vulnerable to the thugs in an organization and community that was otherwise made up of good, decent, and hardworking people. Eventually, I was asked by my most trusted colleagues to step down because they felt (or so they said) that I had not returned to my prestroke condition. I still believe ambition, deceit, manipulation, ignorance, and a lack of character had a lot to do with that perception and my demise. Nevertheless, I am sure you recognize the pain and humiliation that I experienced as I packed my office and hauled it to a local storage facility, while the staff was participating in the back-to-school rally (also described in chapter 3).

Like the high school team that learns to win by losing, I learned to lead by failing. I want to tell you this because I want you to understand that I am not providing this work as a highly successful leadership guru who has mastered the art, craft, and science of leadership. I do not claim to be a leader with unparalleled skill, but I do claim to have studied leadership and worked in that position for more than thirty years. It has not been my experience or honor to provide inspiring and flawless leadership over time. Neither is this work intended as a scientific work. Rather, it is an outgrowth of my teaching, experience, and personal research. The circumstances of my forced retirement were a learning experience. Some have told me that I was highly successful so the jury is mixed. Even so, I did not feel successful. Many of the lessons I have shared have grown out of my own leadership failures. So this writing activity, which has taken two years now, was a real lesson in humility for me. With that context in mind, I would like to leave with you a simple acronym that I believe will serve any leader well. That acronym is FAIR!

Fun:	Create an environment where people want to come to work and enjoy each other by having fun. Initiate a humor committee to insure the proper implementation of fun in the workplace.
Attitude:	Assist colleagues to select an attitude each day that will insure their success.
Involve:	If people are going to be affected by a decision, involve them in the decision-making process. Security requires involvement because it cultivates trust. Trust is the lubrication that provides the lucidity for change. It is critically important that the leader trust the people for participatory decision making to be effective.
Relationships:	There is no real power in position but in relationships only. In a standards-based system, we must be much more thoughtful about building strong and lasting relationships.

IN CLOSING

Use the leadership lessons embedded in this book and inherent in the acronym FAIR, and you will be building on a solid leadership foundation.

NOTE

1. T. S. Eliot, *Collected Poems 1909–1962* (New York: Harcourt Brace, 1963), 208.

Appendix A
Decision by Consensus

Reprinted by permission. Richard A. Schmuck and Philip J. Runkel, *The Handbook of Organization Development in Schools and Colleges*. 4th ed. Prospect Heights, Ill.: Waveland Press, 1994 (pp. 310–311).

DECISION BY CONSENSUS

Techniques to Facilitate Consensus

It is possible to build relationships among the members of a face-to-face group so that decisions can be made effectively by consensus. More effective groups tend to have leaders who allow greater participation, wider initial divergence of expressed judgments, and greater acceptance of diverse decisions (see Torrance, 1975). Moreover, effective leaders have been shown to encourage minority opinions and conflict to a greater extent than less effective leaders. (See Maier and Solem, 1952). Coch and French (1948) have also shown that group participants with little influence over a decision usually are less likely to carry out the decision when action is required.

Stimulation of Minority

In consensual decision making, special care must be taken to uncover minority views that may not easily come to the surface. This can be done by tactfully inviting silent members to express their view. To elicit responses from others effectively, group members can use paraphrasing, summarizing, and checking the feelings of others. Sometimes someone not in the minority can be asked to assume the role of the minority and to express his view to the rest of the group; some members of the minority may then care to say whether the role-taker's expression was accurate.

Taking a Survey

An essential technique for obtaining a consensus is the survey. The full use of this technique involves the following steps. First, someone presents the issue clearly. Then, one or two others clarify it by restating it. Following that, everyone in turn states his reactions to the proposal.

Each person should be as brief as possible while still being clear, but he need not restrict himself to *yes* or *no*. He may say that he is uncertain, that he is confused and wants to hear more, that he is experiencing some pain, or he can simply say that he does not wish to talk about it. A group using the survey should not allow an individual to remain completely silent. If someone does not want to speak, he must at least say explicitly he wants to say nothing. This assures the group of bringing up to date its knowledge of every member's point of view on the question and of doing so through explicit statements, not presumptions.

—Gary Phillips, *Site-Based Governance Training,* Battle Ground, Washington, 1972.

CONSENSUS HANDOUT

Consensus Means That:

- All participants contribute. Everyone's opinions are used and encouraged. Differences are viewed as helpful rather than hindering.
- Everyone can paraphrase the issue.
- Everyone has a chance to express feelings about the issue.
- Those members who continue to disagree indicate that they are willing to experiment for a prescribed period of time.
- All members share in the final decision.

Consensus Does Not Mean That:

- A vote is unanimous.
- The result is everyone's first choice.

- Everyone agrees (only that there is enough support for the decision to be carried out).
- Conflict or resistance will be overcome immediately.

Not all decisions should be made by consensus. The most important point is that everyone agrees on how decisions are to be made.

Instructions for Consensus

Consensus is a decision process of making full use of available resources and for resolving conflicts creatively. Consensus is difficult to reach, so not every ranking will meet with everyone's complete approval. Complete unanimity is not the goal—it is rarely achieved. But each individual should be able to accept the group rankings on the basis of logic and feasibility. When all group members feel this way, you have reached consensus as defined here, and the judgment may be entered as a group decision. This means, in effect, that a single person can block the group if he thinks it necessary; at the same time, he should use this option in the best sense of reciprocity. Here are some guidelines to use in achieving consensus:

1. Avoid arguing for your own rankings. Present your position as lucidly and logically as possible, but listen to the other members' reactions and consider them carefully before you press your point.
2. Do not assume that someone must win and someone must lose when discussion reaches a stalemate. Instead, look for the next-most-acceptable alternative for all parties.
3. Do not change your mind simply to avoid conflict and to reach agreement and harmony. When agreement seems to come too quickly and easily, be suspicious. Explore the reasons and be sure everyone accepts the solution for basically similar or complementary reasons. Yield only to positions that have objective and logically sound foundations.
4. Avoid conflict-reducing techniques such as majority vote, averages, coin flips, and bargaining. When a dissenting member finally agrees, don't feel that he must be rewarded by having his own way on some later point.
5. Differences of opinion are natural and expected. Seek them out and try to involve everyone in the decision process. Disagreements can help the group's decision because with a wide range of information and

opinions, there is a greater chance that the group will hit upon more adequate solutions.

CONSENSUS RULES

1. Everyone participates.
2. Everyone can paraphrase.
3. Everyone has a chance to express feelings.
4. Members who disagree say they will try the solution for a specified period of time.
5. All members share in the final decision.

BRAINSTORMING RULES

1. No criticism
2. No explanation
3. All ideas good
4. Quantity over quality
5. Piggybacks

BRAINSTORMING

Outcomes: 1. Participants develop skill in use of brainstorming.
                 2. Participants experience the power of brainstorming to general ideas.
                 3. Facilitators have evidence of groups' skills in use of brainstorming.
Time: 15–20 minutes
Group Size: Small groups of 5–8 participants
Materials: Flip charts/easel paper for each group, markers
Directions: 1. Facilitator explains purpose of brainstorming and its use in the workshop.
                 2. Facilitator announces that groups will have 2–3 minutes to generate as many potential solutions for the

stated problem as possible and will post them in plain sight of all group members.

3. Facilitator reviews rules of brainstorming:
   - No criticism allowed, no explanation needed.
   - Be freewheeling, anything goes.
   - Seek combinations and improvements.
   - Seek quantity over quality.
4. Facilitator asks groups to select a recorder.
5. Facilitator presents problem and times session #1. Possible practice problems include:
   - Uses for a broom handle.
   - Uses for an old icebox.
   - Uses for empty oatmeal boxes.
   - Uses for a box of ping-pong balls.
6. Facilitator leads reporting of results pointing out a number of ideas and level of creativity or innovativeness.
7. Facilitator leads a second session. Possible problems include:
   - Characteristics of an effective workshop leader.
   - How to publicize an upcoming school event.
   - How to reward and recognize outstanding staff members.
   - Solutions to a problem mentioned by a participant earlier in the day.
8. Facilitator leads a discussion of the activity focusing on:
   - Appropriate uses of brainstorming.
   - Subsequent steps in problem solving.
   - Reactions to the activity.
   - How it could be done differently.

Reflections:
1. It is easy to follow the rules when the topic is fun, harder when the topic is a real problem. Participants should see that brainstorming can work in real situations. It's not just a game.
2. This can be used to identify ideas, topics, or criteria for process observers in a later activity.

Appendix B
Activities

ACTIVITY: INTRODUCTION TO TEAM BUILDING

Outcomes:
1. Participants understand the rationale for team building.
2. Participants establish foundation of facilitator network by beginning colleague relationships with other team members.
3. Participants know some skill groups need to function effectively.

Time: 5–10 minutes

Group Size: Large group, all participants

Materials: None

Directions:
1. Present the lecture below.
2. Hold discussion to a minimum until after the first team-building activity.

Reflections:
1. The trusting relationships that provide the foundation for school improvement are begun here and now.
2. The notions of building trust or building relationships may cause some anxiety as participants wonder what is this sensitivity stuff? There is always some risk in personal exposure, but reassure as appropriate.

Mini-Lecture: The rationale for team building

The early sessions for planning for school improvement rely heavily on small group processes. As with other programs, people often work together on important tasks without being given the opportunity to learn the skills and understandings necessary to work as a team. Typically, such group skills (1) are left to chance, (2) cause problems and delays when they are lacking, more delays than if time were taken to develop these skills early in group settings, (3) need development even in groups that have worked together before. Teams need the following skills if they are to function together effectively: (1) team members need to know and understand one another, they need to know who one another is, how they became the people they are, their interests, hobbies, teaching competencies, and other information that indicates what planning team members can contribute to school improvement in their schools, (2) team members need to understand value differences and similarities, values that might influence school improvement typically focused on such topics as feelings about kids, the importance of discipline in school, grading and evaluation techniques, instructional strategies, how people learn, and the appropriate objectives for learning, (3) team members need to be able to solve problems together, they need to be able to make decisions about such topics as the role of parents and community in the school, the degree of responsibility the students should have for their own learning, the role of teachers in the school, how decisions should be made in the school, how to deal with problem learners, how materials should be selected and evaluated, how to use time in school day, and appropriate goals for the school. Team members must know why cooperation and working toward consensus are important. Team members must learn to effectively use two-way communication. Team members must trust fellow members' motives and abilities and learn to be open and honest. Team members must see differences as strengths.

ACTIVITY: GETTING TO KNOW YOU

Outcomes:
1. Participants know one another better.
2. Participants are more aware of the need to listen to one another.
3. Participants are more aware of values present in the group.
4. Facilitator has evidence of comfort level of participants.
5. Facilitator has evidence of group skills and experience of participants.

Time: 50–60 minutes

Group Size: Small, 5–8 participants per group

Materials: One watch per group

Directions:
1. Facilitator discusses rationale and goals of the activity.
2. Facilitator explains that each member will have 5 minutes to tell their group about themselves, highlighting (1) what helped to make them who they are; and (2) their reasons for attending.
3. Facilitator models process by going first.
4. Facilitator then directs participants to take 2 minutes to write things they want to include in their talk. (This frees the participants to listen, minimizes mental rehearsing.)
5. Facilitator reminds participants to select a timekeeper, emphasizes importance of observing time limits, as participants begin.
6. Facilitator leads group discussion of reactions, learnings. Key questions:
   • What were your reactions as you listened to others? As you talked about yourself?
   • Why is this important?
   • How else might we get acquainted?
   • What did you learn or relearn from this?
   • What strengths did you discover in others?

Reflections: 1. Before asking participants to talk about themselves,
                     you may want to suggest a brief list of topics such as:
                     • Previous work experiences
                     • Family background
                     • Travel
                     • Hobbies
                     • Current/past learning projects
                     • Special events in life
                     • Experience with change
                     • Hopes/expectations for SIP
                  2. Participation should be balanced, hence the impor-
                     tance of timekeeping.
                  3. If participants don't use all their time other members
                     may want to ask questions.
                  4. As you model this, try to reveal something of the real
                     you. Don't model just career history or credential
                     sharing.
                  5. Be positive.

ACTIVITY: HIGH POINTS

Outcomes: 1. Participants know more about other group members.
                  2. Participants continue to identify similarities and dif-
                     ferences among members.
                  3. Facilitator has additional evidence of group comfort
                     level and group skills present.
                  4. Facilitator has additional information about knowl-
                     edge and values of participants regarding SIP.
Time: 30–40 minutes
Group Size: Small, 5–8 participants per group
Materials: High points worksheets
Directions: 1. Facilitator explains goals of activity and distributes
                     worksheets.
                  2. Facilitator directs participants to complete the activity
                     in small groups by:

- Completing worksheets individually (allow 5 minutes for this).
- Sharing high points in groups.
- Being careful to use no more than 4 minutes per person.

3. Facilitator leads discussion of reactions and learnings. Questions:
   - What else did you learn about others?
   - How was this alike or different from previous activity?
   - What similarities/differences are you discovering?
   - What was important to you in the conduct of this? How could you do it differently?
   - What can one learn from this type of discussion?
   - Variations:
   - Use different periods of time or different roles on the high points worksheets.
   - Direct participants to share only three, four, or five of the categories on their sheets.
   - Direct participants to reflect what was heard by repeating information to group members about themselves after all have completed the initial sharing round.

Reflections:
1. Remember that a high point is, above all, positive. It need not be especially significant to others, but it is memorable for the speaker.
2. Abraham Maslow and others claim that it is our high points that have the greatest growth producing impact on our lives. Does your experience support this? What makes a point high anyway?

HIGH POINTS

A high point is defined as any high positive experience one remembers. This experience need not be a unique or unusual experience, but it should be a peak experience to you. It should not be negative.

During the last week:

_____

_____

_____

_____

During the last two years:

_____

_____

_____

_____

Most recent fifth of my life:

_____

_____

_____

_____

Fourth fifth of my life:

_____

_____

_____

_____

Third fifth of my life:

_____

_____

_____

_____

Second fifth of my life:

_____

_____

_____

_____

First fifth of my life:

_____

_____

_____

_____

ACTIVITY: WHIP

Outcomes: 1. Facilitators focus attention of the group.
             2. Facilitators check individual emotional states.
             3. Participants know one another better.

Time: 5–15 minutes

Group Size: Large or small

Materials: None

Directions: 1. Facilitator introduces activity typically at the recon-
                vening of a group by presenting a sentence completion
                task and going first.
             2. Facilitator explains that participants may pass.
             3. Possible WHIP statements include:
                - My childhood ambition was . . .
                - A childhood success I had was . . .
                - My favorite activities as a child were . . .
                - My favorite teacher was . . .
                - My favorite subject was . . .
                - Smells I associate with childhood are . . .
                - My favorite extracurricular activity was . . .
                - Sounds I associate with childhood are . . .
                - Scenes I associate with childhood are . . .
                - An ideal vacation would be . . .
                - An ideal sabbatical (or time of change) would
                  be . . .
                - An ideal evening is . . .
                - Spring is . . .
                - Fall is . . .

- Winter is . . .
- One wish I have is . . .
- One hope I have is . . .
- My favorite animal is . . .
- My favorite color is . . .
- My favorite car is . . .
- My favorite song is . . .

Reflections: 1. This is really a dual-purpose activity. It serves as a warm-up or "sponge" activity and it is a quick check of the condition of the group. Watch for signs of energy or fatigue, eagerness or anxiety, involvement or disengagement.
2. This works best when kept light and quick; if someone stalls for a thought, ask him or her to pass.

ACTIVITY: HUMAN DEVELOPMENT

Human development activities serve to build teams through honesty and understanding.

1. Introductions
2. Feelings or thoughts and behaviors
   - Something that's new and good in my life.
   - One of the nicest things that ever happened to me.
   - Something I feel good and bad about at the same time.
   - Something I enjoy doing that I do well.
   - Something I like to imagine.
   - When I am myself.
   - The most significant gift ever given to me or that I ever gave to someone.
3. Dreaming
   - Craziest dream I ever had.
   - A dream I wish was real.
   - An idea I got from a dream.
   - A dream I've had more than once.
   - Something I solved with a dream.
   - I did something in my dream that I couldn't do otherwise.

4. Values
   - Something someone wants me to be.
   - Two things I believe in that conflict with each other.
   - When I was criticized for doing or saying something I thought was important.
   - The time I stood up for something I strongly believe in.
   - Some qualities that I look for in friends.
   - Something I can't stand.

5. Learning
   - Something I learned that was enjoyable.
   - A time I taught something to someone else.
   - A skill I'm learning now that I didn't have a year ago.
   - A time I learned from failure.
   - Something I want to learn in the future.
   - The best class I ever took.
   - I could learn better if I . . .
   - Something that's getting easier all the time.

6. Communication
   - How I got someone to pay attention to me.
   - Once when someone wouldn't listen to me.
   - A time when I really felt heard.
   - A time when I accepted someone else's feelings.
   - One of the nicest compliments I've ever received.
   - A time when listening would have kept me out of trouble.
   - Someone felt good because of what I said.

7. Trust
   - A place where I feel safe.
   - When someone betrayed my trust.
   - Someone I learned to trust.
   - I didn't trust someone because of what someone else said.
   - A time when I wanted to be trusted.
   - Someone whose opinion I value very much.
   - I could have hurt someone's feelings but I didn't.
   - A person I feel safe with.
   - I kept a promise.

8. Friendship
   - How I made friends and it turned out well.
   - What I like best about the person I like the most.

- What I value in friends of the opposite sex.
- How I handle disagreements with a friend.
- One way I changed to be a better friend.
- If I'm with a friend . . .
- Things I enjoy doing with my friends away from school.

9. Perception
   - An experience I had that caused me to see things differently.
   - A time someone tried to change my perception.
   - Something I see differently than my parents' generation sees it.
   - A time when I tried to put myself in someone else's shoes.
   - A class I took that caused me to see things differently.

10. Being a teenager
    - The best thing about being a teenager.
    - The worst thing about being a teenager.
    - A new responsibility I've assumed.
    - A turning point in my life.
    - A way my personality has changed for the better.
    - The person I want to be in five years.
    - When I feel discriminated against because of my age.
    - When I go off by myself.
    - Self-understanding that I've recently gained.
    - When I like myself most.
    - I felt uncomfortable with the me that emerged in a situation.
    - How I want others to see me.

11. Winning and losing
    - A time I won and loved it.
    - A time I won and felt bad about it.
    - A time I lost and took it hard.
    - A time I lost and felt okay about it.
    - A time I competed with myself.
    - How do you feel about competition?
    - A time I felt like a real winner.

12. Problem solving
    - I solved a problem effectively.
    - When the easy way out made things worse or better.
    - When people try to solve each other's problems.
    - A problem I'd like suggestions for solving.

13. Decision making
    - Looking back on a decision I made.
    - I didn't want to have to make a decision.
    - When I got (or didn't get) to share in making a decision.
    - The most difficult decision I've ever made.
    - I have good judgment.
    - I decided to change something about myself and did.

14. Success and failure
    - They said I couldn't do something, but I could.
    - Something at which I'm getting better.
    - Something at which I'd like to succeed.
    - Something I wish I'd tried.
    - A capability I've recently discovered.
    - Something I enjoy doing because it gives me a sense of accomplishment.
    - I started something and finished it.

15. Accomplishments and goals
    - Something I did (or made) that I'm proud of.
    - A project I've got going right now.
    - Something I've finished that I had a hard time starting.
    - When I get out of high school, I hope . . .
    - If I could accomplish anything I wanted, it would be . . .
    - A goal I'm sure to obtain.

16. Taking charge
    - A time I proved I wasn't helpless.
    - A time I put off until tomorrow . . .
    - I handled a situation well that was like situations that used to upset me.
    - I got my courage up.
    - I made a plan and it worked.
    - I surprised myself when I got it done.
    - How I got what I needed.

17. Influence
    - When one person's mood affected everyone else.
    - Someone tried to make me do something I didn't want to.
    - When someone expected the very best of me.
    - Things I don't like conforming to.

- When someone criticized me.
- Someone did something for me that I really appreciated.
- I went along with the gang.
- I didn't know what group to go with.
- A time when I felt pressured.

18. Assertiveness
    - Later.

19. Feelings are facts
    - A time I remember feeling totally alive and in touch with the world.
    - A time I was alone but not lonely.
    - My feeling label says . . .
    - A time I trusted my feelings.
    - A feeling of sadness I remember.
    - A feeling I've had a hard time accepting.
    - I told someone how I was feeling.
    - A favorite feeling.
    - When someone becomes jealous.
    - When my anger forced me to do something.
    - How my fear helped me realize a danger.
    - A time I remember feeling important.

20. Reality and other realities
    - Something I like to imagine.
    - Someone wouldn't face reality.
    - My reality was different from someone else's.
    - Something unexplainable happened.
    - What's your astrological sign?
    - What else is out there?

21. Responsibility
    - A way I'm independent.
    - An agreement that was hard to keep.
    - My favorite excuse.
    - I didn't do something because I knew it would hurt someone.
    - I did it myself.
    - I didn't want to accept the consequences, but I did.
    - I did it because it needed to be done.

22. Sex roles
    - Things I like about being a young man or young woman.
    - If I were a member of the opposite sex.
    - When I felt I was seen as an object.
    - As a young man or woman, I'm expected to . . .
    - As a young man or woman, I'm never expected to . . .
    - Ways I plan to be different from adults I know.
    - The kind of man or woman I want to be.
23. Parenthood
    - One of the best times I ever spent with my parent(s).
    - Someone I know who is a good parent.
    - Something I think parents should not do.
    - The thing I look forward to most (or least) if I become a parent.
    - Something my parent(s) did that I didn't appreciate at the time but now I do.
    - Something I'm grateful to my parents for.
    - The toughest thing about being a parent.

Bibliography

Alpern, Morton. *The Subject Curriculum: Grades K–12.* Columbus, Ohio: Charles E. Merrill, 1967.

Apex Fitness Group. *Elements of Success: Fitness Handbook.* Middletown, N.Y.: Gold's Gym, 1999.

Bennis, Warren, and Burt Nanus. *Leaders: The Strategies for Taking Charge.* New York: Harper and Row, 1985.

Berliner, David. *The Management Crisis.* Reading, Mass.: Addison-Wesley, 1995.

Blake, P. R., and T. S. Mouton. *The Managerial Grid.* Houston, Tex.: Gulf, 1964.

Blanchard, Ken. *Heart of a Leader.* Tulsa, Okla.: Honor Books, 1999.

Blanchard, Ken, and Sheldon Bowles. *Gung Ho: Turn On the People in Any Organization.* New York: William Morrow, 1997.

Blanchard, Ken, and Paul Hersey. "Leadership Effectiveness and Adaptability Index," *The 1976 Handbook for Group Facilitators.* La Jolla, Calif.: University Associates, 1973.

Blanchard, Ken, and Spencer Johnson. *The One Minute Manager.* New York: Morrow William and Company, 1982.

Blocker, Bill. "How to Get Children to Read." Paper presented at the Institute for the Development of Educational Activities, Harvey Mudd College, Claremont, Calif., July 9–14, 2000.

Bloom, Benjamin. *Taxonomy of Educational Objectives.* New York: Longmans, Green, 1956.

Broad, Eli. "Preparing Leaders for the New Economy," *The School Administrator* (March 2001), 46–49.

Bruner, Jerome S. *The Process of Education.* Cambridge: Harvard University Press, 1977.

Buckingham, Marcus, and Curth Coffman. *First, Break All of the Rules.* New York: Simon and Schuster, 1999.

Carman, Tim. "Leadership Proficiencies and Indicators for District Administrators." Unpublished document, Greater Albany Public Schools, Albany, Ore., December 8, 1989.

Carman, Tim, and Pat Schmuck. Unpublished paper submitted to *The School Administrator.*

Carroll, Lewis. *Alice in Wonderland.* New York: Gilbert H. McKibbin, 1899.

Chait, Richard P., Thomas P. Holland, and Barbara E. Taylor. *Improving the Performance of Governing Boards.* Phoenix, Ariz.: Oryx Press, 1996.

Clifton, Donald O., and Paula Nelson. *Soar with Your Strengths.* New York: Bantam Doubleday Dell, 1992.

Combs, Arthur W. "The Concept of Human Potential and School." Paper presented at the annual meeting of The Montana Association for Curriculum Development, Missoula, Mont., March 1978.

——. *Curriculum and Instruction in the Elementary School.* New York: MacMillan, 1975.

——. "New Concepts of Human Potentials: New Challenge for Teachers. *Four Psychologies Applied to Education.* Ed. T. Roberts. New York: Schenkman Publishing, 1975.

Combs, Arthur W., and Donald Snygg. *Individual Behavior.* New York: Harper and Row, 1959.

Covey, Stephen R. *The Principle Centered Leader.* New York: Simon and Schuster, 1990.

——. *The Seven Habits of Highly Effective People.* New York: Simon and Schuster, 1989.

Danielson, Charlotte. *Enhancing Professional Practice: A Framework for Teaching.* Alexandria, Va.: Association for Supervision and Curriculum, 1996.

Davis, Wynn, ed. *The Best of Success.* Lombard, Ill: Celebrating Excellence, 1992.

Drucker, Peter F. *The Effective Executive.* New York: Harper and Row, 1967.

Eliot, T. S. *Collected Poems, 1909–1962.* New York: Harcourt Brace, 1962.

Epictetus. *The Best of Success,* ed. Wynn Davis. Lombard, Ill.: Celebrating Excellence, 1992.

Feyereisen, K., and John Fiorino, eds. *Supervision and Curriculum Renewal: A Systems Approach.* New York: Meredith, 1970.

Freed, Ron, and Walt Stoll. "Healthy Behavior: The Implications of a Holistic Paradigm of Thinking through Body, Mind Research," *Electronic Journal of Health and Education* 1 (January 1, 1998).

Fullen, Michael. *Change Forces.* New York: Falmer Press, 1993.

Gardner, John. "Self-Renewal." Paper presented at the Aspen Institute for Humanistic Studies, Colorado, 1983.

Goldman, Daniel, Richard Boyatzis, and Annie McKee. *Primal Leadership*. Boston, Mass.: Harvard Business School Press, 2002.

Goodlad, John. *A Place Called School*. New York: McGraw-Hill, 1984.

Gordon, Arthur. *A Touch of Wonder*. New York: Jove Books, 1978.

Halpin, A. W. *The Leadership of Superintendents*. Chicago, Ill.: Midwest Administration Center, University of Chicago, 1959.

Hand, Raymond V., ed. *American Quotations*. New York: Random House, 1989.

Harrison, Roger. "Organizational Culture and Professional Life." Paper presented at the Twentieth Annual Northwest Fire Service and Management Seminar, Portland, Oregon, 1972.

Hass, G., ed. *Curriculum Planning: A New Approach*. New York: Schenkman, 1975.

Henning, Mary Stout. "Organizational Culture and Professional Life." Paper presented at the Twentieth Annual Northwest Fire Service Management Seminar, Portland, Oregon, March 1, 1989.

Holmes, T. H., and R. H. Rahe. "Social Readjustment Rating Scale." *Journal of Psychosomatic Research* 2 (1967): 216.

House Bill 2991, Oregon Legislature, June 1972.

Joyce, Bruce. "Peer Coaching." Paper presented at the annual meeting of the Washington Association for Curriculum Development, Spokane, Wash., June 1972.

Kaufman, Roger. *Needs Assessment*. San Diego: University Consortium for Instructional Development and Technology, 1975.

Kneller, George F. "Behavioral Objectives? No!" *Educational Leadership*, 29, no. 5, February 1972.

Kozol, Jonathan. *Savage Inequalities*. New York: Crown Publishers, 1991.

Lashaway, Larry. *Leading with Vision*. Eugene, Ore.: House of Educational Management, 1997.

Levine, Peter. *Walking the Tiger*. Berkeley, Calif.: North Atlantic Books, 1997.

Lightfoot, Sara Lawrence. *The Good High School: Portraits of Character and Culture*. New York: Basic Books, 1983.

Linhart, Jim, and Garyann Linhart. Conversation with the authors (February 2001).

Marazanno, Robert. *Tactics: A Strategy for Teaching Thinking*. Aurora, Colo.: Midcontinent Regional Educational Laboratory, 1986.

Maslock, Christina. *Burn-Out: The Cost of Caring*. New York: Prentice Hall, 1982.

Maslow, Abraham H. "Some Educational Implications of the Humanistic Psychologies," *Four Psychologies Applied to Education*. Ed. T. Roberts. New York: Schenkman, 1975.

McCarthy, Bernice. *The 4 Matt System, Teaching to Learning Styles with Left/Right Mode Techniques*. Barrington, Ill.: Excel, 1980.

McGinn, Daniel, and Keith Naughton. "How Safe Is Your Job," *Time,* February 5, 2001.

McGreggor, Douglas. *The Professional Manager.* New York: McGraw-Hill, 1960.

Moss, Rosabeth Canter. *When Giants Dare to Dance.* New York: Simon and Schuster, 1989.

Naisbitt, John. *Megatrends: Ten New Directions Transforming Our Lives.* New York: Warner Books, 1982.

Ouchi, William G. *Theory Z: How American Business Can Meet the Japanese Challenge.* New York: William Morrow, 1992.

Parnell, Dale. *Logolearning, Searching for Meaning in Education.* Waco, Tex.: Center for Occupational Research and Development, 1993.

Phillips, Gary. *Site-Based Governance Training.* Battle Ground, Wash.: Institute for the Development of Educational Activities, 1972.

———. "Site-Based Decision Making and School Improvement." Paper presented at IDEA School Improvement Program, Battle Ground, Wash., July 1994.

Popham, James W. "The New World of Accountability: In the Classroom." *Four Psychologies Applied to Education.* Ed. T. Roberts. New York: Schenkman, 1975.

Rogers, Carl R. *Curriculum and Instruction in the Elementary School.* New York: Macmillan, 1975.

———. *Freedom to Learn.* Columbus, Ohio: Charles E. Merrill, 1969.

———. "The Psychology of the Classroom." Paper presented at the annual meeting of The Montana Association for Curriculum Development, Missoula, Mont., April 1969.

Safford, Kim. "Education as an Opportunity." Paper presented at the Northwest Writing Institute, Lewis and Clark College, Portland, Ore, June, 1989.

Schmuck, A., Richard and Phillip J. Runkle. *The Handbook of Organizational Development in Schools and Colleges.* 4th ed. Prospect Heights, Ill.: Waveland Press, 1994.

Sergiovanni, Thomas J. *Leadership for the Schoolhouse.* San Francisco: Jossey-Bass, 1996.

———. *Moral Leadership.* San Francisco: Jossey-Bass, 1992.

Sizor, Theodore. "The American School as a Compromise." Paper presented for the Institute for the Development of Educational Ideas, San Diego, 1971.

Tocqueville, Alexis de. *A Democracy in America.* New York: Vintage Books, 1835.

Watson, Deborah. United Nations agencies document, *Mounting World Hunger.* http:/www.wswsw.org/article/1999/food [October 13, 2001].

Wheatly, Margaret. *Leadership and the New Science: Learning about Organizations from an Orderly Universe.* San Francisco: Berrett-Koehler Publishers, 1992.

Zukav, Gary. *Soul Stories.* New York: Simon and Schuster, 2000.

About the Author

Tim Carman was born in Lewistown, Montana, September 3, 1947, the son of Edward F. and Ann L. Carman. Mr. Carman was married to Donna L. Freier in 1969, and to Barbara A. May in 1989. Tim has one child, Jami Lynn.

Tim's education provided him with a strong background to write this book. He graduated from Glasgow High School in 1965 and from Northern Montana College in 1969 with a B.A. in secondary education and social studies. At Montana State University, Bozeman, he earned an M.A. in history in 1971 and an Ed.D. in curriculum and instruction in 1979.

The experience Carman has acquired over the years makes him extremely qualified to write this book. While he was still studying to become a teacher, he began to teach swimming lessons to students of all ages, from preschool to retired seniors. From 1969 to 1971, he served as a graduate teaching assistant while working on his M.A. degree in history at Montana State University. From 1971 to 1979, he served as a hospital administrator and detachment commander of the 396th Station Hospital, United States Army Reserve Command, in Helena, Montana. From 1971 to 1978, he taught in the social studies department and coached football and track at Sunhaven Intermediate School and Capital High School in Helena, Montana. In 1978 and 1979, he served as a graduate teaching assistant in the department of secondary education and foundations at Montana State University.

From 1995 to 2000, he was the superintendent of schools for the Greater Albany Public Schools in Albany, Oregon. With 19 schools, 7,900 students and about 1,000 full- and part-time employees, the assignment provided

Carman with a rich opportunity to develop a standards-based program of study for children. In 2000, he stepped down to continue a sojourn by taking a much-needed sabbatical to rest, write this book, and to find a place to serve.

Prior to going to Albany, he was the deputy superintendent (six years) of the North Clackamas schools. North Clackamas is a suburb of Portland, Oregon, with 15,000 students. Prior to going to North Clackamas, he was the acting director of the Educational Administration Program, Graduate School of Professional Studies, Lewis and Clark College.

Before that he was the assistant superintendent of schools for the Battle Ground School District (8,000 students). Immediately prior to that, he was the assistant principal and principal at Battle Ground High School (1,300 students). Therefore, he has had two levels of building experience and three levels of district office experience, one of which includes the position of superintendent.

In terms of teaching experience, he has taught across all grade levels from kindergarten to graduate school. He has been an elementary physical education teacher, a middle and senior high school history and social studies teacher, and an assistant professor, and he is currently an adjunct professor at two institutions of higher education.

He is a well-known speaker on school improvement, having made nearly fifty presentations in Oregon, Washington State, and across the nation.